REGNUM STUDIES IN MISSION

Diakonia as Christian Social Practice

An Introduction

Series Preface

Regnum Studies in Mission are born from the lived experience of Christians and Christian communities in mission, especially but not solely in the fast growing churches among the poor of the world. These churches have more to tell than stories of growth. They are making significant impacts on their cultures in the cause of Christ. They are producing 'cultural products' which express the reality of Christian faith, hope and love in their societies.

Regnum Studies in Mission are the fruit often of rigorous research to the highest international standards and always of authentic Christian engagement in the transformation of people and societies. And these are for the world. The formation of Christian theology, missiology and practice in the twenty-first century will depend to a great extent on the active participation of growing churches contributing biblical and culturally appropriate expressions of Christian practice to inform World Christianity.

Series Editors

A full listing of titles in this series appears at the end of this book

REGNUM STUDIES IN MISSION

Diakonia as Christian Social Practice

An Introduction

Edited by

Stephanie Dietrich
Knud Jørgensen
Kari Karsrud Korslien
Kjell Nordstokke

First edition published 2014 by Regnum Books International

Regnum is an imprint of the Oxford Centre for Mission Studies
St. Philip and St. James Church, Woodstock Road
Oxford, OX2 6HR, UK
www.ocms.ac.uk/regnum

09 08 07 06 05 04 03 8 7 6 5 4 3 2 1

British Library Cataloguing in Publication Data
A catalogue record for this book is available from the British Library

ISBN: 978-1-506475-54-7

Typeset by Words by Design
Cover design by Words by Design

regnum

Distributed by 1517 Media in the US and Canada

Contents

Abbreviations

ACT	Action by Churches Together
ARHAP	African Religious Health Assets Programme (now IRHAP, as African has been replaced by International)
Aprodev	Association of World Council of Churches related Development Organizationsin Europe
BIT	Bilateral Investment Treaty/Agreement
CCM	Church City Mission (Norway)
CPE	Clinical Pastoral Education
CPCE	Community of Protestant Churches in Europe
DWI	Diakoniewissenschaftliches Institut
Eurodiaconia	A Pan-European Network of Christian Social and Health Care Providers
FBO	Faith-Based Organisation
FGM	Female Genital Mutilation/Circumcision
HAP	Humanitarian Accountability Partnership
ICCPR	International Covenant on Civil and Political Rights
ICESCR	International Covenant on Economic, Social and Cultural Rights
ICC	International Criminal Court
ILO	International Labour Organisation
INNOSERV	Innovation in Science, Technology and Industry
IOCC	International Orthodox Christian Charities
LWF	Lutheran World Federation
NCA	Norwegian Church Aid
NGO	Non-Governmental Organization
NSC	The Norwegian Seamen's Church
Ortaid	Orthodox Church Aid from Finland
RHA	Religious Health Asset
SADC	Southern African Development Community
UNDP	United Nations Development Project
WARC	World Alliance of Reformed Churches
WCRC	World Communion of Reformed Churches
WCC	World Council of Churches
WHO	World Health Organization

Foreword: Diakonia as Christian Social Practice

Diakonia or service has always been an integral aspect of the life and work of the church. There have been shifts over the decades in approaches to service and from specific departments of the church; service has become professionalised within organisations whose tasks are humanitarian, developmental and advocacy-related.

The validity and justification of *diakonia* are found in the self-understanding of the church and the landscape of poverty and inequality within and between communities and nations. This has spurred shifts in models of *diakonia* and the need for reflection on *diakonia*. This new book on *Diakonia as Christian Social Practice* is divided into three parts: theological perspectives, *diakonia* as social perspective and practical perspectives; it seeks to expound on the theme of *diakonia* from a justice and transformation perspective. A number of writers have written on different sub-topics. As it explores the paradigm shift of *diakonia*, the book views *diakonia* as an integral part of the nature and mission of the church. Furthermore, 'assets' as both tangible and intangible resources are used as a concept for the first time in relation to diaconal action, embracing a new approach to the understanding and definition as well as utilisation of resources. This new definition/understanding of assets clearly makes a shift from the traditional notion of *diakonia* as charity to the suffering, towards mutual interdependence and empowerment of those on the margins and other agencies.

While acknowledging the 'midwifery' role of European churches in the evolution of diaconal teaching, the changing landscape of the welfare state and the need for churches and Christians to be agents of empowerment, the book highlights a new phenomenon, namely, religious minorities and their approach and practice of *diakonia* and not least the notion of 'welcoming'. As regards theory and praxis of *diakonia*, the book analyzes methods in a dynamic and complex field, and underlines the imperatives of empowerment and capacity-building with a view to inform professionalism and practice especially of the vulnerable, excluded, marginalised and disadvantaged people. The book is emphatic about diaconal action being holistic, and rejects the notion of departmentalisation of the human reality and being. By emphasising the holistic approach, the book clearly illustrates the need to root *diakonia* in theological reflection insofar as care and empowerment are concerned, and the need for a prophetic expression of *diakonia* that wrestles with structures and cultures of injustice that generate vulnerability, suffering and marginalisation.

This book is a must-read for academicians, practitioners and leaders in the churches and theological institutions as it brings up new perspectives of *diakonia* in a changing global context. It is an ideal resource book for churches as they nurture and enhance their vision and commitment to *diakonia*, including critiquing their current approaches. The book discusses themes that will inevitably inspire future reflections, consultations and practical work on *diakonia*.

Dr Agnes R. M. Abuom,
Moderator of the World Council of Churches

Introduction
Diakonia as Christian Social Practice

Stephanie Dietrich, Kari Karsrud Korslien,
Kjell Nordstokke and Knud Jørgensen

This book is written within a context of academic reflection on the theory and the praxis of *diakonia*. By academic context is meant postgraduate studies, and this is expressed by the fact that the major part of the authors belong to the faculty of Diakonhjemmet University College in Oslo that offers a Master's Degree in *Diakonia* and Christian Social Practice as well as a PhD programme in *Diakonia*, Values and Professional Practice. The students at this level already have a basic training as professional workers, some of them within the field of health or social work, others as teachers or theologians. The study of *diakonia* at an academic level is marked by an interdisciplinary approach as it aims at bringing together knowledge from different disciplines, primarily theology and the social sciences. The goal is to perform both empirical research related to what is (or could be) designated as diaconal praxis, as well as to elaborate theoretical and normative frameworks when analyzing and evaluating diaconal work. This reflects the fact that most students of *diakonia* are practitioners that are interested in having a better understanding of their work, with the aim of improving their professional competence and adding quality to what they are doing.

Diakonia may be presented as the social ministry of the church and, as an academic discipline, it is often located within the area of practical theology. This is largely in line with the tradition of some Protestant churches, mainly Lutherans, Reformed and Methodists that since the middle of the 19th century have been strongly impacted by what has been named the modern diaconal movement which lead to the formation of communities of deaconesses and deacons, and to the establishment of hundreds of diaconal institutions. This movement started in Germany in the 1830s, but soon spread to neighbouring countries, and later also to other continents. The diaconal institutions became pioneers within the area of health care and social work, and contributed substantially to the development of its professionalism in a way that has had a lasting impact on the development of today's public welfare systems. The position of these institutions as social agents makes it evident that they are important as study objects for social and political research, which supports the claim that *diakonia* as an academic discipline must be done in an interdisciplinary manner, bringing together knowledge from both theological and social sciences.

The concept of *diakonia* has developed over the last decades, especially within the ecumenical movement, to a degree that may be characterised as a paradigm shift. Three main features characterise this change: first, the ecclesial dimension of *diakonia* is now strongly underlined. While *diakonia* was earlier perceived often as the activity of professional diaconal workers or agencies, it is now emphasised that *diakonia* belongs to the nature and the mission of 'being church'. This view has opened a stronger focus on the biblical and dogmatic foundation of *diakonia*, and on its link to missiological themes. Secondly, it affirms that diaconal action must be holistic, taking into consideration the physical, mental, social and spiritual dimension, and rejecting practices that tend to departmentalise sectors of human reality. Thirdly, it enhances bold, some would say prophetic, expressions of diaconal action, in solidarity with marginalised and suffering people, moving away from traditions of conceptualising *diakonia* as humble service.

The authors of this book largely subscribe to this understanding which may be found in contemporary documents from ecumenical organisations such as the World Council of Churches. One such document is *Diakonia in Context: Transformation, Reconciliation, Empowerment*, published by the Lutheran World Federation in 2009. It is frequently referred to in the following presentations. Without giving a strict definition of *diakonia*, this document maintains some fundamental assumptions when elaborating on the understanding of *diakonia*:

> One is that *diakonia* is a theological concept that points to the very identity and mission of the church. Another is its practical implication in the sense that *diakonia* is a call to action, as a response to challenges of human suffering, injustice and care for creation. This rather open-ended understanding of *diakonia* is also due to the fact that the concept itself does not allow for a precise definition, not even when used in the Greek New Testament. The present use of the word has largely been shaped by how Christians have tried to be faithful to the biblical call to be a neighbour throughout the history of the church.[1]

The view is based on the conviction that *diakonia* expresses a biblical call to service. But it also admits that there is no direct link between this concept and its use in the Greek New Testament. Careful interpretation is therefore required. In this book, frequent references will be made to the Australian scholar John N. Collins and his research on the *diak-* words (*diakonia*, *diakonein* and *diakonos*) as used in Greek literature, papyri and inscriptions for

---

[1] Lutheran World Federation, *Diakonia in Context: Transformation, Reconciliation, Empowerment. An LWF Contribution to the Understanding and Practice of Diakonia* (Geneva: LWF, 2009), 8.

the period 400 BC to around 400 AD.[2] His findings show that *diakonia* in the first place means an assignment or mission. The importance of this task and its content relate to the one who authorises and in whose service the *diakonos* is sent as a messenger or as a go-between. According to his research, the *diak*-words themselves have no connotation with charitable (caritative) service or care for the poor, and his careful reading of the passages in NT where these words appear sought to prove this is also the case with the biblical material. Collins therefore concluded that the common interpretation, of both scholars and diaconal practitioners, that *diakonia* meant humble and lowly service directed towards the sick and poor, was based on a misunderstanding. In particular he questioned the interpretation given in the article about *diakonia* in the influential *Theologische Wörterbuch zum Neuen Testament*, published in Germany in the 1930s, later also translated into English.[3]

Collins' interpretations are much discussed. Notwithstanding the results of this discussion on the biblical interpretation, his findings on the broad connotation of the *diak*- words in the NT have stimulated scholars to explore in which way *diakonia* might be understood today, as part of the church's identity and mission. Collins' research has thus contributed to a fundamental reform of how to conceptualise reflection on *diakonia* as theory and praxis, highlighting the fact that a former understanding of *diakonia* as humble service has been misled by a narrow interpretation which had shaped the diaconal movement in the 19th century and the kind of praxis that was established within that particular historical context.

This book is heavily influenced by the reorientation in the understanding of *diakonia* caused by John Collins. Several authors will refer to his findings and use them in the attempt to develop critical reflection on diaconal practice in relation to relevant challenges in today's context. Frequent references are made to the Norwegian (or Scandinavian) context due to the fact that most of the contributors are living and doing their research here, hoping though that the experiences and insight from this part of the world may also be relevant and useful in other contexts. After all, no context exists in splendid isolation; also within the field of *diakonia,* learning processes are mutual and cross-contextual. This is clearly seen in the *Church of Norway Plan for Diakonia*, another document that appears as a frequent point of reference in this book. Its definition of *diakonia* is:

---

[2] Collins, *Diakonia: Reinterpreting the Ancient Sources*.

[3] Gerhard Kittel and Gerhard Friedrich (eds), *Theological Dictionary of the New Testament*, Vols 1-10, 1964-76.

> *Diakonia* is the caring ministry of the Church. It is the Gospel in action and is expressed through loving your neighbour, creating inclusive communities, caring for creation and struggling for justice.[4]

This broad definition can be read in conjunction with Collins' quest for re-interpreting *diakonia*, and also within the development of ecumenical *diakonia*. It articulates two fundamental positions: first, it presents *diakonia* as the Gospel in action. This understanding is held to be in line with the teaching of the NT which announces that Jesus brought the Gospel in words and deeds, and that the disciples were mandated to follow his example. This means that *diakonia* is not just a possible consequence of the proclamation of the Gospel, but an integral part of it, and therefore a core dimension of 'being church'. Secondly, it enlarges the space for diaconal action. In addition to the tradition of caring love for one's neighbour, it points at creating inclusive communities, caring for creation and the struggle for justice. These areas of action indicate that *diakonia* is both faith-based and rights-based. Inclusiveness is focused as a diaconal concern in contexts where people experience mechanisms of exclusion, for social, economic or even religious reasons. They also point in the direction of economic and climate justice as burning issues for diaconal reflection and praxis.

The chapters of this book will deal with a number of these issues. Part 1: *Theological Perspectives* includes the following chapters:

Stephanie Dietrich's opening chapter is entitled *Reflections on Core Aspects of Diaconal Theory*. In this article, the author explores basic aspects of diaconal theory, focusing on the development in the understanding of *diakonia*, moving from Christian social service as acts of charity to its understanding as acts of mutual service in accountability and reciprocity; from post-colonial professional care to autonomy-orientated assistance. The article discusses the ambiguity of these different approaches. She refers to different ethical and feminist approaches concerning the understanding of care, and recent ecumenical studies on the understanding of Christian social service, for the discourse on diaconal theory. Thus, this article is based on an interdisciplinary methodological approach.

Stephanie Dietrich's second article 'Mercy and Truth are met together; Righteousness and Peace have kissed each other' (Psalm 85:10): Biblical and Systematic Theological Perspectives on Diakonia as Advocacy and Fight for Justice focuses on diakonia as advocacy and fight for justice, and the political and prophetic dimension of diaconal theory and practice. The author wants to explore critically the concept of 'prophetic diakonia' by describing some of the main biblical and systematic-theological reasons for the church to engage in

---

[4] An English translation of the plan is available at http://www.kirken.no/?event=doLink&famID=247 http://ask.bibsys.no/ask/action/show?pid=092637698&kid=biblio

societal issues. Her main emphasis lies on biblical anthropology, which forms the basis for her approach to diaconal theory. On this basis, she discusses why and how the church should understand herself as an important and relevant agency in the public sphere, and why diaconal theory and practice should lead towards a distinct critical voice in our societies.

Kjell Nordstokke writes about *Diakonia as Academic Discipline.* This article discusses the understanding of the term *diakonia* in a historical perspective, mainly since its introduction in Germany in the 19th century when it was used to designate church-based caritative work linked with the establishment of diaconal institutions and the formation of deaconesses and deacons. It also gives a survey of how scholars have interpreted this term since then, relating to different historical contexts, ending up with a presentation of 'ecumenical *diakonia*' as this term has been emerging within the ecumenical movement over the last decades.

Hans Stifoss-Hanssen's focus is on *Diakonia as a Professional Practice – Perspectives on Research and Education.* The article focuses on some aspects of the professional practice of the deacons as we know them in the Nordic Lutheran majority churches – as professionals with a higher education in health or social work, and in diaconal theory and practice. They aim for a lifelong career as leaders of the charitable dimension of the parish they work in. The basic argument for this profession is generally taken from sources in theology and church history, which is obviously important. There is, however, even a need for grounding the profession in studies and analyses of the actual performance of the profession in its empirical circumstances. The reason for this is largely the need for providing the deacons with tools to meet practical challenges adequately, but also the growing consciousness of the foundations of professional practices in general. The article discusses a balancing of theological and empirical elements in the basis of the profession of the deacons.

Olav Fanuelsen deals with *Diakonia as Faith-Based Professional Practice.* The question is not whether *diakonia* is a practical activity or a practice per se, but to what extent *diakonia*, as part of the mission of the church, shapes a professional practice which in a particular way is influenced by the basic aspects of the Christian faith: what does it mean that a professional practice is faith-based, and what are the characteristics of that practice? *Diakonia* belongs to the whole church and it is the responsibility of each member of the congregation and of the whole *koinonia* itself. Whether it is professional or general, *diakonia* is of its very nature faith-based. The link between *diakonia* and faith contains different dimensions. In this article the author looks at the concept of what it means to be 'faith-based' and explores the different meanings. Secondly, he looks at different views of professional praxis, in relation to a faith-based diaconal perspective.

Knud Jørgensen writes about *Diakonia and Capacity-building.* Equipping for service designates the biblical understanding of capacity-building.

Capacity-building is therefore the primary task of servant leaders. In other words: capacity-building is at the very heart of *diakonia* and diaconal leadership. The article looks at capacity-building as part of organisational development in a rapidly changing society, using models to illustrate the complexity of capacity-building and the holistic nature of being equipped for service. Secondly, capacity-building for *diakonia* is not a separate entity; different contexts will require specific capacities and capabilities – theological, practical, political, networking, redressing imbalances of power, etc. There is a variety of forms of *diakonia* and therefore also a variety of areas to be covered by capacity-building. Thirdly, learning in *diakonia* applies to all levels of the church to enable and empower people to see *diakonia* as something they know and own, and in which they participate. Finally, the article expands on the need for developing a relevant leadership and on the challenge to include *diakonia* in the curriculum of theological education.

Carlos Ham's contribution is entitled *Empowering Diakonia: A Perspective from the World Council of Churches.* Focusing on a methodology that the author has called the *Five Dimensions of Empowering Diakonia*, the article will address the theoretical and practical tools for *diakonia* as Christian social practice. From the perspective of the World Council of Churches, the article will unpack the visional, normative, need-oriented, contextual and transformative dimensions of this methodology in order to explore and construct the concept and practice of the Empowering Diakonia model. The article will also analyze how empowerment lifts the natural gifts and dignity of human beings, taking place in mutuality, in partnership, in a spirit of power-sharing. From the standpoint of the Judæo-Christian tradition, it will explore empowerment as a process of reaching out to the other with the love of the triune God; it is, therefore intrinsically attached to *diakonia*, which affirms the power-service in Christ's way, towards transformative justice, as part of God's mission.

Part 2 includes chapters on *Social Perspectives*. The first chapter on *Diakonia as Rights-based Practice,* written by Hans Morten Haugen, explores three questions: first, what are the actual implications of viewing diaconal work as rights-based? Secondly, how and where is rights-based diaconal work promoted? Thirdly, what are the main limitations in a rights-based approach? It applies as a theoretical framework the human rights-embedded moral philosophy of Thomas Pogge, exploring how global institutions currently do not promote global justice. The empirical material is from international *diakonia*, particularly Norwegian Church Aid, applying a so-called integrated approach, where emergency, development and advocacy activities are guided by human rights. The article has three findings to each of the three questions. First, there are no contradictions between human rights principles and diaconal principles. Secondly, advocacy work can be directed at various powerful agencies, and there is a mutual reciprocal relationship between having a rights-based platform and devoting resources to advocacy. Thirdly, there are tools and principles derived from human rights treaties that can be more actively applied by diaconal organisations.

Annette Leis-Peters writes about *Diaconal Work and Research about Diakonia in the Face of Welfare Mix and Religious Pluralism in Sweden and Germany*. Diaconal work is affected by the welfare system within which it is operating and by the way the relationship between the state and religion is organised. Different contexts influence the ways in which diaconal work is organised, conducted and perceived. At the same time, diaconal agencies are facing similar global trends such as religious pluralism and growing welfare mix solutions. Do similar social changes result in comparable strategies in diaconal work? How is research mirroring these processes? The article gives some indications of how the questions could be answered by taking a closer look at the Swedish and German contexts, and at two research projects which were conducted within and about them. The role of diaconal work is discussed both from the perspective of church-based welfare institutions and of church social work at the local parish level.

Olav Helge Angell's chapter is on *Diakonia and Hospitality*. It relates the two concepts *diakonia* and 'hospitality' to each other, the former from the Church of Norway Plan for Diakonia, the second from Luke Bretherton's discussion of the concept in his doctoral thesis. Hospitality as actively welcoming the stranger may be specified further to involve welcoming 'those with the least status': the imperative to welcome the weak and the vulnerable serves as a constant reminder to see and hear those members of society who are most easily marginalised, oppressed and rendered invisible. We may apply this principle for social practice more generally, also to encompass neighbourly love, irrespective of whether the neighbour shares the person's or the collective's moral values or not, whether the neighbour is marginalised, oppressed or not. In the discussion the author draws on empirical material from a study of The Norwegian Seamen's Church.

Anders Bäckström focuses (*Religion Between the Private and Public - about Diaconal Studies as an Academic Field)* on the need to widen the study of diaconia though the examples of two research projects conducted in thirteen municipalities in twelve countries in Europe; Welfare and Religion in a European Perspective, funded by the Bank of Sweden Tercentenary Foundation, and Welfare and Values in Europe: Transitions related to Religion, Minorities and Gender funded by the European Commission Sixth Framework Programme. The projects explore how majority churches and minority religions engage in welfare, how they experience public welfare provision and how interaction in welfare contributes to social cohesion. The article sketches the most important results of the projects and analyses them from the perspective of diakonia. The author argues that this kind of research is one of many examples of the new conditions for research if diakonia wants to become a discipline of its own within the scientific community.

Part 3 includes *Practical Perspectives.* Kari Jordheim's chapter on *The Role of the Deacon in Church and Society* is based on research done during a World Assembly arranged by the Diakonia World Federation in the summer of 2013 in Berlin. The Diakonia World Federation's members are associations, organisations and communities of deaconesses, deacons, diaconal brothers and sisters, diaconal ministers and other church workers. Forty-eight people volunteered to answer a questionnaire. The informants represented twenty different countries from all continents and 22 different church denominations. The two main questions were: 'What are the most important tasks in your job?' and 'How would you describe your role as a deacon/deaconess in the church and in society?' Many of the answers talk about being a bridge-builder: building bridges between the church and local society, between the daily life of the people in the community and the liturgy in the church, between individuals in the community. The article therefore discusses the role of the deacon as one who 'goes between'.

Kari Karsrud Korslien's chapter is called *Diakonia as Action – Some Perspectives on Diaconal Professional Practice*. It discusses *diakonia* as action. On the basis of five characteristics for progressive *diakonia* given by Nordstokke and Collins (2011), the author reflects on how a methodological approach can help enhance personal skills and relevant professionalism in an increasingly complex field of *diakonia.*

Kjell Nordstokke has put together a chapter on *Mapping out and Mobilising Diaconal Assets* in which he explores the term 'asset' as related to diaconal action, and especially to activities of church-based organisations engaged in international development work. 'Assets' are understood as tangible and intangible resources that are activated in diaconal practice and that make a difference in the performance of activities. It is assumed that such assets represent added value in the work of diaconal agencies, that they facilitate local participation and acceptance, and thus contribute to sustainability. The aim of the article is to map such assets and discuss how diaconal agents can mobilise them as part of their professional work.

The last chapter is written by Edwina Ward and Anneliese Schäpers on *Christian Care and Counselling in a Multicultural Context.* This article offers some guidance to prospective pastoral care-givers working in an intercultural environment away from their country of origin. Christian care and cross-cultural counselling in a multicultural society presents us with the need for knowledge of culture and how culture affects what ministry can take place between two people in a counselling context. An intercultural approach to pastoral counselling is proposed which promotes respect for the uniqueness of each individual.

The above presentation of the various contributions affirms the opening statement of the introduction that most of the authors of this book do their research in contexts that are familiar with the concept of *diakonia.* This may not be the case with all its readers, either because the term is largely unknown, or if the related title 'deacon' is used, its use may reflect quite a different understanding.

In the end, it may be claimed that whatever term we choose for designating the social practice of the church is not that important; it is more important 'to walk the walk' than 'to talk the talk'. Even so, terminology matters; it is therefore our hope that the following chapters may contribute to a broader understanding of the concept of *diakonia* and its potential for expressing an important and integral dimension of the church's mission in today's world.

Part 1

Theological Perspectives

Reflections on Core Aspects of Diaconal Theory

Stephanie Dietrich

Introduction

Diakonia is a term which is used frequently and increasingly in the ecumenical world, describing the church's social action and engagement locally, in society and globally. Some traditions, like the European Protestant tradition, have used it frequently, especially during the last 200 years; others, like the Anglican, Orthodox or Roman Catholic traditions are not used to this connotation of *diakonia* and would use other words, like *caritas* in the Roman Catholic tradition, or they associate *diakonia* mostly with the deacon's ministry as a first stage on the way to priesthood as in the Anglican, Roman Catholic and Orthodox traditions, with merely liturgical functions. What does *diakonia* actually mean? Is it about service for each other in mutuality, including empowerment and advocacy work, humble service for people in need, acts of mercy and charity performed by 'good Christian people'?

In this article, I want to discuss basic aspects of diaconal theory. Diaconal practice includes acts of mercy and mutual service in accountability and reciprocity. This article wants to give an example how today's understanding of *diakonia* can embrace different theories on human interaction, shaped by personal engagement to show 'acts of mercy' for the sake of the other, and shaped by fundamental acts of reciprocity and mutual empowerment, communal sharing *and* respect for the individual's autonomy. Methodologically, the article will draw on theological and philosophical resources to highlight core aspects of diaconal theory. Of specific interest will be the principles of autonomy and *Ubuntu*, the discussion of imbalances of power in diaconal acts, empowerment as an important method based on my reflections concerning mutuality and reciprocity in *diakonia*, and a fresh look at the understanding of care in the light of modern feminist approaches.

Paradigm Shift

There has been a fundamental move concerning the basic paradigm of care within different scientific approaches to professional care. There has been a move from post-colonial professional care to autonomy-orientated assistance. Within social work, the focus today is not on offering help, but on partnership and empowerment. Within international aid, one has moved from a main emphasis on offering help to those in need, to a basic understanding of partnership between donors and recipients.

Also within church-based social work (*diakonia*) there has been a profound move in the understanding of what it means to offer and to receive help, referred to as a 'new paradigm of *diakonia*'.[1] The main emphasis today is on mutuality, helping each other because we are a part of the community of human beings called to share with each other. We are not merely 'donors' or merely 'recipients' of help, but, bound together in this community, we are both at the same time – sometimes more as givers, sometimes more as recipients.

The basic call to help other people in need, arising in human beings as a part of their human identity, conscience, religious faith or other moral obligations, is a profound and necessary aspect of human interaction, and should go hand in hand with respect for the other's autonomy and right to decide on their own. Therefore, this article will also focus on and discuss critically the concept of autonomy in relation to diaconal theory. The article will also reflect on the understanding of care, emphasising that care for other people should not only be professionalised and institutionalised, but also be motivated personally and related to the community in which it is embedded.

Autonomy and Interdependency Related to Diaconal Theory

The principle of autonomy is important for the development of diaconal theory today. Autonomy can be described as the capacity of a rational individual to make an informed, un-coerced decision. In moral and political philosophy, autonomy is often used as the basis for determining moral responsibility and accountability for one's actions. Though it has been criticised as focusing too much on the individual and not on the community, and from a feminist perspective as being a merely male concept, the principle of autonomy nevertheless is relevant for the understanding of *diakonia*. Within medical ethics, the principle of autonomy is the central premise of the concept of informed consent and shared decision-making. Within the concept of *diakonia*, everybody's right to autonomy is based on the fundamental understanding of human dignity. Created in the image and likeness of God, everybody is given a uniqueness and value which forms the basis for acknowledging autonomy from a Christian ethical perspective. Based on the principle of autonomy, the receivers of help or care in a diaconal setting are not merely *objects* of diaconal service, but always also *subjects* of their own life. Thus, every kind of service offered to another person should take into account that this person has a basic right to autonomy. Even if a person needing help has reduced capacities to take

[1] Kjell Nordstokke, *Liberating Diakonia* (Trondheim: Tapir Akademisk Forlag, 2011), 46.

care of their own autonomy actively, the one who is offering help needs to be aware of this basic demand and right to autonomy.

The principle of respect for everybody's autonomy plays a prominent role in the field of ethics, especially medical ethics. Within the discussion on death-hastening decisions, it is one of the main arguments used when it comes to underline every individual's right to decide on their own life and death. "The notion of autonomy as self-determination and the possibility to pursue one's aspirations, interests and preferences, is more uniformly used to back up justification of euthanasia as a morally acceptable practice."[2] Also within the field of *diakonia* as Christian social service, the principle of respect for everybody's autonomy plays an important role. This also indicates a move from paternalistic patterns of Christian social service towards the understanding that such service should *assist* the individual in living out their autonomy.

Nevertheless, there has been an ongoing discussion within different sciences on negative implications, which this principle of autonomy may have. Some of the critical arguments refer to the discussion on autonomy as a negative freedom, a freedom from moral obligations and dependencies which somehow may lead into a narrow understanding of the individual person. The question might be whether human interaction based on the principle of every individual's autonomy can take sufficiently into account the fact that every human being depends on others, and that this dependency may have both negative and positive consequences.

In particular, modern feminist theologians have argued for the need to relate autonomy and interdependency in inter-human relationships. Decisions on life and death, but also every human interaction, always include an aspect of *interdependence*. Autonomy and self-determination stand side-by-side with dependency on 'the other' as constitutive elements of human existence.[3] Thus,

---

[2] *A time to live, and a time to die. An Aid to Orientation of the CPCE Council on Death-hastening Decisions and Caring for the Dying.* Community of Protestant Churches in Europe (CPCE) (Vienna, 2012), 71.

[3] The concept of 'the Other' has been an important theme within the history of philosophy and until today. Prominent exponents exploring the concept were philosophers like Levinas, Derrida and Kierkegaard. Ethically, for Levinas, 'the Other' is superior or prior to the self; the mere presence of the Other makes demands before one can respond by helping them or ignoring them. The Danish philosopher Søren Kierkegaard related the concept of the other as the concept of 'you' and 'I' to the philosophy of love: "There are a you and an I, and there is no mine and yours! For without a you and an I, there is no love, and with mine and yours there is no love but 'mine' and 'yours'. These possessive pronouns are, of course, formed from a 'you' and an 'I' and as a consequence seem obliged to be present wherever there are a you and an I. This is indeed the case everywhere, but not in love, which is a revolution from the ground up. The more profound the revolution, the more completely the distinction 'mine and yours' disappears, and the more perfect is the love." *Works of Love: Kierkegaard's Writings,* Vol. 16, trans. Howard V. and Edna H. Hong (Princeton University Press,

autonomy should be understood as relational self-determination or autonomy in dependency. As human beings, everybody is dependent on other human beings. Everybody's life is to some degree interwoven with other peoples' lives and also accommodates social arrangements such as family, friendship, or other human relationships. Human life involves a dialectic of dependence and independence, and this does not stand in contradiction to the basic claim for respect for everybody's autonomy. Thus, interdependency is a positive aspect of human identity. Everybody depends on other human beings.

For *diakonia* as social service, this includes the basic realisation that all those involved in the act of *diakonia* are agencies in interdependency, and not merely subjects or objects or helpers or recipients of help. "Perpetuating narcissistic illusions of independence – including non-interference – carries tremendous moral risks for a culture that idolises independence and autonomy in every sphere of life, as ours does."[4]

For diaconal practice, these reflections might have several implications: those who are providing help or offering diaconal service should do so in a way of respecting the autonomy and integrity of the other, and avoid creating relationships shaped by uneven dependencies. This principle is relevant both at an interpersonal level, for instance, when providing financial support to individuals, and at a more structural level, as in international aid, where longstanding relationships of dependency should be avoided. Thus, diaconal service should focus on reducing dependencies, supporting independence, and activating the other person's own resources to cope on their own in the long run. Autonomy and interdependence are not opposites, but are related to each other dialectically and complementarily. It belongs to the basic structure of human life both to rely on help from other people and at the same time to be able to help others. This is especially a reminder to the 'professional helpers', who often do not see themselves as mutually dependent and thereby risk paternalising the other person.

Based on this emphasis on everybody's interdependency, diaconal work should always keep in mind the importance and necessity of supporting people through their communities and networks and families, being aware of the power which lies in the personal relationships everybody is involved in and bound into.

Johannes Nissen argues along the same line, when saying: "The basic ontology of human existence is interdependency. The ethical demand springs from this interdependency, requiring human beings to take care of others

---

1998), 266. The concept of 'You' and 'I' is developed as the core principle of Martin Buber's philosophy. *Ich-Du* ('I-Thou' or 'I-You') is a relationship that stresses the mutual, holistic existence of two beings. In Buber's philosophy, it forms the ground for all inter-human interaction. Martin Buber: *I and Thou.* Trans. (1937) Ronald Gregor Smith (Edinburgh, T&T Clark), 1923.

[4] Harry R. Moody, 'The Cost of Autonomy, the Prize of Paternalization', in R. Disch et al (eds), *Dignity and Old Age* (New York), 111-27, 121.

without taking responsibility for them … Interdependency means that every one of us holds some of the life of the other in our hand."[5]

The Principle of *Ubuntu*

Autonomy is not necessarily a merely individualistic principle. Different definitions of autonomy place the individual in a social context. The principle of 'relational autonomy' defines a person through their relationships with others.[6] The principle of 'supported autonomy'[7] suggests that in specific circumstances it may be necessary to temporarily compromise the autonomy of the person in the short term in order to preserve their autonomy in the long term. Nevertheless, the demand for respecting the other's autonomy is present even if the individual person cannot make an explicit claim for her autonomy by herself.

From a diaconal point of view, the principle of autonomy should be respected and at the same time also reflected on critically. Historically, autonomy is a typical western philosophical principle, emphasising the individual's rights and demands embedded in Kantian philosophy.

Other traditions, like the African philosophy of *Ubuntu*, which is closely linked with South Africa's modern history, would emphasise much more the community dimension of social interaction. The word comes from African languages and means that a person is only a person in relationship with others.

According to Michael Onyebuchi Eze, the core of *Ubuntu* can best be summarised as follows:

> 'A person is a person through other people' strikes an affirmation of one's humanity through recognition of an 'other' in his or her uniqueness and difference. It is a demand for a creative inter-subjective formation in which the

[5] Johannes Nissen, 'Towards a transformation of power: New Testament perspectives on diaconia and empowerment', in *Diaconia. Journal for the Study of Christian Social Practice,* 3:1, 2012 (Göttingen: Vandenhoeck & Ruprecht), 26-43.

[6] See Mackenzie, Catriona and Stoljar, Natalie (eds), *Relational Autonomy: Feminist Perspectives on Autonomy, Agency, and the Social Self* (OUP, USA, 1999). This anthology includes a number of articles exploring the social and relational dimensions of individual autonomy, drawing on feminist critiques of autonomy to challenge and enrich contemporary philosophical debates about agency, identity and moral responsibility.

[7] Richard Bouwmeester, Wilmar Harpe and Diana Polhuis, 'Supported autonomy', in *The Journal of Cognitive Rehabilitation*, Fall 2010, 4-10. "Supported autonomy means that there is no longer a patient but an autonomous person who is being supported in functioning within society. The term 'supported autonomy' is a dialectic term because it expresses someone's dependence as well as his or her independence. In supported autonomy a client is supported in such a way that he or she can function as autonomously as possible … Supported autonomy is a central term in all sorts of care and assistance" (5).

> 'other' becomes a mirror (but only a mirror) for my subjectivity. This idealism suggests to us that humanity is not embedded in my person solely as an individual; my humanity is co-substantively bestowed upon the other and me. Humanity is a quality we owe to each other. We create each other and need to sustain this otherness creation. And if we belong to each other, we participate in our creations: we are because you are, and since you are, definitely I am. The 'I am' is not a rigid subject, but a dynamic self-constitution dependent on this otherness creation of relation and distance.[8]

The concept of *Ubuntu* has become well known all over the world, not least due to its use by Archbishop Desmond Tutu, whose identification with *Ubuntu* has given rise to the idea of '*Ubuntu* theology' – where ethical responsibility comes with a shared identity. If someone is hungry, the *Ubuntu* response is that we're all collectively responsible. There is a spiritual as well as practical dimension to this. This includes also the idea that all humans are part of a long chain of human experience, linking them with previous and future generations.

Undoubtedly, modern diaconal theories would emphasise the importance of a community-based approach, supporting very much the idea that no one is a mere recipient or a mere donor of services, but that we are all intertwined as human beings with the same value and dignity. In the document from the Lutheran World Federation called *Serving the Whole Person*, it is underlined that this community aspect, which is core to the *Ubuntu* principle, is of the utmost importance for an adequate understanding of *diakonia*: "The mutual sharing inherent in the communion of the church can transform the unjust power relationships that often are present in diaconal work, such as between 'wealthy givers' and 'poor recipients.' In *diakonia*, those served and those serving are both transformed."[9]

The principle of *Ubuntu* might also contribute to the critique of a narrow interpretation of the principle of autonomy. Nevertheless, one might question whether the *Ubuntu* principle – as opposed to the principle of autonomy – also cements characterisations and stereotypes about what is perceived to be an African culture on the one hand, or a western culture on the other. As described above, the principle of autonomy can and should also be developed through approaches like the feminist philosophy of relational autonomy, which do not necessarily stand in contradiction to a so-called '*Ubuntu* model'. It should also be considered how far 'romantic' descriptions of cultures are in accordance

---

[8] Michael Onyebuchi Eze, *Intellectual History in Contemporary South Africa* (Palgrave Macmillan, 2010, 190-91). For a general description of *Ubuntu*, see Willem H.J. de Liefde, *Ubuntu: in der Gemeinschaft Lösungen finden und Entscheidungen treffen* (Signum, 2006) (own tranlsation: "Ubuntu: finding common solutions and decisions").

[9] Kjell Nordstokke (ed – in collaboration with Frederick Schlagenhaft), *Serving the Whole Person. The Practice and Understanding of Diakonia within the Lutheran Communion* (Minneapolis, MN: Lutheran University Press, 2009), 16.

with the complexities of the different worlds we are living in, in both the global South and the global North.

Thus, the philosophical principles of autonomy, and methods developed within the field of social work, which are based on these principles, and more contextual approaches like the *Ubuntu* principle, offer an important contribution to the development of diaconal theory and methodology, together with more communal approaches.

Imbalance of Power in *Diakonia*

Without any doubt, all diaconal acts include aspects of power. Whenever somebody performs any kind of service, and somebody receives a service, there is an imbalance in power. This imbalance in power is not negative in itself, as long as there is a profound consciousness about it on behalf of the diaconal agencies, and as long as one reflects critically on it. Roy Kearsley asks in his book *Church, Community and Power* for a church culture which is self-critical and develops a huge sensitivity to power structures in itself. He also relates a critical perspective on power asymmetries in the church to the concept of empowerment, which will be discussed later in this article:

> Theological resources here especially value desires to empower and enable others as Jesus did under his 'power' to transform for good. With more attention to this, true power could genuinely pervade the community, even in its characters as sociological. Everyone on the way to the *koinonia* would be empowered to play their part in community decision-making and action, and ready to realise power in the strength of the shared Spirit of power.[10]

The goal for diaconal action is not to elude power relationships, but to develop awareness about imbalances, not least in diaconal actions shaped by the spirit of neighbourly love and charity. Philosophical attempts to promote that as the ultimate goal should be a total balance of power in an ideal relationship between human people representing a more theoretical model than life experience can provide. Thus, when the philosopher Jürgen Habermas promotes a 'power-balanced dialogue',[11] based on symmetrical and dialogical social relationships, this possibly does not take sufficiently into account the fact that imbalances of power belong to life's realities and are not in themselves to

---

[10] Roy Kearsley, *Church, Community and Power* (Cardiff University, and Farnham, UK: Ashgate, 2008), 225.

[11] "The structure of the ideal speech situation (which means that the discourse is) immunised against repression and inequality in a special way … The structures of a ritualised competition for the better arguments… The structures that determine the construction of individual arguments and their interrelations", *Theory of Communicative Action – Volume One: Reason and the Rationalization of Society*. Trans. Thomas A. McCarthy (Boston, MA: Beacon Press, 1984 [first published in 1981]), 25.

be condemned, but should rather be handled in an ethically accountable way. The question of power balance and imbalance, symmetry and asymmetry in human relational acts, has also been discussed in different theological studies. The New Testament scholar Gerd Theissen underlined: "Helping is always an asymmetric relation. The helper has more power than the one that needs help, otherwise he couldn't help."[12] The problem in the relationship is not the imbalance of power as such, but the attitude towards it, and the way power can be misused as a means of disregard of the other's autonomy. Power cannot be reduced to its negative implications of misuse of forces or to its potential to 'em-power' people, but must be recognised in its ambivalence, with the possibilities and dangers of misuse. In particular, workers within the field of *diakonia*, where a certain relationship with a godly authority as the sending power is presupposed for the action, should be careful concerning the use and misuse of power. Using power when proclaiming that it is God's will to use this power may easily lead to misuse of power and suppression, covered by a mantle of piety.

The use of power in diaconal actions is inevitable. Nevertheless, it is not power over somebody, as dominion, but power which is supposed to improve the possibilities of governing the lives of those who are served on their own. The misuse of power, often reflected in paternalistic practices of professional care, is well known in the history of *diakonia*, as in professional development practices towards the so-called 'third world countries' or in the practice of several diaconal institutions in Central Europe during the 20th century.

As indicated earlier in this article, there has been a paradigm change in different areas of social care, moving from a paternalistic connotation of care, towards an understanding which focuses on care as assistance to achieve autonomy. Within the German-speaking discourse on the understanding of *diakonia*, Johannes Degen is one of the scholars who have argued vehemently for a self-critical dealing with questions of power balance within *diakonia*. He asks for a professional practice which is conscious about an ethos of care that acts *together* with the person, and not only acts for or on behalf of another person.[13] Degen argues: "The former diaconal ethos of care has come to an end. The former 'for' needs to be transformed to a 'together-with' culture in care relationships. A new conception of diaconal care needs to understand itself as a means of assistance towards a self-governed life ..."[14] This concept of being an

---

[12] 'Die Bibel diakonisch lesen: Die Legitimitätskrise des Helfens und der barmherzige Samariter', in V. Herrmann and M. Horstmann (eds), *Studienbuch Diakonik, Bd.1: biblische, historische und theologische Zugänge zur Diakonie* (Neukirchen-Vluyn (2.Aufl.), 88-116, 90 (own translation: 'Reading the Bible in a diaconal perspective: the crisis of legitimacy in professional care and the Good Samaritan').

[13] Johannes Degen, *Freiheit und Profil. Wandlungen der Hilfekultur – Plädoyer für eine zukunfstfähige Diakonie* (Gütersloh: Leiten-Lenken-Gestalten. Theologie und Ökonomie, Bd.13, 2003), 20.

[14] Degen, *Freiheit und Profil*, 37 (own translation).

assistant also brings a different perspective to the understanding of professional help. Professional care-givers are assisting and supporting others, helping them to fulfil their projects. Helping the other means assisting the other and walking together with them in order to help them to manage their own life. Such a perspective has also an impact on the understanding of professionalism; it is not the professional which has the final answer on what should be the right choice for an individual, but the professional can assist the individual in finding her own way. Interestingly enough, this is very much in accordance with a basic principle in New Testament theology based on Jesus' encounter with people in situations of need.

Diakonia as Empowerment

Within a modern ecumenical understanding of *diakonia*, as presented by the Lutheran World Federation's study document *Diakonia in Context*,[15] empowerment has become a core aspect of diaconal theory and practice: "As a theological concept, empowerment refers to the biblical understanding of creation that every human being is created in the image of God, with capacities and abilities, independent of their apparent social situation."[16]

Methods of empowerment are widely used within all areas of social science. There are numerous studies on empowerment theories and practices from the field of social work which are relevant also within the context of Christian social work. Notwithstanding the many different approaches and theories on empowerment, all theories are influenced by specific values and anthropologies which shape ita understanding. Concerning empowerment as a key concept within *diakonia*, its understanding should be developed within the concepts of Christian anthropology. As outlined above, the concepts of dignity, autonomy, communality and interdependency also play a profound role for the understanding of the theory and practice of empowerment within *diakonia* as Christian social service.

Empowerment may be defined as a multi-dimensional social process that helps people gain control of various aspects of their lives and participate in the community with dignity. It is a process that fosters power in people for use in their own lives, their communities and in their society, by acting on issues they define as important. J. Rappaport, one of the most prolific authors in the field of empowerment, offers a definition of the term: "(Empowerment) suggests a sense of control over one's life in personality, cognition, and motivation. It expresses itself at the level of feelings, at the level of ideas about self worth, at the level of being able to make a difference in the world around us … We all have it as a potential."[17]

---

[15] LWF, *Diakonia in Context.*

[16] LWF, *Diakonia in Context*, 45.

[17] Julian Rappaport, *The power of empowerment language*, Social Policy 16 (2), 1985,

D. Solomon defines empowerment as –

> a process whereby the social worker engages in a set of activities with the client … that aim to reduce the powerlessness that has been created by negative valuations based on membership in a stigmatised group. It involves identification of the power blocks that contribute to the problem as well as the development and implementation of specific strategies aimed at either the reduction of the effects from indirect power blocks or the reduction of the operations of direct power blocks.[18]

Rappaport's concept of empowerment "conveys both a psychological sense of personal control or influence and a concern with actual social influence, political power and legal rights".[19] Summarising different strands within the research on empowerment theories and practice, empowerment is described as relevant at three levels: at the personal level, where empowerment is the experience of gaining increasing control and influence in daily life and community participation;[20] at the small group level, where empowerment involves the shared experience, analysis and influence of groups on their own efforts; and at the community level. The concept of community empowerment is especially relevant within international work and development work. In 2013, the WHO defined community empowerment in the following way:

> Community empowerment refers to the process of enabling communities to increase control over their lives … 'Empowerment' refers to the process by which people gain control over the factors and decisions that shape their lives. It is the process by which they increase their assets and attributes and build capacities to gain access, partners, networks and/or a voice, in order to gain control … It assumes that people are their own assets, and the role of the external agent is to catalyse, facilitate or 'accompany' the community in acquiring power. Community empowerment, therefore, is more than the involvement, participation or engagement of communities. It implies community ownership and action that explicitly aims at social and political change. Community empowerment is a process of renegotiating power in order to gain more control … Community empowerment necessarily addresses the social, cultural, political and economic

---

15-21.

[18] B. Solomon, *Black Empowerment: Social Work in Oppressed Communities* (New York, 1976).

[19] Rappaport, 'Terms of empowerment/exemplars of prevention: Toward a theory for community psychology', in *American Journal of Community Psychology* (1987), 15 (2), 121-48, 121.

[20] Cf Keiffer, C., 'Citizen empowerment: A developmental perspective', in *Prevention in Human Services* (1984), 3 (16), 9-35.

determinants that underpin health, and seeks to build partnerships with other sectors in finding solutions.[21]

Johannes Nissen highlights the ambiguity of the concept of empowerment in relation to its use within the field of *diakonia*. He uses New Testament texts to interpret and reinterpret the concept, emphasising that the notion of power is a principal key to an appropriate use of the concept of empowerment within the diaconal field of work. Nissen emphasises that *diakonia* should develop power concepts "where the sharing with others ... makes the other person more autonomous in the centre of both practice and theory".[22] He emphasises that power within *diakonia* should not be power *over*, but power *to*, *with* and *within*, including a reversal of the roles of givers and receivers: "The aim of any form of help should be that the power is shared with the other person so that this person might have the experience of being more autonomous. In other words, a power that helps must be a liberating power."[23]

Kjell Nordstokke develops this concept of empowerment as a diaconal approach further through a description of its use in ecumenical contexts and documents. He puts specific emphasis on the pneumatological reflection on *diakonia* as empowering practice.[24] In his article, specific attention is given to the fact that empowerment should be seen as a process of mutual transformation which emerges from within and from below. Thus, processes of empowerment also include and require a shift of power. According to Nordstokke, empowerment has "a God-given goal (*telos*) of energising people to participate in God's project and realising God's good intention for creation and human society: of mutual love and care, and of promoting human dignity and justice".[25]

Empowerment theories are highly relevant for the concept of *diakonia* because they bring together the basic understanding of everyone's dignity and the emphasis on diaconal acts as a means of assisting the other to help herself without patronising her. They can contribute to improving the diaconal agencies' competencies in helping other people in a way that helps them to use their own power. Empowerment theories are based on a fundamental respect for the capacities and resources of all human beings which also serve as a basic principle within *diakonia*. Even though *diakonia*, in the same way as social work and health care, often takes place in asymmetric relationships of help, including a gap of power, empowerment theories are helpful in reminding the

[21] World Health Organization, Track 1: *Community empowerment*: www.who.int/healthpromotion/conferences/7gchp/track1/en/ (28 March 2014).

[22] Nissen, 'Towards a transformation of power', 26.

[23] Nissen, 'Towards a transformation of power', 42.

[24] Kjell Nordstokke, 'Empowerment in the perspective of ecumenical diakonia', in *Diaconia. Journal for the Study of Christian Social Practice,* Vol. 4, 2013 (Göttingen: Vandenhoeck & Ruprecht), 185-95.

[25] Nordstokke, 'Empowerment', 194.

agencies to recognise this gap of power and encouraging them to contribute to a gain of power, i.e. empowerment, of the 'receiver' of diaconal service. All diaconal action should therefore orientate itself towards the concept of 'help to self-help'.

Modern Theories of Care – Inspired by Feminist Philosophy

Based on interdisciplinary reflections on autonomy, empowerment and communality related to the theory of *diakonia*, the paradigm shift from paternalistic charity to autonomy-orientated care as empowerment should be warmly welcomed, especially within the field of church-based professional care. This contributes to an empowerment of the care-givers to become actors, and not merely objects, within their lives.

Nevertheless, the aspect of personal engagement for the other person who is suffering or needs help and assistance should not be neglected when discussing the understanding of *diakonia* today. Charity, as a result of personal concern for the other person who needs help, must not be rejected, but redefined thoroughly.

In the 1980s, the theory of care became relevant when Carol Gilligan[26] emphasised that women tend to think and speak in a different way from men when they confront ethical dilemmas. This theory also suggests the feminine ethic of care and the masculine ethic of justice. Though Gilligan's theories have been highly discussed and criticised, not least concerning gender stereotypes, her emphasis on care as a relevant concept within social practice has been most important for the development of ethical approaches during the last thirty years. The concept of care emphasises that every human being is intertwined in relationships with other human beings, and that we are not merely autonomous individuals. Feminist philosophers have also emphasised that interactions of care between human beings need to bring together cognitive aspects and emotional aspects, like empathy, compassion, sympathy and goodwill. The new concept of care, as developed by feminist philosophers, forms an important addition to an emphasis within professional care on rationality and professionalism, by saying that basic inter-human care and solicitude at eye-level should stand side-by-side within the field of professional care. The concept of care does not only become relevant within the field of professional care, but it becomes relevant wherever human people depend on each other and each other's help and service. In principle, all human beings depend on each other and on each other's help, sometimes more, sometimes less. Thus, care-relationality and mutual interdependency form the basic condition of human life.

---

[26] Carol Gilligan, *In a Different Voice. Psychological Theory and Women's Development* (Harvard University Press, 1982).

The German philosopher Elisabeth Conradi describes the development of different feminist philosophical approaches towards the concept of care since Carol Gilligan's decisive publication in the 1980s.[27] This includes a profound critique of the traditional deontological ethical approaches, like John Rawls' *A Theory of Justice*.[28] Conradi emphasises two aspects of the concept of care: first, the interrelatedness of human beings, and secondly, the concrete action of care. Conradi proposes, as an alternative to the deontological concept of respect, a concept of carefulness (*Achtsamkeit*), which is based on an understanding that human beings are basically reliant on each other and thus called to take care of each other. This carefulness is an act of mutuality and reciprocity; at the same time it is a duty and a gift. Conradi underlines that this principle of carefulness is based on the understanding that all human beings rely and depend on each other.[29]

Thus, the feminist ethicists have made an important contribution to the understanding of care interpreted as an act of mutuality, in communality. Their approach can also be related to the concepts and theories of *diakonia* concerning these issues.

A basic understanding of care as gift and mutuality is emphasised in Anika Christina Albert's interdisciplinary study *Helfen als Gabe und Gegenseitigkeit*.[30] Albert develops an understanding of *diakonia* as care, understood as an act of relational communication (*Beziehungsgeschehen*). Theologically, according to Albert, the doctrine on justification helps to overcome inter-human asymmetries since it emphasises that all human beings are receivers and donors at the same time.[31] Albert's study gives an example of how diaconal research is based on an interdisciplinary discourse, including both philosophical and theological approaches, when analyzing the concept of care as gift and mutuality. Albert concludes by referring to the fundamental human condition of being receivers. All human action is, in this perspective, a reply to the given-ness of life. God's call into life and God's gift of grace to mankind thus forms the final background for mankind's answer to God, implying service in mutuality and love. According to Albert, the doctrine of justification leads towards an emancipation from false authorities, and gives a

---

[27] Elisabeth Conradi, *Take Care. Grundlagen einer Ethik der Achtsamkeit* (Frankfurt/New York: Campus Verlag, 2001).

[28] John Rawls, *A Theory of Justice* (Belknap Press, 1999).

[29] Conradi, *Take Care*, 238-39.

[30] Anika Christina Albert, *Helfen als Gabe und Gegenseitigkeit. Perspektiven einer Theologie des Helfens im interdisziplinären Diskurs.* Veröffentlichungen des Diakoniewissenschaftlichen Institut Band 42 (Heidelberg: Universitätsverlag Winter, 2010).

[31] Albert, *Helfen als Gabe*, 372: "As elaborated on above, the meaning of the doctrine of justification leads towards the emancipation from false authorities … leads towards authenticity and enables people to act" (own translation: "Care as Gift and Mutuality: Perspectives of a Theology of Care in an Interdisciplinary Discourse").

new authenticity and growth in the capacity to act in the world. Helping each other in this sense is not only giving, but a 'replying giving' (*ein antwortendes Geben*).[32]

Concluding Remarks

In this article I have tried to explore the theory of *diakonia* in the light of different philosophical and theological approaches. It became obvious that *diakonia* cannot be described by merely one concept, but gains through including a multidimensional perspective. Different approaches to the understanding of *diakonia* contribute to enrich its understanding. *Diakonia* includes acts of mercy and mutual service in accountability and reciprocity. Thus, the article has contributed to underline why today's understanding of *diakonia* should embrace different aspects of human interaction, both shaped by personal engagement to show 'acts of mercy' for the sake of the other, and shaped by fundamental acts of reciprocity and mutual empowerment, communal sharing and respect for the individual's autonomy.

Bibliography

A time to live, and a time to die. An Aid to Orientation of the CPCE Council on Death-hastening Decisions and Caring for the Dying (Community of Protestant Churches in Europe (CPCE), Vienna, 2012).

Bouwmeester, Richard, Wilmar Harpe and Diana Polhuis, 'Supported autonomy', in *The Journal of Cognitive Rehabilitation*, Fall 2010, 4-10.

Buber, Martin, *I and Thou,* trans. (1937) Ronald Gregor Smith (Edinburgh: T&T Clark), 1923.

Conradi, Elisabeth, *Take Care. Grundlagen einer Ethik der Achtsamkeit* (Frankfurt/New York: Campus Verlag, 2001)

Degen, Johannes, *Freiheit und Profil. Wandlungen der Hilfekultur – Plädoyer für eine zukunfstfähige Diakonie* (Gütersloh: Leiten-Lenken-Gestalten. Theologie und Ökonomie, Bd.13, 2003), 20.

Eze, Michael Onyebuchi, *Intellectual History in Contemporary South Africa* (Palgrave Macmillan, 2010).

Gilligan, Carol, *In a different voice. Psychological theory and women's development* (Harvard University Press, 1982).

Habermas, Jürgen, *Theory of Communicative Action, Volume One: Reason and the Rationalization of Society,* trans. Thomas A. McCarthy (Boston, MA: Beacon Press, 1984) (first published in German in 1981).

Kearsley, Roy, *Church, Community and Power* (Cardiff University, and Farnham, UK: Ashgate, 2008).

Keiffer, C., 'Citizen empowerment: A developmental perspective', in *Prevention in Human Services* (1984), 3 (16), 9-35.

Kierkegaard, Søren, *Works of Love: Kierkegaard's Writings, Vol. 16*, trans. Howard V. and Edna H. Hong (Princeton University Press, 1998).

[32] Albert, *Helfen als Gabe*, 372.

Lutheran World Federation, *Diakonia in Context: Transformation, Reconciliation, Empowerment. An LWF Contribution to the Understanding and Practice of Diakonia* (Geneva: LWF, 2009).

Mackenzie, Catriona, and Natalie Stoljar (eds), *Relational Autonomy: Feminist Perspectives on Autonomy, Agency, and the Social Self* (OUP, USA, 1999).

Moody, Harry R., 'The Cost of Autonomy, the Prize of Paternalization', in R. Disch et al (eds), *Dignity and Old Age* (New York), 111-27, 121.

Nissen, Johannes, 'Towards a transformation of power: New Testament perspectives on diaconia and empowerment', in *Diaconia. Journal for the Study of Christian Social Practice,* 3:1, 2012 (Göttingen: Vandenhoeck & Ruprecht), 26-43.

Nordstokke, Kjell, 'Empowerment in the perspective of ecumenical *diakonia*', in *Diaconia. Journal for the Study of Christian Social Practice,* Volume 4, 2013 (Göttingen: Vandenhoeck & Ruprecht), 185-95.

Nordstokke, Kjell, *Liberating Diakonia* (Trondheim: Tapir Akademisk Forlag, 2011).

Nordstokke, Kjell (ed), *Serving the Whole Person. The Practice and Understanding of Diakonia within the Lutheran Communion.* LWF Documentation 54/2009 (Minneapolis, MN: Lutheran University Press, 2009).

Rappaport, Julian, *The power of empowerment language,* Social Policy 16 (2), 1985, 15-21.

Rappaport, Julian, 'Terms of empowerment/exemplars of prevention: Toward a theory for community psychology', in *American Journal of Community Psychology* (1987), 15(2), 121-48, 121.

Solomon, B., *Black Empowerment: Social Work in Oppressed Communities* (New York, 1976).

Theissen, Gerd, 'Die Bibel diakonisch lesen: Die Legitimitätskrise des Helfens und der barmherzige Samariter', in Herrmann V. and Horstmann, M. (eds), *Studienbuch Diakonik, Bd. 1: biblische, historische und theologische Zugänge zur Diakonie* (Neukirchen-Vluyn – 2.Aufl.), 88-116, 90.

World Health Organization, Track 1: *Community empowerment,* www.who.int/healthpromotion/conferences/7gchp/track1/en/ (28 March 2014).

'Mercy and Truth Are Met Together; Righteousness and Peace Have Kissed Each Other' (Psalm 85:10): Biblical and Systematic Theological Perspectives on Diakonia as Advocacy and Fight for Justice

Stephanie Dietrich

Introduction

How can the *church*[1] relate to the world? Is it a part of the world and of our societies, or is it opposed to the world as a somehow 'heavenly space' or alternative space on earth? How should *Christians* relate to the world and to their societies? Is it the church's or the Christian's task to be involved in their societies, perhaps even involved in advocacy work and the fight for justice, or should Christians concentrate on sharing the Gospel and leave the social and political engagement to politicians and other professional people who have dedicated their work to that specific task?

There is no easy answer to these questions. Different theological traditions and contexts give different answers. The answers often rely on different contexts and historical circumstances as well as profound theological choices. Nevertheless, when studying diaconal literature from past decades, one can see that there is an increasing focus on the church's duty to engage in the world, often called *diakonia* as fight for justice, or *prophetic diakonia.*[2] This is not seen in contradiction with the church's self-understanding as being a "congregation of saints, in which the Gospel is rightly taught and the sacraments are rightly administered" (Confessio Augustana VII), but as an important and non-negotiable aspect of the church's identity.

In my opinion, theology and ecclesiology play a core role for the understanding of *diakonia* and should neither be excluded nor monopolised in

---

[1] In this article, I use the term 'church' in the singular, well knowing that the Christian church appears in a number of different shapes and bodies and confessional identities all around the world. 'Church' does not therefore stand only for my own church, the Church of Norway, but for the Church as it becomes visible and concrete in different contexts.

[2] Cf. Böttcher (ed), *Prophetic Diakonia: 'For the Healing of the World'*. Report Johannesburg: South Africa (Geneva: Lutheran World Federation, November 2002).

diaconal studies. Thus, in this article the focus will be on biblical and systematic theological aspects of *diakonia* as I try to come to terms with the understanding of 'prophetic *diakonia*'.

Here, I want to explore basic aspects of biblical and systematic theology, which are relevant for the understanding of *diakonia*. There will be a specific emphasis on *diakonia* related to advocacy and the fight for justice, the so-called 'prophetic *diakonia*', and its biblical foundation.

> Rather than merely rendering humble service to the poor, *diakonia* needs to be viewed and enacted within the context of Jubilee and Sabbath dynamic of relief and social intervention which aims at restoring the dignity of human beings. It involves taking a stand and the willingness to take risks. It touches and engages us personally and requires a spirituality that includes confession of our own culpability and the acknowledgement that we are not heroes or saviours of the poor.[3]

Diakonia, Ecclesiology and Multidiciplinarity

Why should we use *diakonia* as a core term for describing the church's task to get involved in 'worldly struggles'? As a theologian, I am concerned that *diakonia* is not just a mere practice or a concern of 'Practical Theology'; *diakonia* is both about the theory *and* practice of Christian social service in our societies and in the world, and it is about ecclesiology. The theory of *diakonia*, what can be called 'science of *diakonia*', is not merely a practical study about 'How to do it', but interrelates with different theories and disciplines. The science of *diakonia* is in its essence interdisciplinary. It includes different methodological approaches, such as theological, ethical, philosophical and legal disciplines, etc. This multidisciplinary identity of *diakonia*, and thus ability to relate theory and practice, makes the concept extraordinarily useful in the encounter between church and world. Because the science of *diakonia* includes both a profound analysis of the context, theoretical multidisciplinary reflections and competencies on professional practice, it is notably useful when dealing with the church's responsibilities in and towards the world.

Diakonia is not an easy term to define. As Psalm 85:10 says: "Mercy and truth are met together; righteousness and peace have kissed each other." *Diakonia* is about mercy – God's mercy for mankind and mankind's mercy for one another; it includes the call to stand up for justice and truth in society, to advocate the rights of the poor and underprivileged, and to work for peace in the world. *Diakonia* is a multidimensional term and cannot therefore be placed in an easily understood and one-dimensional category.

---

[3] Molefe Tsele, 'Prophetic Task of the Church: A Listener's Response', in Böttcher (ed), *Prophetic diakonia*, 53.

Many scholars differentiate between political *diakonia* and prophetic *diakonia*, highlighting both the differences and the close connection between the two concepts.[4] Nordstokke emphasises that they should be differentiated, pointing out that political *diakonia* "must be conscious of its socio-political role and be ready to speak out when it's necessary",[5] while prophetic *diakonia* has a somehow more theological and biblical emphasis, since prophecy is a theological term indicating that *diakonia* belongs to God's mission. "It relates to the intrinsic theological nature of *diakonia*, affirming the prophetic task as a part of the mandate and authority that God has given the church and its *diakonia*."[6]

Biblical Background and Old Testament Tradition

Without attempting to cover fully the broad spectrum of biblical theology of *diakonia*, it is important to highlight some *core aspects of biblical theology*, which are basic for the understanding of *diakonia* in the wide spectre of inter-human interaction of care and fight for justice.

We find in the *Old Testament* some profound principles concerning the relationship between God and mankind, and between human beings, which should be highlighted.

The theology of creation and humankind's inherent dignity

The theology of creation clearly teaches that every human being is created in the image and likeness of God and thus has an intrinsic dignity, which forms the basis for humankind's call to treat one another as human beings, with the same dignity, value and right for protection and a meaningful life as oneself. Thus, anthropology, which is based on this basic principle, forms the background for our emphasis on mutuality and respect as a diaconal paradigm. Everybody is created by God, with the same value and dignity. This dignity is neither based on humankind's abilities and resemblance, nor on its own merits and capacities. It is based and founded on the basic relationship between God the creator and all human beings and it is given as a gift, not a merit. God's power to call into life marks the centre of human dignity. When God calls humankind into being and into community and relationship with God himself and one another, God at the same time calls us into responsibility for each other, and care for one another. Nobody is worthless in God's eyes; therefore, nobody should be worthless in humankind's eyes. Not respecting this basic

---

[4] See Nordstokke, *Liberating Diakonia*, 51; Kjetil Fretheim, 'Dimensions of diakonia: the public, political and prophetic', in *Diaconia* Vol.4, 2013, 67-80.

[4] *A Moment of Truth. A word of faith, hope, and love from the heart of Palestinian suffering* (Kairos Palestine 2009), 78.

[5] See Nordstokke, *Liberating diakonia*, 51.

[6] Nordstokke, *Liberating diakonia*, 51.

principle of equal value of all human beings, may inevitably lead into degrading other human beings, discrimination or racism. In many contexts, specific concern needs to be given to the life conditions of women, as they suffer discrimination in male-dominated societies and structures of power, and also in Christian churches. Thus, the basic Christian belief that men and women are created equally in the image and likeness of God should force diaconal agencies to fight for gender equality and gender justice.

A basic responsibility for the well-being of other human beings, which could be termed 'diaconal responsibility', finds its foundation in the theology of creation. God's call for stewardship of the whole world includes the call to take care of each other and of the creation. "The Lord God took the man and put him in the Garden of Eden to work it and take care of it" (Genesis 2:15).

The need for companionship and the church for 'the other'

The Old Testament also emphasises the *need for companionship* right from the beginning: "It is not good for the man to be alone" (Genesis 2:18). A clear aspect of reciprocity concerning human relationships based on God's call into life can be outlined in this context. As human beings created in the image and likeness of God, everybody is called to community and mutual care. A Christian understanding of humanity will therefore reject individualism where people feel responsible only for themselves, following the principle 'What's in it for me?' Being called into fellowship means being called into communion and care for each other. This mutual care is to be offered to everybody and is part of the basic condition of being human, irrespective of one's background or religion, gender, age or identity. This implies that Christian acts of *diakonia* should concern everybody, not only those who belong to the Christian community.

Another biblical story, which deserves to be mentioned in this context to underline that human companionship is a godly gift and call, is the story of Cain and Abel (Genesis 4:1-16). Even when Cain had killed his brother Abel, God continually called him and asked him where his brother was. Even a person who was outside God's covenant, who tried to disappear and quit the community, was still called by God to stand responsible for 'the other'.

From the 1950s, many theologians have referred to a term shaped by Dietrich Bonhoeffer, 'Church for Others'.[7] Bonhoeffer emphasised that the church can only be church in the real sense when it is there for other people. The 'other people' are all those who do not belong to the church as an

---

[7] Cf. Ottmar Fuchs, 'Church for Others', in *Concilium: Diakonia. Church for Others,* Norbert Greinacher and Norbert Mette (eds), (Edinburgh: T&T Clark Ltd, 1998), 41-54. Bonhoeffer writes about the 'Church for others' in his famous *Letters and Papers from Prison* (*Widerstand und Ergebung: Briefe und Aufzeichnungen aus der Haft*), Christian Gremmels, Eberhard Bethge, Renate Bethge, Ilse Tödt (eds), (DBW 8, München: Christian Kaiser 1998), 560.

institutional or doctrinal community of faith, especially those who are counted as 'unbelievers, sinners, outsiders' – all those who are suffering. Bonhoeffer himself did not intend to draw a contrast between church and world, rather the opposite.[8] He argued against the Lutheran doctrine of the Two Kingdoms of God. He taught that the doctrine of the Two Kingdoms of God led into a false dichotomy between the church and the world. Bonhoeffer himself, fighting against the Nazi regime and imprisoned, realised the dangers of a theological approach which contributed to the fact that most of the governing church structures at his time chose to accept and co-operate with the totalitarian regime, instead of fighting against it. In his understanding, the church needed to become radically secular and through this emerge as the church in its real sense.

Nevertheless, the way Bonhoeffer's understanding has been used by theologians later on, especially in relation to the social task of the church,[9] might somehow have been misleading. One might ask whether this understanding, in spite of Bonhoeffer's good intentions, has not contributed to creating new dichotomies between those who are 'inside' and those who are 'outside' the church. Due to my ecclesiological approach, based on a biblical concept of mutuality and reciprocity, of community and fellowship, there should not be a conception of 'we, the church', and 'them, the outsiders'; but an ecclesiological approach focusing on a 'we' who embraces everybody and calls everybody into the communion of the church and into fellowship with Jesus Christ. That does not mean that everybody becomes 'anonymous Christian', as in Karl Rahner's understanding, but it means that everybody as created in the image and likeness of God deserves to be respected and supported when needing help.

Bonhoeffer addressed in his ecclesiology his own evangelical church, which he saw as shaped by a bourgeois middle class self-goodness, where 'the other' was mainly an object for charitable goodness in order to comfort one's own conscience. In this way, Bonhoeffer's approach according to its intention might become highly relevant for an understanding of *diakonia* today. Bonhoeffer's ecclesiology and incarnational theology argue vehemently for the church's and every Christian's duty to live in the world, in their specific societies, engaging in them as Christians. The Christian congregation is called to serve the world

---

[8] "The reality of God is not just another idea. Christian faith perceives this in the fact that the reality of God has revealed itself and witnessed to itself in the middle of the real world. In Jesus Christ the reality of God has entered into the reality of this world. (…) From now on we cannot speak rightly of either God or the world without speaking of Jesus Christ. (….) In Christ we are invited to participate in the reality of God and the reality of the world at the same time, the one not without the other. The reality of God is disclosed only as it places me completely into the reality of the world." Dietrich Bonhoeffer, *Ethics*, 54-55.

[9] Internet research (accessed 13 May 2014) linking the term 'Kirche für andere' and 'Diakonie' gave more than 900,000 hits.

and society, whether people are Christian or not. While those who are not baptised or do not belong to the church are certainly not members of the church, they are nevertheless part of the community all human beings belong to, both 'inside' and 'outside' the church, and thus everybody is responsible for each other and bound to each other in their common humanity.

Contemporary concepts of *diakonia*, as for example presented at the World Council of Churches (WCC) Assembly 2013 in Busan, South Korea, even emphasise that the church and its identity should be defined from the 'underside of history', from below, and not least from those living in the global South.[10] At a Conference in Colombo, Sri Lanka, in June 2012, on Theological Perspectives on *Diakonia* in 21st Century, it was underlined that *diakonia* derives its basic starting-point and perspective from marginalised people.

> The world may tend to see the margins as places of disgrace and powerlessness; however, the biblical witness points towards God who is always present in the struggles of those unjustly pushed to the margins of society. It gives several accounts of God's attention and caring love to people in situations of oppression and consequent deprivation. God hears the cry of the oppressed and responds by sustaining and accompanying them in their journey towards liberation (Exodus 3:7-8). This is the *diakonia* of God: a *diakonia* of liberation as well as of restoring dignity, and ensuring justice and peace.[11]

Based on this faith in God the Creator and humankind as created in God's image and likeness, it also becomes clear that helping each other and receiving help are acts of mutuality, and there are no mere givers and recipients when everybody has the same basic value.

This basic understanding of mutuality and reciprocity is echoed concretely in Church of Norway's plan for *diakonia*, as presented in the introductory chapter in this publication.

Social responsibility

The Old Testament also emphasises the *communal aspects of responsibility in society*. The OT tradition of law includes the emphasis on a corporal responsibility of the faithful for those who are in need, and today's diaconal emphasis on the responsibility for all the people one is living together with, also those who are slaves or strangers, finds its roots in the OT texts showing how God asked the people of Israel to uphold this duty, through clear rules and official laws, and through story-telling and prophetic speech. The book of

---

[10] WCC, *Theological Perspectives on Diakonia in 21st Century*, from the conference jointly organised by Justice and Diakonia, Just and Inclusive Communities, and Mission and Evangelism programmes of the World Council of Churches in Colombo, Sri Lanka, 2-6 June 2012. Resource document from the WCC programmes for the WCC Assembly 2013, Busan.

[11] WCC, *Theological Perspectives on Diakonia,* §11.

Leviticus is often referred to when one speaks about the Old Testament laws regarding the poor, the widows, the orphans and the alien. Leviticus 19:9-10 asks the Israelites to plough their fields only once so that the poor may come and harvest food for themselves. The Year of Jubilee, which is pronounced in Leviticus 25:8-55 has become an important theme for today's understanding of global justice. Interestingly enough, one might say that these texts are very much in accordance with modern concepts of self-help when establishing policies which enable the poor to provide for themselves through their own work. The Israelite landowners were asked to give access to their land to non-owners so that these marginalised and oppressed people could pick what was left and feed themselves through their own labour. The Jubilee tradition prevents people remaining permanently landless, no matter what the reason for their former land loss.

The covenant between God and mankind

In this context, the biblical tradition of *covenant* also plays an important role. There are different groups of covenants in the Old Testament, like the Noahic Covenant, the Abrahamic covenant, the Mosaic covenant, the Priestly Covenant, and the Davidic covenant. All these covenant traditions, though having different emphases, underline that God has bound God himself to humanity; that God has a mission for humankind and uses humankind through sending it and obligating it to follow God's will. In the New Testament, the covenant belief is related to Jesus' death and resurrection, establishing what can be called the *new covenant* linked with Jesus' life, proclamation and deeds, and his death. Luke 22:20 speaks about the new covenant related to the Last Supper and the institution of the Eucharist: "This cup that is poured out for you is the new covenant in my blood." The concept of covenant is important for our understanding of *diakonia*, because it links mankind's life to its mission and sending by God and shows that God has a clear will and intention for his creation, namely, to follow God's call and to be faithful to God under all conditions. Further, it is important that the covenant in the biblical tradition is not about the relationship between God and individuals, but is grounded in God's relationship with a *community* of people. In our understanding of *diakonia*, it is important that diaconal action, in distinction to merely charitable activities, which are often individualised, is a collective concept and thus demands organisational and collective structures above the level of individual motivation.

Prophetic diakonia

The tradition of *diakonia* has often somehow narrowly focused on humble service, based on historical circumstances in the 18th century and a narrow reading of the New Testament tradition.[12] Nevertheless, this concept of humble service, often described as acts of charity, should not be totally discarded. As Molefe Tsele underlines:

> God is charitable to his entire creation. Society as a whole needs to be made more charitable. We must resist turning charity into a dirty word, an undertaking viewed with suspicion. However, the ultimate objective of *diakonia* is restorative: it aims to restore the dignity of the poor. In doing so, *diakonia* unites the giver and the receiver, and leaves neither of them unchanged. Thus it is liberating and transforming.[13]

Within diaconal literature from the last decade, the term 'prophetic *diakonia*' turns up regularly in order to describe the proactive dimension of *diakonia*. Prophetic *diakonia* addresses and takes a stand against injustice. The prophets in the Old Testament were clear in their messages, which were often unexpected and unpopular. The prophets claimed that their message was received from God, and they spoke bravely about injustice and the peoples' misbehaviour, irrespective of the personal dangers that could ensue for them. The prophets criticised the establishment sharply, as in Amos 5:12: "For I know how many are your offenses and how great your sins. There are those who oppress the innocent and take bribes and deprive the poor of justice in the courts." In Amos 6:4-6 the prophet argues against the immoral lifestyle of the governors:

> 4 "You lie on beds adorned with ivory
> and lounge on your couches.
> You dine on choice lambs
> and fattened calves.
> 5 You strum away on your harps like David
> and improvise on musical instruments.
> 6 You drink wine by the bowlful
> and use the finest lotions,
> but you do not grieve over the ruin of Joseph."

The prophets also criticised the cultic practice of the establishment, pointing out that all worship has to be in accordance with the basic insight that Yahweh, the God of justice, claims justice from his people. Thus, the prophets made it clear that people's faith, worship and lifestyle must be consistent with one another. There is no true service or worship of God without service to humankind, especially those who are in need. The prophets did not only point to the past, but also to the future. The hope for a future shaped by a just

---

[12] See the introductory chapter in this publication on the exegetical renewal following John Collins' research.

[13] Tsele, 'Prophetic Task of the Church', 54.

communal life and a new creation became the motivation for their prophecies to fight against injustice (cf. Isaiah 49:7-13).

Prophets in the Old Testament were visionary, critical against the misuse of power in their societies and guiding role models for their people concerning ethical and moral choices in life.[14] In this way, one could say the prophets can be seen as role models for a diaconal church. The prophets were individuals chosen by God to speak a prophetic word to those in power who were deviating from God's purposes. The prophetic aspect of *diakonia* refers to its task in dismantling injustice and fighting for the poor and marginalised people. In the New Testament, Jesus is conceived of and described as a prophet (Matthew 21:11; John 4:19; etc.), because of both his proclamation and his deeds.

Promoting the term 'prophetic *diakonia*', one has to be aware that there is a danger of false prophecy and power misuse, when people, especially within church contexts, claim to speak with the authority of God's voice and thus cannot be 'wrong'. A problem might also be in communicating the terminology in secular contexts, where there might be no clear reference or acceptance for a religious dimension, which is linked with the 'prophetic' terminology. Thus, the terminology 'prophetic' might be more useful inside the Christian church as an internal tool to explain one's diaconal engagement and mission in e.g. the fight for justice, than it might be in the context of society or politics.

Nordstokke rightly underlines that "*diakonia* and its prophetic expression must be contextual".[15] *Diakonia* has both a theological and ecclesiological foundation, and is at the same time deeply rooted in specific contexts, which demand a socio-political analysis and an interdisciplinary approach. He differentiates between political *diakonia*, acknowledging the political implications of *diakonia* in general, and prophetic *diakonia*, referring more to the theological nature of *diakonia* as a task mandated and given authority to by God, as a part of God's mission.[16] Nordstokke makes it clear that "to be prophetic therefore, means to defend justice. Consequently, diaconal action should by its very nature include the task of unmasking injustice and promoting justice".[17]

As indicated above, one should nevertheless ask whether the term 'prophetic *diakonia*' in the end turns out to be the most useful term when trying to underline the need for involvement and engagement in societal issues, fighting for justice, doing advocacy work, etc. First, the term 'prophetic' can be difficult to understand and communicate vis-à-vis secular institutions not relating themselves to a Christian self-understanding. Secondly, it might be misleading

---

[14] For a summary on biblical and exegetical aspects of prophetic diakonia, see Herbert Haslinger, *Diakonie. Grundlagen für die soziale Arbeit in der Kirche* (Paderborn: Ferdinand Schöning, 2009), 234-37.

[15] Nordstokke, *Liberating Diakonia*.

[16] Cf. Nordstokke, *Liberating Diakonia*, 51.

[17] Nordstokke, *Liberating Diakonia*, 52.

because it claims to speak with a God-given authority, which it is difficult to question.

Kjetil Fretheim[18] develops the concept of *diakonia* based on an analysis of the Kairos Palestine document[19] from 2009. Fretheim claims that the public, political and prophetic can and should be combined in Christian social work, even if there are nuances. Fretheim underlines that "concern for the excluded and marginalised represents a key contact between public and prophetic theologies".[20]

> While public *diakonia* is concerned with inclusive and empowering participation, and political *diakonia* deals with policy implementation, prophetic *diakonia* shares the important characteristics of prophetic theology, being radically visionary, critical and morally committed to liberation and justice.[21]

Fretheim and many others underline the link between prophetic theology, prophetic *diakonia* and liberation theology, which interprets the teachings of Jesus Christ in relation to liberation from unjust economic, political, or social conditions. The principal methodological innovation of liberation theology is seeing theology from the perspective of the poor and the oppressed.

Among many other famous liberation theologians from the Latin-American context, one should mention Gustavo Gutiérrez, who gave the movement its name with his book *A Theology of Liberation* (1971).[22] Gutiérrez shaped the phrase 'preferential option for the poor', which became a slogan of liberation theology. Drawing from the New Testament motif on the poor, Gutiérrez asserted that God is revealed as having a preference for those people who are 'insignificant,' 'marginalised,' 'unimportant,' 'needy,' 'despised' and 'defenceless.' This motif becomes a core motif in today's diaconal theory, which is strongly influenced by liberation theology.[23]

> If we are aware of its prophetic nature, and able to integrate *diakonia* with a prophetic vision, diaconal work moves beyond charity towards social transformation, pointing to the reign of God. As churches become more aware of *diakonia*'s prophetic dimension, God's mission in the world will be furthered.[24]

---

[18] Fretheim, 'Dimensions of diakonia'.

[19] *A Moment of Truth. A word of faith, hope, and love from the heart of Palestinian suffering* (Kairos Palestine, 2009).

[20] Fretheim, 'Dimensions of diakonia', 75.

[21] Fretheim, 'Dimensions of diakonia', 78.

[22] Gustavo Gutiérrez, *A Theology of Liberation: History, Politics, and Salvation* (15th anniversary edition with new introduction by author), trans. Caridad Inda and John Eagleson (Maryknoll, NY: Orbis, 2012).

[23] Böttcher (ed), *Prophetic diakonia*, 16.

[24] Böttcher (ed), *Prophetic diakonia*, 16.

The New Testament Tradition

Jesus' holistic ministry

Coming to the *New Testament*, Jesus himself summarised his message with the words recorded in Matthew 22:34-40:

> 'Love the Lord your God with all your heart and with all your soul and with all your mind.' This is the first and greatest commandment. And the second is like it: 'Love your neighbour as yourself. All the law and the prophets hang on these two commandments.

Jesus was referring to and quoting from the OT law as found in Deuteronomy 6:5 and Leviticus 19:18. Neighbourly love, love of God and loving oneself are bound together and cannot be separated. This includes respect towards our neighbours as autonomous persons, not mere objects of charity. The profound respect for the other's identity and integrity is the basis for our diaconal approach today, placing a specific emphasis on the call for mutuality and reciprocity in all human relationships.

Taking into account Jesus' own example in his encounter with other people, the picture is multifaceted. What is striking in many of the New Testament stories about Jesus' interaction with the people he met in different circumstances is his *holistic approach* towards them. He did not only tell them what to do and what was right, or preach for them, but took care of them in a holistic way, healing their diseases, offering forgiveness and inclusion into his fellowship, turning traditional values in society upside-down and having table fellowship with sinners. Thus, one could easily say that Jesus' ministry integrated a model of respect and care for other human beings, despite their status in society, treating them as autonomous human persons deserving to be met with God's healing power through Jesus' encounter with them. Acts 10:38 tells how Jesus "went around doing good and healing all who were under the power of the devil, because God was with him". Healing the sick and showing solidarity with the weak were integrated parts of Jesus' life and Messianic service.

Jesus did not only offer help to those who were in despair; he also felt sorry for them (Mark 1:41) and was touched by their condition, and at the same time empowered them through his liberating and uplifting power. Thus, following Jesus' model of *diakonia*, professional care should always keep in mind that the care-giver's personal engagement in the other person is an important part of the act of care-giving, and not a sign of non-professionalism. Jesus never became so 'professional' that he was not touched personally by the encounter with other people. Also in professional practice, there should be room for compassion and personal engagement.

Within the studies of *diakonia* and Christian social service, it is important to remind ourselves of these basic structures of the encounter between Jesus and his fellow human beings, because Jesus' ministry is an important starting-point and model for today's understanding of *diakonia*. When discussing the 'ethos of diaconal service' later in this chapter it will become clear that the New Testament provides us with an understanding of *diakonia* which is based on mutuality and interdependency, which also predominates in modern approaches to the understanding of *diakonia*.

Focus on people in need

Jesus focused especially on those in need. Thus, the aspect of focusing on those who are in need in different ways, the outcasts of communities and societies, should be a core aspect of the theology of *diakonia*. Jesus' encounter with people in need did not mean mere acts of charity, but included empowerment and the challenge to change one's life. Even if today's diaconal emphasis concentrates primarily on mutuality and reciprocity, one should keep in mind that people who are suffering in different ways deserve specific concern for help and should be given priority. This also includes the fact that sometimes there is within diaconal action an imbalance of power caused by the realities of suffering in the world. This imbalance of power in diaconal service calls for a huge amount of consciousness for all people involved in the act of diaconal service.

Focus on empowerment and gender equality

The stories about Jesus in the New Testament also show his focus on the *empowerment* of people, asking them what they want him to do for them (Mark 10:51). In the encounter with the blind man, Jesus did not take for granted that the man wanted to be healed, but asked him first what he wanted him to do for him. Respect for the autonomy of every human being, and faith in people's ability to think on their own and contribute to changes in life, should also shape today's professional diaconal encounter between people. Jesus encouraged people to stand up, take their bed and go. Thus, diaconal authority should contribute to empower people to manage their own lives. The New Testament stories about Jesus' encounter with people with different challenges show Jesus' respect for people's autonomy. According to Mark 10: 43-45, Jesus made clear that serving each other in mutuality is the duty of his followers:

> Whoever wants to become great among you must be your servant, and whoever wants to be first must be slave of all. For even the Son of Man did not come to be served (*deaconed*), but to serve (*deacon*), and to give his life as a ransom for many.

Reading the New Testament in an 'empowerment perspective', one could see that Jesus' holistic ministry includes the empowerment of both women and men. The Gospels of the New Testament often mention Jesus speaking to women publicly and openly against the social norms of the time. The New

Testament includes a number of stories about Jesus' encounter with women, which can be seen as ground-breaking and extremely radical for contemporary Judaism. Even though there is no specific teaching on the role of women, the mere fact that Jesus treated every woman as a person in her own right and dignity should be noticed explicitly and included as an important principle and model for the outline of diaconal theory and practice.

In many societies, especially in the global South, one can measure a 'feminisation of poverty', showing that women are trapped in discrimination and exploitation. Of the 1.3 billion people worldwide in extreme poverty, 70% are women or girls. Women work two-thirds of the world's working hours, but earn only 10% of the world's income, and own less than 1% of the world's property.[25] A recently published survey made by the European Commission[26] showed that 33% of women have experienced physical and/or sexual violence from the age of 15. That corresponds to 62 million women. The report also showed that violence against women remains largely under-reported and relatively under-researched. The survey on which the report is based makes clear that a wide variety of groups need to take action to combat violence against women, including employers, health professionals and internet service providers. Thus, a gender perspective should be included as a non-negotiable part of diaconal studies. Prophetic *diakonia* in its fight for justice always needs to have a specific concern for injustice and violence forced by gender discrimination.

Remarks on John Collins' research

There has been an ongoing discussion on the understanding of *diakonia* based on the interpretation of the terms *diakonia*, *diakonein* and *diakonos* on the New Testament and the New Testament context, mainly inspired by the Australian theologian John Collins.[27] As described in the introductory chapter, Collins criticised the narrow interpretation of these terms as related to mere humble

---

[25] According to statistics provided by PCI: www.pciglobal.org/womens-empowerment-poverty/ accessed 3 June 2014.

[26] See http://fra.europa.eu/sites/default/files/fra-2014-vaw-survey-main-results_en.pdf (accessed 3 June 2014). "The survey asked women about their experiences of physical, sexual and psychological violence, including incidents of intimate partner violence ('domestic violence'), and also asked about stalking, sexual harassment, and the role played by new technologies in women's experiences of abuse. In addition, it asked about their experiences of violence in childhood. What emerges is a picture of extensive abuse that affects many women's lives, but is systematically under-reported to the authorities. For example, one in 10 women has experienced some form of sexual violence from the age of 15, and one in 20 has been raped. Just over one in five women has experienced physical and/or sexual violence from either a current or previous partner, and just over one in 10 women indicates that they have experienced some form of sexual violence by an adult before they were 15 years old" (p.3).

[27] Collins, *Diakonia: Reinterpreting the Ancient Sources.* See his introductory chapter for further details on Collin's impact on the development of diaconal theory.

service. Collins' interpretations are highly discussed, both amongst New Testament scholars and among scholars in the field of *diakonia* research and education.[28] They have been criticised by some scholars, and warmly welcomed by others.[29] Notwithstanding the results of this discussion on biblical interpretation, Collins' findings on the broad connotation of the *diak-* words of the New Testament might encourage theologians to explore ways in which *diakonia* might be understood *today*, as part of the church's identity. Collins' research contributed thus to a fundamental reform within the understanding of *diakonia*, highlighting the fact that a former understanding of *diakonia* as humble service was very much based on the narrow interpretation of *diakonia* which shaped the diaconal movement in the 18th and 19th centuries and its respective historical context.

In our context, I want to underline critically that today's understanding of *diakonia* as the social practice of the church cannot only be based on a narrow interpretation of the semantic connotation of the *diak-* words in the New Testament, but has to be interpreted much more broadly, in the light of biblical theology in general and modern multidisciplinary studies on *diakonia* as Christian social practice. Based on this biblical interpretation, and taking into account the development of *diakonia* within church history until today, we may have a fresh look at the understanding of *diakonia*, not least in the light of ecumenical theology focusing on the church's social service and modern multidisciplinary approaches to social service and care.

Thus, Collins' biblical semantic research is helpful in dismantling a historically far too narrow interpretation of the meaning of the NT *diak-* words, but it turns out to be insufficient as a tool for defining today's understanding and interpretation of diaconal theory and practice.

The relationship between church and state

The relationship between church and state, the Christian as believer and part of the Christian community, and the Christian as citizen with rights and duties in different societies, has been discussed throughout church history. The discussion has always, and still is, shaped by specific historical circumstances and contexts. Within the Lutheran tradition, there has been an ongoing discussion on the interpretation of the Doctrine of the 'Two Kingdoms' or 'Two Governments (Regiments)',[30] and its meaning for today's church life.

---

[28] See Ismo Dunderberg (2007): 'Vermittlung statt karitativer Tätigkeit? Überlegungen zu John N. Collins' Interpretation von diakonia', in Volker Herrmann and Heinz Schmidt (eds), *Diakonische Konturen im Neuen Testament* (DWI-INFO Sonderausgabe 9, Heidelberg, 2007), 177 (own tranlsation: "Proclamation instead of chatitable deeds? Reflections on John N. Collins' interpretation of diakonia").

[29] See Anni Hentschel: *Diakonie im Neuen Testament* – see footnote 89.

[30] The 'Two kingdoms doctrine' teaches that God is the ruler of the whole world, and that he rules in two ways. God rules the worldly or left-hand kingdom through a secular, but nevertheless Christian, government, by means of law (i.e. the sword or compulsion),

The doctrine has been criticised vehemently, because it sometimes contributed to pacify church members in their engagement with the world and in civil society, and led to quietism. Historically, to some degree, it functioned in a mono-cultural and mono-religious world, where governors understood themselves as led by God's will, but not in today's multicultural and multi-religious secular state systems. In many European countries, like the Nordic countries, which to a large degree are historically shaped by Lutheran state religion, the state has, over the centuries, taken over the social roles of the church, leading to a generally secularised public sphere.

Other theological traditions, such as the Roman Catholic tradition, emphasise natural law as the main basis for their understanding of the relationship between church and state, or, like the Protestant reformed tradition, argue for a political model, which operates with one kingdom, and where political leadership is shaped by the Christian faith. Notwithstanding the variety in approaches and models of understanding, the approach chosen has a significant impact on the understanding of the church's and Christians' involvement in societal issues and concerns, and thus there is a need to be aware of the theological models and one's own tradition and context.

Conclusion: Individuality and Communality – Charity and Justice

Over many centuries, the church's *diakonia* has understood itself primarily as charity towards individuals in need. The story of the Good Samaritan, taking care of the injured person along the road, has become a core story for Christian *diakonia*. This kind of charity does not need any organisation or structures. It is based on the individual's motivation and care for the one who is in need of help. One should not underestimate this aspect of personal motivation for diaconal care. Nevertheless, it is worth reflecting on how a Good Samaritan *today* would and should have acted. Certainly, there would have been the need for 'first aid', but immediately, the need to call for an ambulance and professional help would have arisen. Today's health and welfare systems lead to an additional perspective on the story of the Good Samaritan, the co-operation between the individually motivated *diakonia* arising from the true-to-life encounter with pain and the societal *diakonia* taken care of by structures and institutions in our societies. There need not be any contradiction between these approaches to *diakonia*, but there should be a vital co-operation between

and in the heavenly or right-hand kingdom, his spiritual kingdom – that is, the Church and its members – through the gospel or grace. The doctrine is derived from the Lutheran core principle of discerning Law and Gospel. In affirming the two kingdoms doctrine, God is understood as ruling all human institutions and activities, but ruling them in two fundamentally different ways: God rules the church (the spiritual kingdom) as a redeemer in Jesus Christ, and rules the state and all other institutions (the civil kingdom) as creator and sustainer, and thus these two kingdoms have significantly different functions and modes of operation.

institutional, structural, political and individual *diakonia*. These existing structures would certainly vary in different contexts and countries, both within and between the global North and within the global South. Immediate and spontaneous *diakonia* as help for one another is still relevant and important. In addition, there is a need for structural and communal approaches to *diakonia*. Such structures are not to be seen as a lack of charity and help for each other, but may represent a form of collective solidarity and mutuality. The Old Testament background shows us that there is a strong biblical tradition supporting the need of societal structures and communal approaches, also to avoid individual dependencies. This leads us forward to an understanding of *diakonia* as 'prophetic *diakonia*', where the diaconal actors very much relate to and co-operate with existing structures in society.

Diakonia in this sense extends the biblical insight that *diakonia* is much more than feeling pity with other people and helping them when they are in need. The communal and rights-based approach, which can be derived from the biblical tradition, supports the development of a sustainable culture of mutual care where those who are in need of help are respected and supported to find ways to solve their problems. Mere charity creates dependency, while a rights-based approach contributes to creating secure and safe spaces for those who are in need, without claiming any specific 'goodwill' from those offering help.

Thus, for those who are in need of help and support, institutional structures and rights-based constituencies give freedom to individuals and groups. In the long run, it is important for everybody to have predictable structures, and not merely acts of free charity depending on individuals' varying motivations and engagements. This also implies that the church in its engagement with people in need should not only focus on the individual's motivation to provide help, but also address structures of power and political stakeholders in order to create just legal systems and support people in the official societal structures. As the EKD underlined in its document on *diakonia* from 1998: "The duty to help must become the claim for rights for those who are in need of help. Only then a partnership between care-givers and the recipients of care can be realised" (own translation).[31] Thus, *diakonia* implies both voluntary help and care

---

[31] *Herz und Mund und Tat und Leben,* in Denkschrift der EKD Nr. 143 (Hanover: Kirchenamt der EKD), 1998, §67: (Own translation: Heart and mouth and life, in: Report from the EKD nr. 143, Hanover: EKD Church Council, 1998, §67: "Based on biblical anthropology, we conclude that receiving help and offering help is not like receiving or sharing alms, but that those who are in need of help have a right for help. The dignity of those who are in need of help will be ruined, if their understanding is reduced to being mere beggars. The duty to help must become the legal claim of the helpless. Only when the duty to help becomes a legal claim, there can be a real partnership between the helpers and those who are in need of help. Only a legal claim can put those who are in need of help into the position, to choose the helpers and the help. Diakonia is co-responsible for these structures, which contribute to a life in dignity for those who are in need of help."

offered by individuals based on their own motivation, and socio-political *diakonia* focusing on just structures in society and proactive work. These are not alternatives, but both sides complement each other. Within the field of *diakonia*, acts of care on the level of interpersonal interaction must be supplemented by engagement for creating just societal structures through an engagement for rights-based democratic systems. The biblical tradition makes it clear that, from the very beginning, these complementary aspects of *diakonia* are important for an adequate understanding of the church's social service today. Through supporting the creation of structures of social justice and solidarity, *diakonia* contributes both in co-operation with and sometimes in opposition and protest towards the modern welfare state. This protest can also be summarised by what earlier was described as 'prophetic *diakonia*'.

Bibliography

Böttcher, Reinhard (ed), *Prophetic Diakonia: 'For the Healing of the World'*. Report Johannesburg: South Africa (Geneva: Lutheran World Federation, November 2002).

Bonhoeffer, Dietrich, *Ethics*. Translated from the German Edition ed. By Ilse Tödt, Heinz Eduard Tödt, Ernst Feil and Clifford Green. English edition ed. Clifford J.Green. (Dietrich Bonhoeffer Works Vol. 6. Minneapolis: Fortress Press, 2005).

Bonhoeffer, Dietrich, *Widerstand und Ergebung: Briefe und Aufzeichnungen aus der Haft*. Christian Gremmels, Eberhard Bethge, Renate Bethge, Ilse Tödt (eds), (DBW 8, München: Christian Kaiser, 1998).

Collins, John N., *Diakonia: Reinterpreting the Ancient Sources* (New York: OUP, 1990).

Dunderberg, Ismo, 'Vermittlung statt karitativer Tätigkeit? Überlegungen zu John N. Collins' Interpretation von diakonia', in Volker Herrmann and Heinz Schmidt (eds), *Diakonische Konturen im Neuen Testament* (DWI-INFO Sonderausgabe 9, Heidelberg, 2007).

Fuchs, Ottmar, 'Church for Others', in *Concilium: Diakonia. Church for Others*. Norbert Greinacher and Norbert Mette (eds), (Edinburgh: T&T Clark Ltd, 1998).

Gutiérrez, Gustavo, *A Theology of Liberation: History, Politics, and Salvation* (15th anniversary edition with new introduction by author), trans. Caridad Inda and John Eagleson (Maryknoll, NY: Orbis, 2012).

Haslinger, Herbert, *Diakonie. Grundlagen für die soziale Arbeit in der Kirche* (Paderborn: Ferdinand Schöning, 2009).

Hentschel, Annie, *Diakonie im Neuen Testament, Studien zur Semantik unter besonderer Berücksichtigung der Rolle von Frauen*. Wissenschaftliche Untersuchungen Zum Neuen Testament 2/226 (Tübingen: Mohr/Siebeck, 2007).

Herz und Mund und Tat und Leben, in Denkschrift der EKD Nr. 143 (Hanover: Kirchenamt der EKD, 1998).

Kairos Palestine, *A Moment of Truth. A word of faith, hope and love from the heart of the Palestinian suffering* (Palestine: Kairos, 2009).

Nordstokke, Kjell, *Liberating Diakonia* (Trondheim: Tapir Akademisk Forlag, 2011).

Tsele, Molefe, 'Prophetic Task of the Church: A Listener's Response', in Reinhard Böttcher (ed), *Prophetic Diakonia: 'For the Healing of the World'*. Report Johannesburg: South Africa (Geneva: Lutheran World Federation, Nov 2002), 53-55.

WCC. *Theological Perspectives on Diakonia in 21st Century,* from the Conference jointly organised by Justice and *Diakonia*, Just and Inclusive Communities, and Mission and Evangelism programmes of the World Council of Churches in Colombo, Sri Lanka, 2-6 June 2012. Resource document from the WCC programmes for the WCC Assembly 2013, Busan.

The Study of Diakonia as an Academic Discipline

Kjell Nordstokke

Diakonia as an Emerging Ecumenical Concept

Since 2011 Diakonhjemmet University College in Oslo has offered an English Master's degree in *diakonia*. The intention of the programme is to 'produce graduates who qualify for both practical and leadership positions within diaconal activities and institutions as well as value-based social service agencies, whether they are Christian or public-welfare based'.[1] The study provides theological and hermeneutical knowledge, ethical competence, management and leadership skills, research skills, inter-cultural and inter-religious skills, and interdisciplinary working proficiency, and is based upon the understanding of *diakonia* as church- or faith-based practice, especially in the form of service delivery within the areas of health care, social work, or education, at the level of local congregation or professional social institutions.

The concept of *diakonia* may not belong to the vernacular of many churches; instead, they more frequently use terms as 'social ministry' or 'social action' when referring to their involvement in this kind of work. These terms can, however, be perceived as rather secular, without the ability to express the distinctively Christian nature of such activity. In addition, they may give the impression that this kind of work is mostly due to external conditions and challenges, and that the church may opt for being involved or not. For that reason, some prefer the biblical word *diakonia* as this concept holds together an understanding of what we *are* and what we *do* as Christians and as churches when serving people in need, and when assuming a role as agent in civil society promoting human dignity and the well-being of all. From this understanding, diaconal work is not optional for the church, but an integral part of its being and mission to the world.

Within the ecumenical movement, the term *diakonia* has been given increased attention over the last decades, affirming its ecclesiological and missiological dimension. This was strongly affirmed at a World Council of Churches consultation held in Colombo, Sri Lanka, in June 2012:

1 www.diakonhjemmet.no/DHS/Studiehaandbok/Direkte-publisering/Studiekatalog/Informasjon/Master-s-Degree-in-Diakonia-and-Christian-Social-Practice

> The Church, as a community called into being through baptism and led by the Holy Spirit, participates in this (God's) mission through its very being, proclamation and service. Commonly understood as service, *diakonia* is a way of living out faith and hope as a community, witnessing to what God has done in Jesus Christ.[2]

A similar position is held by the Lutheran World Federation (LWF). In their study document *Diakonia in Context*, it is stated that "*Diakonia* is a theological concept that points to the very identity and mission of the Church" and "a call to action, as a response to challenges of human suffering, injustice and care for creation".[3] The view is that *diakonia* refers both to theological reflection and to church-based action, with the consequence that a theoretical reflection on *diakonia* should encompass theological disciplines: not only practical theology and social ethics, but also systematic theology and biblical interpretation. At the same time, it should study forms of social action and their relevance as a response to challenges of human suffering and injustice in today's world.

It is a fact that only a few theological seminaries have addressed *diakonia* as an academic theme. There may be many reasons for this. One is that the concept of *diakonia* is not often used in theological English; for that reason, some seminaries may use other words for the same area of study, such as 'social ministry'. Several churches are acquainted with the title 'deacon', either as the first step in the ordained ministry, as is the case in the Roman Catholic and the Anglican churches, or as a voluntary lay service related to tasks in the local congregation. This use has however not implied the introduction of the term *diakonia*. In parts of the world, mainly Germany and the Nordic countries, *diakonia* has become quite a well-known word due to the work of numerous diaconal institutions over the last 150 years. Here *diakonia* is mainly conceived of as professional health or social work, and therefore not a serious matter for theological study, unless as a possible sub-theme within practical theology. It should however be noted that training institutions for diaconal workers in these countries normally employ theologians as teachers, and that lately an increasing number of professorships in the science of *diakonia* have been established.

The emergence of *diakonia* as an ecumenical concept, emphasising its ecclesial, missiological and prophetic dimensions, has stimulated scholars and church leaders to give the term new attention and include it in the theological vernacular, and eventually develop study programmes that include reflection on *diakonia* as a theological theme and church-based action. In 2005 the LWF organised a consultation on *diakonia* and development for Asian church leaders in Bangkok, and the participants challenged seminaries to:

---

[2] WCC, *Theological Perspectives on Diakonia*, 105.

[3] LWF, *Diakonia in Context*, 8. The document was received by the LWF Council in 2009 and was thereby given semi-official status within the Lutheran Communion.

a) Strengthen diaconal education at all levels of the churches and introduce *diakonia* studies in the seminaries.
b) Produce relevant biblical and theological foundation for praxis.
c) Strengthen diaconal understanding leading to the publication of books and other reading materials in the area of *diakonia*, preferably in local languages.[4]

Two Distinct Approaches to the Study of *Diakonia*

As already indicated above, there are two main approaches to the academic study of *diakonia*. One starts with diaconal praxis, activities commonly named *diakonia*. Such work, and the manner in which it is performed, is then made the object for empirical research. This may include diaconal activities organised by a local congregation, or diaconal institutions such as hospitals or homes for elderly people. According to this approach, the theory of *diakonia* basically becomes a critical reflection on such diaconal praxis, and presents questions like: What makes this praxis good? How is the diaconal identity expressed? Is there a diaconal distinctiveness in what is performed, or is it done in the same way as any other professional work? The advantage of this approach is that it is reality-oriented: it roots theory in praxis. The limit, however, is that it may seem irrelevant in contexts where the concept of *diakonia* is not used or even unknown. It could lead to the conclusion that there is no need for reflecting on *diakonia* in churches that are not accustomed to using the term in their daily work.

The other approach starts with the concept of *diakonia* and studies it in its biblical and theological setting. The mere fact that the *diak-* words (διακονια, διακονειν, διακονος) are used around 100 times in the New Testament indicates their importance, even more so when we see that they appear in important passages, both in the gospels and in the letters of Paul. The vantage point of this approach is the theological focus that is given to a concept, correcting the notion that it mainly refers to a European tradition, perhaps irrelevant in other contexts. This theological focus may provoke a new understanding and also new practices in the church.

The two approaches should in my understanding be considered complementary, and not conflicting. They help us to uphold a sound dialectic tension between theory and praxis. If theology ignores practice, it runs the risk of becoming idealistic, losing its relevance in the reality where churches carry out their mission. On the other hand, theology must be critical: its task is not just to affirm what is preached and practised in the churches. Thus the academic study on *diakonia* is challenged to respond to fundamental positions of Reformation theology, of the hermeneutical principles of *sola scriptura* and *sola fide*, committing itself to clarifying the faith base of diaconal action, and at

[4] Nordstokke (ed), *Serving the Whole Person*, 57.

the same to the principle of *ecclesia semper reformanda*, asking how this challenges the church to renew its life and work in today's world.

In this article I shall use both approaches. In the following, I shall first present some examples of how *diakonia* has been reflected theologically over the last 150 years, mainly in the German context where the diaconal movement grew from the 1830s. Then I shall bring in a few other contributions, expressing new research and also different ecumenical perspectives.

The Diaconal Movement in Germany in the Nineteenth Century

Whereas care for the sick and the poor always been an integral part of the life and ministry of the church, it was the so-called diaconal movement in Germany that reintroduced the concept of *diakonia* for activities within this field, in the first place by establishing fellowships of deaconesses and deacons who were trained as nurses, teachers and social workers. The movement was pioneered by Protestant pastors like Theodor Fliedner (1800-64) and Johann Hinrich Wichern (1808-81).[5] The first served a local congregation in Kaiserswerth, close to Düsseldorf in western Germany, being deeply challenged by the suffering of the poorest in a time of growing industrialisation and social marginalisation. In 1833 he opened a home for the homeless, released female prisoners, and soon after opened another home for orphans, and in 1836 a training institution for deaconesses, and finally a hospital. Similar institutions were established all over Germany and also spread to neighbouring countries, together with so-called 'motherhouses' to which the deaconesses were affiliated as a communion of sisters. In many ways they appeared similar to Catholic convents of nuns; like them, evangelical deaconesses committed themselves to celibacy, poverty and obedience. Flieder also travelled to America and established diaconal institutions there, and at the time of his death in 1864 no less than thirty motherhouses had been founded and 1,600 deaconesses were working at 400 institutions. Since then too, the movement of deaconesses was brought to other continents, for instance Asia where communities were established in India, Indonesia, Korea, Japan and the Philippines.

While Fliedner is remembered as the pioneer of the deaconess movement, Wichern focused on young men and offered them training as a way out of poverty. In 1833 he opened *Rauhes Haus* in Hamburg, at first as a kind of home where poor boys were included as family members; this soon developed into a fellowship of brothers, and eventually those trained were called deacons. In Wichern's vision for a renewed church, these deacons would play a key role: in a time of growing social need and also revolutionary fermentation they

[5] The history of the diaconal movement in Germany in the 19th century is broadly presented in Erich Beyreuther, *Geschichte der Diakonie und Inneren Mission in der Neuzeit* (Berlin: CZV-Verlag, 1983) (3., erw. Aufl.).

would contribute to developing a church that cared about the poor and needy. According to Wichern, this was a missionary task, so it was soon given the name of 'Inner Mission'. At the same time, it was considered a strategic option for making the church relevant in that historical context.

Wichern himself became the leading figure of the Inner Mission, and it became a strong lay movement. Deeply influenced by Pietism, it promoted individual conversion and discipleship. But most of all, it became an important area of action, both as an expression of following the example of Jesus who cared for the sick and the poor, and as a way of saving the needy from the powers of sin and destruction.

In 1848, the same year the Communist Manifesto was published by Marx and Engels, Wichern spoke to the Synod of the Evangelical Churches that met in Wittenberg and urged them to commit themselves to the task of Inner Mission. This resulted in the establishment of a Central Committee for Inner Mission. Later, in 1855, Wichern presented his vision for *diakonia* at a conference in the Monbijou Palace in Berlin, called together by King Friedrich Wilhelm IV, as a preparation for a general church synod to be held later. Interpreting *diakonia* as 'loving care for the poor' (*den Armen zugewendete Liebespflege*), Wichern differentiated between three forms of diaconal action: the 'free', the church-based, and the 'civil'.[6] According to his understanding, the 'free' referred to the many activities and institutions initiated by the Inner Mission, independent of official church structures. By 'civil' was meant the public care for sick and poor, as assumed by the state or by local government. The real concern of Wichern, however, was to re-establish the church-based *diakonia* that in his understanding had been a part of the apostolic tradition, but had been lost in the course of church history. Through its *diakonia* the church should take a leading role in developing services of care for people in need, thus being a model for the civil *diakonia*. In order to assume this task, the church should educate and ordain deacons. According to Wichern, an organic relationship existed between God's revelation in the old and the new covenant and *diakonia*. The ministry of the deacon he saw modelled in the ministry of Jesus, in his saving love. *Diakonia* as a theological task therefore required a fourfold academic reflection: on the concept of God, on being human, on situations of need, and on how to assist – in other words, a comprehensive and interdisciplinary approach.

Wichern's ideas were not given the attention that he had hoped, and his proposals regarding a church-based *diakonia* were not realised. Instead, the Inner Mission remained an independent undercurrent in the life of the church. It remained the key diaconal agency in Germany; diaconal institutions therefore grew and developed independently of official church structures. As public

[6] Johann Hinrich Wichern, 'Gutachten, die Diakonie und den Diakonat betreffend', in *Johann Hinrich Wichern. Ausgewählte Schriften, Band 1: Schriften zur sozialen Frage.* Herausgegeben von Karl Janssen (Gütersloh: Carl Bertelsmann Verlag, 1956), 138.

welfare services began to be introduced in some of the north European countries by the end of the 19th century, it became natural for diaconal institutions to co-operate with them, and also for diaconal workers to find work there, with the consequence that in some cases more links were developed between *diakonia* and the state than between *diakonia* and the official church.

The diaconal movement became a leading force in developed professional health and social services in Europe in the 19th century. In addition, it was a pioneer in giving women education and respectful work. Nevertheless, this significant public action in the name of the church was largely ignored by the scholars at theological faculties. They did not find much reason for addressing diaconal work in their academic research, even if some of them might have supported it privately. There might have been many reasons for this: an obvious one is that the theological faculties educated mainly pastors, with the consequence that practical theology was in the first place conceived of as enabling pastors for their future ministry. The diaconal workers received their professional training in schools run by the diaconal movement; here theological subjects would of course be part of the curriculum, but not always at an academic level.

The separation between the church and the diaconal movement, and consequently between academic theology and diaconal training, may also have been caused by a mutual suspicion between the two. The leaders of the Inner Mission were critical towards the kind of liberal theology that dominated most German universities at that time. Similarly, the programme of the Inner Mission was rejected by many university theologians for not responding to the challenges of modernity, and for focusing too much on individual conversion and spirituality.

Diakonia remained largely a non-theme in academic theology until after World War II. Some few exceptions can be noted. Gerhard Uhlhorn (1826-1901), who had a doctoral degree in church history, chose to work as director of a new diaconal institution in Hanover, not following the invitation of King George V, to assume leading positions in the church. He published a two-volume history of the Christian action of love (*Die christliche Liebesthätigkeit*) that for decades should be the standard work on the history of *diakonia.*[7] In the same period, Theodor Schäfer (1846-1914) who pioneered diaconal work among people with disabilities people, formulated the concept 'Diakonik' – proposing that a new theological discipline with this name should be developed. His idea was brought to the public in a handbook for the theological sciences (*Handbuch der Theologischen Wissenschaften*) published by Otto Zöckler in 1885, but it was not followed up in the academic world of theology. What came nearest was the Institute for Social Ethics and Science of Inner Mission (*Institut für Sozialethik und Wissenschaft der Inneren Mission*) that the

[7] Gerhard Uhlhorn, *Die christliche Liebesthätigkeit in der alten Kirche*. 2 Bände (Neukirchen: Neukirchener Verlag, 1959 [1882-84]).

University of Berlin established in 1927 under the leadership of Reinhold Seeberg, a prominent professor of systematic theology. Due to pressure from the Nazi government, this institute was closed in 1938.

Philippi reflects on this lack of interest and lists various reasons why the study of *diakonia* was not included in academic theology.[8] In his opinion, one of the main factors was the heritage of the Reformation and its focus on justification by faith which has often led to a lack of interest, if not suspicion, in addressing the theme of good works and consequently diaconal action.

Understanding *Diakonia* in the Aftermath of World War II

The period of the Nazi regime in Germany (1933-45) in many ways became a time of profound trial for the diaconal movement. It turned out that the diaconal institutions largely adapted to the dominant ideology and found no difficulties in co-operating with the authorities.[9] Some few resisted, as did Friedrich von Bodelschwingh (1877-1946), the director of an institution for people with mental disabilities. He did his best to protect them against the Nazi's euthanasia and sterilisation policies. But he was an exception, as was the case of most professional health workers at that time: many deaconesses and deacons openly supported the inhuman measures taken by the regime that resulted in the murder of vulnerable groups.

In the mood of self-examination after the war, some explained this lack of opposition to the Nazi ideology came as a result of a lack of critical theology. *Diakonia* had mainly been conceived of as humble service, which had relegated it to a form of servility, not questioning those in power. Now churches in Germany were confronted by new diaconal challenges: in the first instance, assisting the victims of war, among them millions of refugees and other homeless people, and after that, contributing to the reconstruction of national welfare services. How could the diaconal mandate be renewed, also in the sense of being given a more solid theological platform? As initiatives were taken to reorganise diaconal work with its institutions into a nationwide co-ordinating structure, the need to establish an academic institution with the purpose of providing theological reflection on *diakonia* was also strongly felt. This was realised in 1954 when the Institute for Diaconal Studies (*Das Diakoniewissenschaftliche Institut – DWI*) was established as part of the University of Heidelberg; since then, DWI has played an important role in

---

[8] Paul Philippi, *Christozentrische Diakonie. Ein theologischer Entwurf* (Stuttgart: Evangelisches Verlagswerk, 1963), 5-20.

[9] The history of diakonia in Germany under the Nazi regime has been broadly documented in Theodor Strohm and Jörg Thierfelder (eds), *Diakonie im 'Dritten Reich'* (Heidelberg: Heidelberger Verlagsanstalt, 1990).

educating diaconal leadership as well as of promoting research; it has since produced an impressive number of studies on *diakonia.*[10]

Paul Philippi had already joined the Institute for Diaconal Studies in 1954 and later became its director (1971-86). As a scholar of systematic theology, his prime concern was to contribute to the ecclesiological and Christological foundation of *diakonia.* In his opinion, *diakonia* should not in the first place be understood as action responding to external social need, but as a fundamental structure of what constitutes the church. In his major study on Christ-centred *diakonia* (*Christozentrische Diakonie*) from 1963, Philippi claims that such a diaconal structure can be found in the New Testament narratives of the ministry of Jesus, and that this structure also determines the way of 'being church'. The communion around the table has a central place as the theological *locus* in this understanding as it announces the presence of Christ, the true Deacon; at the same time, it is here the congregation is qualified and empowered for diaconal service.

In Philippi's view the local congregation is where *diakonia* has its beginning and main arena of action. "Who wants to speak right about *diakonia,* must speak about the right congregation" reads one of his statements.[11] This opinion may be considered as rather narrow in the sense that the diaconal response is mainly oriented by church-centred motifs and practices, withdrawing from the public arena and its challenges. This was not however Philippi's intention: his main concern was to root diaconal action in the diaconal identity of the church. His position may be understood as a way of overcoming a deficit in Lutheran ecclesiology that had interpreted the teaching of the 'two kingdoms' in a manner that restricted the mandate of the church to the 'spiritual realm': that of preaching the gospel and administrating the sacraments, while the diaconal task was conceived of as belonging to the 'worldly realm' – in other words, to the political authorities. Philippi's main point is that this practice empties the congregation of its diaconal identity and mandate, with the result that it is not able to respond to its vocation in the world.

While Philippi's concern was to equip the local congregation with solid theological arguments for diaconal service, others would consider his approach as inadequate in responding to the burning social issues with which the diaconal institutions and their leaders were wrestling. They claimed that disciplines such as social ethics, more than dogmatics, should be given attention when reflecting theologically on *diakonia.*

One of the strongest voices in this endeavour is that of Heinz-Dietrich Wendland. He sought to embed *diakonia* in his concept of a 'theology of society' (*Theologie der Gesellschaft*) in which the diaconal action establishes a

---

[10] For instance, the book series edited by Theodor Strohm, *Diakoniewissenschaftliche Studien* (Heidelberg: Diakoniewissenschaftliches Institut – DWI), 1993f.

[11] Philippi, *Christozentrische Diakonie*, 249.

kind of link between church and society.[12] In Wendland's concept, the church is mandated to contribute to the formation of a responsible society. While this apparently requires social and ethical reflection, and evidently assumes a different epistemological and methodological approach from the one proposed by Philippi, it nevertheless builds on a vision of the cosmological diaconate of Jesus, in the sense that his ministry as Servant and Lord has changed the course of the history of the world. Wendland holds together the concepts of διακονος and δουλος (slave), giving especial attention to the Christological hymn in Philippians 2:5-11 where Jesus is announced as the slave who was "obedient to death – even death on a cross" and thereby became the Saviour of the world. On the one hand, becoming δουλος implied a free renouncing of the position of "being in very nature God" (εν μορφη θεου), taking upon him the condition of being a human, including enslavement to the powers of this world. On the other hand, it points to his victory over the same powers and his exaltation as Lord (κυριος) 'in heaven and on earth and under the earth.'[13]

From this understanding, Jesus is presented as the cosmological deacon, or the primordial deacon of the world (*Urdiakon der Welt*). How does this relate to the *diakonia* of the church and to Christians committed to diaconal work? Although the *diakonia* of Jesus is unique, only he is the Saviour of the world, the *diakonia* of the church is performed 'in Christ', empowered by the gifts of his diaconal presence in the church. But Christ's presence in the world cannot be limited to the church. As the deacon of the world, Christ is present where people suffer and are victims of injustice and poverty, although hidden, as told in Matthew 25:31-46.

In Wendland's concept, the arena of diaconal engagement is in the world, promoting freedom, equality and human dignity. In that sense, he urges diaconal agencies to overcome positions that belong to the past, especially those that affirmed hierarchical structures of submission and obedience. Diaconal workers should be moved by freedom, not by obligation. On the other hand, such freedom is for the world and should assume the task of 'political *diakonia*', of promoting social responsibility and well-being.[14]

Jürgen Moltmann has, in his writing on *diakonia*, added another perspective, namely, that of hope as the motivation and driving force in diaconal action.

---

[12] Dierk Starnitzke, *Diakonie als soziales System. Eine theologische Grundlegung diakonischer Praxis in Auseinandersetzung mit Niklas Luhmann* (Stuttgart et al: Kohlammer, 1996), 50.

[13] Heinz-Dietrich Wendland, 'Christos Diakonos – Christos Doulos. Zur theologischen Begründung der Diakonie', in Heinz-Dietrich Wendland, Artur Rich, Herbert Krimm (eds), *Christos Diakonos. Ursprung und Auftrag der Kirche* (Zürich: EVZ-Verlag, 1962), 13-29.

[14] Heinz-Dietrich Wendland, 'Diakonie zwischen Kirche und Welt', in Christine Bourbeck and Heinz-Dietrich Wendland (eds), *Diakonie zwischen Kirche und Welt. Studien zur diakonischen Arbeit und Verantwortung in unserer Zeit* (Hamburg: Furche-Verlag, 1958), 17-36.

Invited to present a lecture on the occasion of the anniversary of a diaconal institution, in which diaconal work had been shaped by professional standards, and where the distinctiveness of a Christian worldview may be difficult to spot, he challenged his audience by asking: "Do we hope for the realisation of God's Kingdom that in the presence and the spirit of Jesus already seizes, liberates and prepares for service? Or do we wait for the end of this world of unavoidable suffering and basically hopeless work as its overcoming?"[15]

In Moltmann's understanding, *diakonia* is following Jesus, the Crucified, and in the horizon of the inbreaking Kingdom of God. Both references are fundamental in order to understand *diakonia* in its holistic meaning. To follow Jesus implies walking as he did, embracing the poor and the sick, and bringing them healing, salvation, hope and a future, as announced in his 'manifesto' in Luke 4:18-19. In the same manner, the mission of the church must be holistic: any separation between mission and *diakonia* would contradict the unity that is expressed in the mission of Jesus, to which his disciples were also called. At the same time, this is the way of the Crucified: wounds are healed by wounds, as is said in Isaiah 53:5: "By his wounds we are healed." So also *diakonia* is a calling to follow Jesus by taking up the cross (Mark 8:35) and suffer in solidarity with those who are in need.

Diakonia thus becomes a way of living (*Lebensform*) that marks the life of the Christian congregation, making it overcome ethnic, social and gender differences (Galatians 3:28). Moltmann distinguishes between a general *diakonia*, the diaconate of all believers, and a specialised *diakonia*, that of attending demanding challenges – as, for instance, caring for mentally disabled people through institutional and professional work. Such distinctions should not however lead to separation, as often has happened, and he strongly advocates the 'becoming-diaconal of the congregation as well as the becoming-congregational of *diakonia*'.[16] Taking *diakonia* away from the congregation will simply weaken the congregation.

This conclusion sounds very similar to the one made by Philippi, and it should be remembered that this was written in a period (the 1960s and 1970s) when the number of diaconal institutions was increasing in Germany due to the expansion of the welfare system.[17] In many ways, Moltmann points to the same importance of Christological and ecclesiological foundation in a theology of *diakonia*, but his approach is different since the vision of hope directs his perspective. The congregation is certainly affirmed as a sign and anticipation of what is hoped for. However, God's inbreaking Reign cannot be limited to the

[15] Jürgen Moltmann, *Diakonie im Horizont des Reiches Gottes* (Neukirchen-Vluyn: Neukirchener Verlag, 1984), 22.

[16] Moltmann, *Diakonie im Horizont*, 36.

[17] Since then it has continued to grow. Today, *Diakonisches Werk*, the social welfare organisation of the Protestant churches in Germany, encompass over 28,000 independent institutions employing more than 450,000 people and providing over one million care placements.

church, as God's Spirit acts according to God's good intention and promise for the whole of creation. This view clearly affirms the close link between *diakonia* and social ethics. This was strongly emphasised by Theodor Strohm who was the director of DWI from 1986 to 2000.

Holding the above positions together, they all reflect the background of the German context and intention to overcome the tendency of separation between church and *diakonia*, and of understanding diaconal work as professional health and social services separated from the mandate given to all Christians. Although their contributions, together with those of others, must be evaluated as both substantial and timely, their impact nevertheless remains rather limited, both in relation to diaconal praxis and to theology as an academic study. In 1983 the theological journal *Pastoraltheologie* dedicated a whole issue to the question why *diakonia* had never been included in the vernacular of academic theology. In one of the articles, Philippi continues to elaborate on the reasons why.[18] Perhaps, he states, it has to do with the literalism that dominates Protestant theology which tends to reduce the word (λογος) to what is said, and which has been linked to a form of Hellenist docetic spirituality that pays little interest to real human life. Philippi challenges preachers to address this issue, and to expand their theological understanding of *diakonia* and apply it in their sermons. Again, this is another reason for including *diakonia* in the theological curriculum.

The Reinterpretation of *Diakonia*

The German scholars referred to above all subscribed to the understanding of *diakonia* as active Christian love for one's neighbour (*Nächstenliebe*). This had been stated in Kittel's influential *Theological Dictionary of the New Testament*: in the first German edition from 1935 H.W. Beyer maintained that, in the New Testament, *diakonia* means 'waiting at table' or in a rather wider sense 'provision for bodily sustenance', and also 'discharge of service' in genuine love.[19] This reading was in line with the interpretation given by Wilhelm Brandt who in 1931 had published his doctoral thesis on the concept of service in the New Testament.[20] In many ways, their position affirmed the understanding of *diakonia* that had been developed within the diaconal movement, as humble service and as care for people in need, following the example of Jesus.

---

[18] Paul Philippi, 'Diakonik – Diagnose des Fehlens einer Disziplin', *Pastoraltheologie*, No 4, 1983, 177-86.

[19] H.W. Beyer, 'διακονέω'. *Theologisches Wörterbuch zum Neuen Testament,* Kittel (ed), (Stuttgart: Kohlhammer, 1935), 81-93.

[20] Wilhelm Brandt, *Dienst und Dienen im Neuen Testament* (Gütersloh: Carl Bertelsmann Verlag, 1931).

The Australian scholar John N. Collins has proved that this reading is based on a misinterpretation. After studying a large number of Greek texts from the time that the New Testament was written, he concluded that *diakonia* is never used in the sense of charitable or humble service. Rather, it designated an honourable task or mission given to a person, that of being an envoy, a spokesperson, or a 'go-between' who is entrusted with important tidings. In other instances it means a mediator, a person given a commission on behalf of someone in authority and fulfilling a vital task.[21] With this in mind, Collin examines all biblical passages that contain the *diak-* words, and concludes that none of them refer to services for the sick and poor.[22] When related to Jesus, it refers to his Messianic mandate "to give his life as a ransom for many" (Mark 10:45); in other words, as Saviour to fulfil the mission given to him by the Father. In a similar manner, the Apostle Paul writes about his *diakonia* as the ministry in which he takes pride (Romans 11:13), and which is "received in the Lord" (Colossians 4:17). In some few instances, deacons are referred to as a specific order of ministry (Philippians 1:1 and 1 Timothy 3:18), but in none of these passages is any indication given that they are responsible for charity work; in the first place, they seem to be designated to assist the bishop.

Collins' reinterpretation of the term *diakonia* is now supported by many New Testament scholars, including many in Germany.[23] It has been broadly discussed what consequences his findings may have for diaconal work today. If the word *diakonia* has been misinterpreted and has wrongly influenced the concept of the diaconal mandate, does this mean that it does not make sense to use it any more, and that other terms should be found for what some churches define as *diakonia*? How then to understand the diaconal ministry? Should deaconesses and deacons conclude that their service is based on a misunderstanding? This is clearly not the conclusion Collins draws; on the contrary, the reinterpretation of the biblical meaning of *diakonia* presents new perspectives on this term that can be used as points of reference when elaborating a theology of *diakonia*.[24]

In the first place, *diakonia* should not be conceived of as humble service or as self-effacing care for people in need. Much more, its biblical background presents it as bold action that announces good news for the poor. Secondly, *diakonia* cannot be limited to professional work; it belongs to the mandate given by the triune God to the church as an integral part of its mission. As such, the reinterpretation of *diakonia* has reconfirmed its ecclesiological and missiological nature. And thirdly, its performance is modelled by the one who

[21] Collins, *Diakonia: Re-interpreting the Ancient Sources*, 194.

[22] Collins, *Deacons and the Church. Making connections between old and new* (Leominster, UK: Gracewing, 2002), 27-85.

[23] A noteworthy study that fully supports the views of Collins was published by Anni Hentschel, *Diakonia im Neuen Testament* (Tübingen: Mohr Siebeck, 2007).

[24] Kjell Nordstokke, *Liberating Diakonia*, 41-47.

has given the diaconal mandate, as in John 20:21: "As the Father has sent me, I am sending you." In other words, as the sending of Christ encompassed words and deeds, so also the mission of the church is mandated to include proclamation and acts of healing, reconciliation, advocacy and inclusion; or, as Collins describes the tasks of the deacon, assuming a ministry of 'go-between' or as mediator.

Ecumenical *Diakonia*

In many ways, ecumenical *diakonia* corresponds to the manner in which *diakonia* is now understood within the ecumenical movement. But here also a notable change has taken place. When the World Council of Churches (WCC) was founded in 1948, it soon addressed *diakonia* as a major preoccupation, defining it as "responsible service of the gospel by deeds and by words performed by Christian in response to the needs of people".[25] Two main tracks were followed in the work by the WCC in the first decades of its existence, one of concrete action in the form of inter-church aid providing assistance to refugees and victims of war and poverty, another of engagement in social and ethics issues promoting 'responsible society'. The first led to the development of large aid programmes, while from the 1960s it included development work in Africa and Asia. The second corresponded in many ways to Wendland's view regarding political *diakonia*, and this position was given even more emphasis after the WCC Uppsala Assembly in 1968. One controversial example was the *Program to combat racism* that expressed solidarity with and support for the liberation movements in Southern Africa which, according to some critics, implied acceptance of armed struggle in achieving political goals.

By the 1990s, this way of performing *diakonia* ecumenically was to be changed.[26] It was no longer possible to uphold an understanding of *diakonia* that operated with donors and beneficiaries as two separated groups, or between rich churches in the North and poor receivers in the South. Both theological and political arguments were presented in order to reorient diaconal action as a shared responsibility, mandated by a common call to witness and serve.

Within this perspective, new dimensions of *diakonia* were emphasised. An important moment of reorientation was the WCC consultation in Larnaca, Cyprus, in 1986 that stressed the ecclesial nature of *diakonia*, rejecting that its action belonged to some few specialists. Instead it belongs to the whole people

---

[25] Teresa Joan White, *'Diakonia'*, in *Dictionary of the Ecumenical Movement,* Nicholas Lossky et al (eds), 2nd edn (Geneva: WCC, 2002), 305-10: www.oikoumene.org

[26] Richard D.N. Dickinson, 'Diakonia in the Ecumenical Movement', in John Briggs, Mercy Amba Oduyoye and Georges Tsetsis (eds), *History of the Ecumenical Movement, Vol. 3, 1960-2000* (Geneva: WCC, 2004), 403-31.

of God, and in particular to the local church.[27] On this occasion also, the political implications of diaconal work was affirmed: diaconal action should consider the root causes of poverty and suffering; it should become more comprehensive, preventative and liberating. Or, as noted above: bold action as mediation and 'go-between'.

The growing acknowledgment of the political implication of *diakonia* contributed to the framing of the theme 'prophetic *diakonia*' which urged diaconal agencies to stand up against injustice, and promote the rights of the poor and marginalised. In November 2002, the LWF organised a global consultation on 'Prophetic *diakonia*'. In the letter from that meeting the participants acknowledge with gratitude the many kinds of diaconal work that the church has carried out through the centuries, and then affirm:

> This work is now challenged to move toward a more prophetic form of *diakonia*. Inspired by Jesus and the prophets who confronted those in power and called for changes in unjust structures and practices, we pray that God may empower us to help transform all that leads to human greed, violence, injustice and exclusion.[28]

This perspective is maintained in the already mentioned LWF study document *Diakonia in Context*. It emphasises the ecclesial, the holistic and the prophetic dimensions of *diakonia*. This is also expressed when transformation, reconciliation and empowerment are determined as basic directions of diaconal work.[29] Clearly, the notion of *diakonia* has moved beyond that of humble and menial service.

Developing Curriculum on *Diakonia*

As we have seen, most theological institutions have not included *diakonia* in their study programmes. The fact that *diakonia* is a rather new discipline may cause uncertainty regarding its content and how to organise it as an academic discipline.[30]

This issue was addressed by a working group convened by the WCC in Geneva in December 2012. The working group did not intend to establish a fixed curriculum for the study of *diakonia*. Instead it identified four elements that were considered fundamental: theology, social analysis, scientific approach or methodology, and personal competence. The two first elements point to the

---

[27] Klaus Poser (ed), *Diakonia 2000: Called to be Neighbours. Official Report of the WCC World Consultation on Inter-Church Aid, Refugee and World Service, Larnaca, Cyprus, November 1986* (Geneva: WCC, 1987)

[28] Lutheran World Federation, *Prophetic Diakonia: 'For the Healing of the World'. Report Johannesburg, South Africa, November 2002* (Geneva: Lutheran World Federation, 2003), 6.

[29] LWF, *Diakonia in Context,* 43-47.

[30] Nordstokke, *Liberating Diakonia*, 29-39.

interdisciplinary nature of *diakonia*; diaconal action requires both knowledge of basic theological issues and the ability to analyze the social, political, economic, and cultural context. The third element refers to how this study is made – for instance, linking theory and praxis, discovering 'silent' knowledge, and using the hermeneutics of suspicion. The last element related to the development of professional competence, of leadership and management skills, and also of the identity as diaconal worker.

Indeed, some steps have been made in the process of developing *diakonia* as an academic discipline. New steps are needed, above all, in the endeavour to root *diakonia* in the life and the mission of local churches.

Bibliography

Beyer, H.W., διακονέω. *Theologisches Wörterbuch zum Neuen Testament,* Gerhard Kittel (ed), (Stuttgart: Kohlhammer, 1935), 81-93.

Beyreuther, Erich, *Geschichte der Diakonie und Inneren Mission in der Neuzeit* (Berlin: CZV-Verlag, 1983) (3., erw. Aufl.).

Brandt, Wilhelm, *Dienst und Dienen im Neuen Testament* (Gütersloh: Carl Bertelsmann Verlag, 1931).

Collins, John N., *Diakonia: Re-interpreting the Ancient Sources* (New York/Oxford: OUP, 1990).

Collins, John N., *Deacons and the Church. Making connections between old and new* (Leominster, UK: Gracewing, 2002).

Dickinson, Richard D.N., 'Diakonia in the Ecumenical Movement', in John Briggs, Mercy Amba Oduyoye and Georges Tsetsis (eds), *History of the Ecumenical Movement. Vol. 3, 1960-2000* (Geneva: WCC, 2004), 403-431.

Hentschel, Anni, *Diakonia im Neuen Testament* (Tübingen: Mohr Siebeck, 2007).

Lutheran World Federation, *Prophetic Diakonia: 'For the Healing of the World'. Report Johannesburg, South Africa, November 2002* (Geneva: Lutheran World Federation, 2003).

Lutheran World Federation, *Diakonia in Context: Transformation, Reconciliation, Empowerment. An LWF Contribution to the Understanding and Practice of Diakonia* (Geneva: LWF, 2009).

Moltmann, Jürgen, *Diakonie im Horizont des Reiches Gottes* (Neukirchen-Vluyn: Neukirchener Verlag), 1984.

Nordstokke, Kjell (ed), *Serving the Whole Person. The Practice and Understanding of Diakonia within the Lutheran Communion* (Minneapolis, MN: Lutheran University Press, 2009).

Nordstokke, Kjell, *Liberating Diakonia* (Trondheim: Tapir akademisk forlag, 2011).

Philippi, Paul, *Christozentrische Diakonie. Ein theologischer Entwurf* (Stuttgart: Evangelisches Verlagswerk, 1963).

Philippi, Paul, 'Diakonik – Diagnose des Fehlens einer Disziplin', *Pastoraltheologie*, No. 4, 1983, 177-86.

Poser, Klaus (ed), *Diakonia 2000: Called to be Neighbours. Official Report WCC World Consultation Inter-Church Aid, Refugee and World Service. Larnaca, 1986* (Geneva: WCC Publications, 1987).

Starnitzke, Dierk, *Diakonie als soziales System* (Stuttgart: Kohlhammer, 1996).

Strohm, Theodor, and Jörg Thierfelder (eds), *Diakonie im 'Dritten Reich'* (Heidelberg: Heidelberger Verlagsanstalt, 1990).

Strohm, Theodor (ed), *Diakoniewissenschaftliche Studien* (Heidelberg: Diakoniewissenschaftliches Institut – DWI), 1993f.

Uhlhorn, Gerhard, *Die christliche Liebesthätigkeit in der alten Kirche*. 2 Bände (Neukirchen: Neukirchener Verlag, 1959 [1882-84]).

Wendland, Heinz-Dietrich, 'Diakonie zwischen Kirche und Welt', in Christine Bourbeck and Heinz-Dietrich Wendland (eds), *Diakonie zwischen Kirche und Welt. Studien zur diakonischen Arbeit und Verantwortung in unserer Zeit* (Hamburg: Furche-Verlag, 1958), 17-36.

Wendland, Heinz-Dietrich, 'Christos Diakonos – Christos Doulos. Zur theologischen Begründung der Diakonie', in Heinz-Dietrich Wendland, Artur Rich, Herbert Krimm (eds), *Christos Diakonos. Ursprung und Auftrag der Kirche* (Zürich: EVZ-Verlag, 1962), 13-29.

White, Teresa Joan, *'diakonia'. Dictionary of the Ecumenical Movement*. Nicholas Lossky et al (eds), (Geneva: WCC, 2002), 305-10.

Wichern, Johann Hinrich, 'Gutachten, die Diakonie und den Diakonat betreffend', in *Johann Hinrich Wichern. Ausgewählte Schriften, Band 1: Schriften zur sozialen Frage*. Herausgegeben von Karl Janssen (Gütersloh: Carl Bertelsmann Verlag, 1956), 130-204.

World Council of Churches, *Theological Perspectives on Diakonia in the Twenty-First Century*, in *Resource Book, Busan, 2013, WCC 10th Assembly* (Geneva: WCC, 2013), 103-11.

Diakonia as a Professional Practice: Perspectives on Research and Education

Hans Stifoss-Hanssen

Introduction

This article will discuss the challenge to diaconal studies that consists of its character of being a relational, social practice, and whether the educational processes and research that accompany this practice provide the best possible match for such a practice.

First, two different but related meanings of the term *diakonia* need to be addressed:

- There is the meaning of *diakonia* as the caring and empathic approach of the churches, that is essential to the identity of the churches, and that rests on every Christian body and individual as a necessary characteristic.
- And then, there is *the professional practice of the deacon*, understood in the context of the churches, where a certain person is dedicated (and consecrated) to the inspiration and leadership of this caring and empathic process in the church. The deacon we are talking about is typically equipped with higher education for the task; she or he is employed full-time and has entered the deaconate as a lifetime vocation.[1]

The second meaning of *diakonia* – the professional practice of the deacon – is obviously intimately linked with and derived from the first meaning. But there is also a distinct difference where all Christians and churches have a responsibility for the needs and challenges they observe, the professional deacon enters the same field with a leadership role, competence, professional ethics, and paid time set aside for taking this responsibility. This similarity/difference has parallels in many other social processes: all of us have a responsibility to care for and help the weak and suffering, but home nurses and social workers respond professionally to the same needs; we all have a

---

[1] This distinction is entered for the clarity of the argument, but there are also some deacons, and persons in deacon-related functions, who work in organisations and institutions. Those persons share many tasks with parish deacons, and they will be well served by similar knowledge in the field of Christian social service.

responsibility to teach children and adolescents useful things in order to have a good life, but teachers have a special responsibility for the education of the next generation, and so on.

This article deals with *diakonia* based on the second meaning, on *diakonia* as the practice of the professional deacon, and more specifically on how *the knowledge base* – training and research – is or should be constructed to provide an adequate and effective context for becoming and staying a good professional practitioner of *diakonia*.

Diakonia, Values and Professional Practice: A Research Field

In Diakonhjemmet University College (DUC), our most recent and important investment in diaconal knowledge construction has been the development and implementation of the PhD programme in *Diakonia*, values and professional practice. During our work in DUC in constructing the programme, an effort was also made to present principles for the academic activity that could be called 'The science of diakonia', the academic activity that accompanies the professional practice of the deacon. The reflections aimed at directing the academic activities more towards research on practices: "Academically, the diaconal tradition has primarily been dealt with as a theological discipline and to a large extent from a theological-normative or a systematic-theological viewpoint. The diaconal academic work is usually presented as diaconal research or diaconal sciences. The PhD Programme in Diakonia, Values and Professional Practice at Diakonhjemmet University College, aims at contributing towards the *expansion and development of the diaconal sciences through studies with a focus on professional practice in health and social services, and churches and other faith communities*. The PhD studies will thus characterise the design of diaconal sciences with an empirical and multiple- and interdisciplinary profile, a view from within and a practice-oriented goal". This implies that the *diakonia* term used in the PhD programme is mainly operational and empirical. The study programme aims to renew, expand and support the establishment of an empirical and practice-oriented diaconal scientific tradition.[2]

The PhD programme points to a general reflection on how diaconal studies could preferably be shaped with an increased focus on *diakonia* as a professional practice and on empirical studies of diaconal practices as the core element.

---

[2] Programme description: www.diakonhjemmet.no/DHS/Studiehaandbok/Direkte-publisering/Studiekatalog/Information/PhD-program/Structure, 4.

The Role of Empirical Studies

One consequence of this line of argument is to place great emphasis on relevant and solid knowledge about the diaconal practices, the users, and the relational processes in the profession. Here, empirical research methods should play an important role, since this knowledge about practice should be acquired in a methodically transparent way. Such knowledge will be useful in revealing structural conditions and connections, and such knowledge can help evaluate the actions and strategies of the professionals and the parishes. Systematic studies of practices can also contribute towards improving strategies, developing reflection on practice (= theory), and establishing links between theory and practice.

When using the term 'empirical' about studies, it is important to point out that this is not an empiricist position or a positivistic view on methodology. Linking this field of studies with a particular empirical methodological perspective is obviously counter-productive. The aim of such studies is to keep diaconal practices faithful to good quality, and these practices by their nature transcend limits between fields, professions, data types, etc. Diaconal practices aim at a holistic profile; hence studies of these practices need to be methodologically flexible, preferably with combinations of different methodical tools of a qualitative and quantitative nature.

From Scandinavian parish *diakonia*, Ch. Engel's thesis provides a very interesting example.[3] In short, her research indicates that there is a tension between the explicit diaconal aims of the church and the diaconal activities and practices at the parish level. In the parishes she studied, activities and resources were to a large extent dedicated to church-active, middle class parishioners, whereas the diaconal programmes of the church clearly stated that *diakonia* should prioritise marginalised and underprivileged persons and groups. Engel interprets these findings as different strategies to encounter the challenge of secularisation and the possible loss of importance by the church. She thinks national elites prefer to portray the church as a progressive social force in Swedish society, whereas those responsible for local activities feel they need to prove themselves relevant to the groups that might continue their membership in the church. This research provides a good example of the value of empirical research for *diakonia*, producing knowledge we did not and could not otherwise have had. On the other hand, the appropriation of this piece of knowledge is not that simple. It needs to inspire (and it already has inspired) a broad reflection on a series of issues in the interface between diaconal ideals, theory and practice. In our context, the example is included to illustrate how

---

[3] C. Engel, 'Social Work in the Church of Sweden – For whom and why? A religious-sociological study of a deaconry dilemma', in Charlotte Engel; *Svenska kyrkans sosiale arbete – för vem och varför? En religionssosiologisk studie av ett diakonalt dilemma* (Ersta Sköndal Högskola /Uppsala Universitet, PhD Diss, 2006).

empirical knowledge needs to be integrated into the model for constructing a knowledge base of diaconal activities.

A Renewed Interest in Empirical Studies in *Diakonia*

In the invitation to the fifth biennial conference on the research and study of *diakonia* and Christian social practice, held in Stockholm in 2014, the centrality of empirical studies was underlined:

> The value of empirical studies of diaconal and Christian social practice will be emphasised and put into focus. One central theme will be such empirical studies of *diakonia* in relation to the changing economic, social, cultural and religious contexts. The presentation of research and evaluation studies of local contexts and practices from a broad variety of countries both within and beyond Europe will hopefully serve as the base for new and shared knowledge; a first step in mapping out the empirical picture of the international diaconal field and the varieties in adapting to or counteracting the challenges from marketisation and from increasing marginalisation for already vulnerable and exposed groups and communities.[4]

In similar words, the Society behind the conference calls its scientific journal a journal of 'Christian social practice'.[5] And the faculty of theology, University of Oslo, presents this definition of the science of *diakonia*: "A study and interpretation of certain practices and of the social context in which these practices occur."[6] These developments among academics who work with the construction of the field of diaconal studies seem to point to a turn in the field. Not in particular towards practice, since studies of *diakonia* have to a large extent been supplemented by internships and discussions of practices in the profession, but towards a systematic empirical analysis and appropriation of diaconal practices and their contexts, and a stronger integration of such analyses into the knowledge base of *diakonia*, into diaconal studies.

Nordstokke: Theological Motives for Including Empirical Studies in the Knowledge Base

It has been indicated that the diaconal tradition has normally been dealt with from a theologically-normative starting-point.[7] This is not the only option of how to deal with diaconal studies theologically, not even the most preferable

---

[4] www.esh.se/index.php?id=1842

[5] www.v-r.de/en/magazine-0-0/diaconia_journal_for_the_study_of_christian_social_practice-500059/

[6] www.tf.uio.no/forskning/vi-forsker-pa/diakonivitenskap/mer-om-diakonivitenskap.html

[7] above in this chapter p 63.

alternative. In his book *Liberating diakonia*, Kjell Nordstokke recommends that diaconal studies and the theory of *diakonia* should be composed of empirical and theological knowledge, in a model clearly related to professional practices.[8]

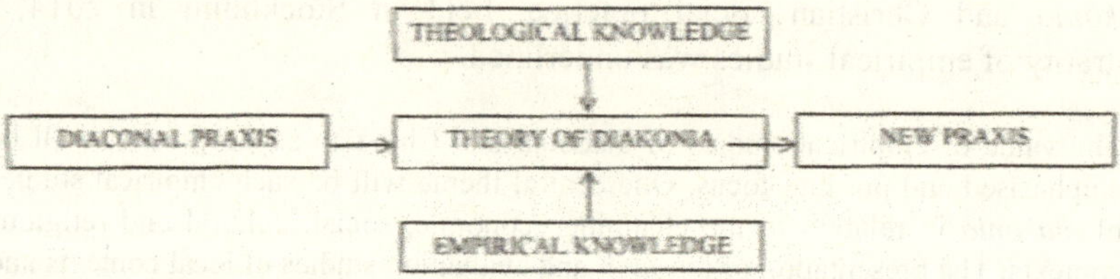

In his paper "Reflections on the theology of *diakonia*",[9] Nordstokke presents the idea of the field of *diakonia* being constructed along three tracks: a contextual track which is the immediate response to observed needs, an ecclesiological track which takes seriously *diakonia* as a feature of the Christian tradition and communities, and a 'praxeological' track: "Connecting the three tracks is not an easy task. It implies bringing together knowledge from theology and the social sciences and opening up a dialogue between theory and praxis."[10] The praxeological track "has its point of departure in the concrete praxis of *diakonia*. The theology of *diakonia* must critically reflect the diaconal practice in which the church is already involved and set priorities for the use of its limited resources. It is only then that the theology of *diakonia* becomes practicable in the sense of meaningful action, of strengthening vision and commitment, of empowerment and mobilisation".[11] This praxeological track of *diakonia* must be dealt with in diaconal studies using empirical methods as we may learn about them from social sciences. This chapter, the one you are reading now, should be seen as an attempt to specify that 'third track'. Further on, it points to a programme for what could be called 'Diaconal science' (*Diakoniewissenschaft, diakonivitenskap*). The application of such methodology (see Nordstokke's model above) has the function of helping the church "critically reflect the diaconal practice in which the church is already involved" (cited above), by providing some tools that can help understand the practices in a systematic and transparent way. Practical experience in itself does not provide sufficient knowledge and a basis for action. The example made by Engel, mentioned above, is only one out of many, of knowledge

---

[8] Kjell Nordstokke, *Liberating Diakonia*, 67, 2011a.

[9] Nordstokke, 'Reflections on the theology of diakonia', in *Diakonian Tutkimus*, No. 2, 2011b.

[10] Nordstokke, 'Reflections on the theology of diakonia', 2011b, 224-25.

[11] Nordstokke, 'Reflections on the theology of diakonia', 2011b, 225.

generated through systematic methodical work on data, knowledge that was not achieved on the basis of singular experiences alone.

In my judgement, such a reflection is particularly important in relation to the construction and maintenance of the diaconal profession. Those professionals who are dedicated to the practice of the diaconal profession in a faith community, need and deserve the support and assistance of a practice-based knowledge-constructing community of colleagues, teachers and researchers. This need is accentuated by the fabric of social welfare in our communities, where provision of welfare and care is carried out by groups of professionals practising on the basis of practice-based knowledge, or if you will, on empirical and practice-based studies and research. Such knowledge must be appropriated by the reflexive process in the construction of a knowledge base for *diakonia*, a work that will be positive to the field's work on theory-praxis challenges. Deacons who study their own profession through material built on empirical studies of deacons' professional practices and the field of diaconal work, will be better equipped for dealing with the theory-practice challenge, and show good judgement and discretion in practical work situations.

The parallel between the professional deacon and the nurse, social worker, medical doctor, teacher, and so on, is obvious. It calls for a systematic "bringing together knowledge from theology and the social sciences and opening up a dialogue between theory and praxis" – repeating the quote from Nordstokke.

Hermeneutical Parallels

This logic has much in common with the recent theological hermeneutics of emancipation, liberation and contextual theologies, feminist theology, and so on.[12] These hermeneutical influences have already affected theological work in Scandinavia to a great extent; they have contributed to an altered status for experiential material in theological work, and have (consequently) made empirical methods from the social sciences and psychology inevitable and welcome in theology.

These theologies have in common their tendency towards focusing on the local, the unique, and the contextual aspect – frequently expressed through the norm of "the epistemological privilege of the marginalised".[13] These tendencies

---

[12] S.B. Bevans, *Models of contextual theology* (New York: Orbis, 1992); G. West, *Biblical Hermeneutics of Liberation – modes of reading the Bible in the South African context* (Pietermaritzburg, RSA/New York: Cluster/Orbis, 1995); Sturla Stålsett, *The crucified and the Crucified. A study in the liberation Christology of Jon Sobrino* (New York/Oxford: Peter Lang, 2003); J. Salomonsen, 'Fra hedendom til kristendom – eller er vi fortsatt "hedningekristne"? En argumentativ revy over nyere norrøn religionsforskning og dens utfordringer til teologien' (*Norsk teologisk tidsskrift, No.* 3, *2003*).

[13] West, *Biblical Hermeneutics of Liberation*, 87.

gain importance at the cost of religious universalism, and they often lean heavily on teachings of creational theology and incarnation. A diaconally relevant instance of such a theology could be N. Eiesland's work on "The Disabled God",[14] documenting the failure of the American Lutheran Church to open up to disabled persons. The example of Eiesland, and that of Engel, both show that systematic analysis and reflection on practice very often has a critical element, and must be critical.

Theologically speaking, making space for systematic empirical knowledge in the base of diaconal studies does not need to represent weakness or secularisation. On the contrary, it can be seen as representing a different kind of theological argument, which not only communicates well with our colleagues in the welfare professions, but which is also in line with important theological ideals – like meeting the real needs of real people in adequate ways. A central inspiration to this theological perspective comes from the so-called New Practical Theology founded by D. Browning,[15] followed up by other theological researchers like J. van der Ven,[16] who among other things founded the "Journal of Empirical Theology".[17] This hermeneutical tradition, which currently influences several research projects with relevance to *diakonia*, has as its basic aim organising theological work as a hermeneutical circle that always takes empirical studies of real-life church challenges as its starting-point. The work process then invites heuristic and normative contributions from biblical studies, history and systematic theology, and concludes with a strategic suggestion to meet the original challenge. Following the implementation of the strategic suggestion, this model implies evaluation of the practical changes and follows the issue through more tours through the circle. The thinking of those theologians is inspired by the idea of 'theological correlations' in Paul Tillich's works, which is further developed by D. Tracy.[18]

The Deacon as a Professional Practitioner

The argument in this paper, and especially the development of thinking in the PhD programme in *Diakonia*, Values and Professional Practice, points evidently to an understanding of the role of the deacon as a professional practice, as a clear parallel to nurses, social workers, teachers – but also lawyers, medical doctors and ministers. This shaping of the work of the deacon

---

[14] N. Eiesland, *The disabled God. Toward a liberatory theology of disability* (Nashville, TN: Abingdon Press, 1994).

[15] D. Browning, *A fundamental practical theology. Descriptive and Strategic Proposals* (Minneapolis, MN: Augsburg Fortress Press, 1996).

[16] J. van der Ven, *Practical theology: An empirical approach* (Kampen: Pharos Publishing House, 1993).

[17] www.brill.com/journal-empirical-theology

[18] Browning, *A fundamental practical theology*.

has recently been clarified and argued by Nygaard.[19] The role of the parish deacon is a profession. According to professional studies, a profession is characterised by some performative aspects. First, a professional provides services, like comfort, counselling, the opportunity of company, or something similar. Secondly, a professional relates to clients or users, persons who ask for some assistance or service. This is true also of diaconal practices, even if the church is very conscious of de-escalating uneven power relationships – at the heart of Christian social practice is the vision of equal relationships. Thirdly, a professional tries to solve problems presented by persons (clients, users). Much time is spent by deacons trying to help individuals solve problems. The next feature of a profession is the attempt to create change, which is fundamental. Change has to do with trying to assist in problem-solving, but it also points to more basic changes, to avoid a return of the same problem. Lastly, and most important in the context of this article, is the characteristic that has to do with the profession's knowledge base. A professional performs on the basis of a systematic base of knowledge, and what I am mainly discussing here is the construction of this knowledge base for the deacon. Generally, the knowledge base should contribute to the professional's ability to assess a situation, to analyze what choices are available, and make a decision. The knowledge base is of crucial importance to the professional's conception of the relationship between theory and practice, and hence to the feeling of professional proficiency in the professional.

Example: Nursing Science

Looking at the construction of nursing studies (or nursing science) which is a parallel relevant to the diaconal profession, we can observe that a quite similar discussion takes place. Based on M. Kirkevold's work,[20] it seems clear that the composition of the knowledge base of the profession is influenced by a long range of factors of a practical and theoretical nature. Nursing is strongly influenced by the medical profession, but where medicine seems to operate on a rather monolithic scientific base, nursing is to a greater extent, historically, based on normative models of caring relationality. But nursing has undergone a transformation under the influence of the focus on evidence-based professional practices, like other professions. This has inspired work in the direction of making a coherent theory of the profession, and in connection with that, towards accumulating a body of empirical research that can provide underpinning to the models, and present a transparent demonstration of the

---

[19] M.R. Nygaard, 'Diakoners profesjonsvilkår i Den norske kirke', in *Halvårsskrift for Praktisk Teologi*, No. 2, 2011; M.R. Nygaard and G. Afdal, 'Deacons' professional practice as knowledge creation – taking 'see-judge-act' a step further', in *Prismet*, No. 2, 2013.

[20] M. Kirkevold, *Vitenskap for praksis?* (Oslo: Gyldendal akademisk, 2002).

theory-practice relationship in professional practice.[21] Kirkevold follows the American nursing scientist H.S. Kim and points to the areas or domains of client conditions, nurse-client interaction, practical operations in the work, and contextual factors, as necessary foci of empirical research in order to cover the field of nursing in a way that will help construct a knowledge base.[22] This systematising of the working field will most likely sound familiar to many who practice the diaconal profession. Kirkevold discusses models representing the content and structure of nursing science; they all lean on systematic empirical research, typically as a significant portion of the model.[23] Antagonistic positions also exist among the nursing theorists, prioritising alternatively empirical or theoretical dimensions, but not without an empirical foundation.

Compared with the division of diaconal theory in three tracks by Nordstokke, this situation of nursing studies comes out as quite similar. Like the other professions in our society, deacons and nurses perform on the basis of shared norms of justice, compassion, human rights, and so on. And at the same time, their dedication to people (clients, confidents, patients, residents, pupils …) requires a tested and systematic knowledge base that is to a significant degree taken from the actual experience of those people, and from practices with those people – i.e. empirical research. From the perspective of society at large, it is reasonable to conceive of professional practices as interfaces where the population can gain from the cost that society has spent on research, demonstrating that it is worth the price. For the churches and the diaconal research bodies, this is equally true. The work of universities, colleges and researchers can be expected to generate a base of knowledge that takes material in a systematic way from the practice field and contributes to quality in it.

The Research Fields

I have mentioned a few studies of diaconal practices that can show elements of the empirical knowledge body we need in *diakonia* to develop our theoretical and empirical model of diaconal studies. I will also present some reflections on what studies we should prioritise and what data we could preferably collect in order to strengthen the empirical dimension of the model of *diakonia*. To some extent, such studies obviously exist already, so my point is partly to initiate new studies, but partly also to systematise existing and new studies, and integrate them more explicitly into the construction of diaconal science. The following can be seen as a suggestion of how to specify the 'praxeological track' in diaconal theory introduced by Nordstokke.[24] It may be expected that students of *diakonia* and deacons will be helped by seeing that the theory of

[21] Kirkevold, *Vitenskap for praksis?* 143.
[22] Kirkevold, *Vitenskap for praksis?* 146.
[23] E.g. model in Kirkevold, *Vitenskap for praksis?* 139.
[24] Nordstokke, 'Reflections on the theology of diakonia'.

their profession is communicating transparently with the practice field in its complexity.

To the extent that we shall have the opportunity to plan and initiate research in diaconal professional practice, I suggest that the following three directions are taken into consideration:

(1) *Mapping out exploratory studies in the field of church and society*. Looking in this direction, we should study which groups in society are marginalised: their conditions, locations, numbers, etc. But we should also see to what extent and in which ways churches, deacons and parishes serve or interact with those people. If such contact is sparse or non-existent, a challenge on many levels is identified. But we should also produce overviews of the work of deacons, diaconal practices in parishes and faith communities, including the number of hired deacons, of volunteers, and different kinds of groups and practices. Such material alone can provide important insights into issues regarding the relationship between theory and practice in diaconal work. In this area, numerous studies already exist,[25] and also systematised statistical reports.[26] But there is much left in the area of systematic analysis and regarding the quality of statistics.

Integral to this exploratory perspective is also the study of religious and spiritual dimensions in the lives of people, especially in coping with crises and with major life events. The churches and faith communities should undoubtedly aim to play a role in relation to this kind of challenge; this is demonstrated in, for instance, research into public mental health and existential issues.[27] The move of many societies towards more religious and cultural pluralisation certainly makes this perspective of study increasingly relevant.

The study of religious and spiritual coping in the population is obviously a huge challenge, which goes far beyond the capacity of diaconal research alone, but in this area there are several active researchers and institutions. The challenge to diaconal research is to contribute, to co-operate, and to follow, the research activities as a whole with the aim of producing analyses that can help develop diaconal theory and practices.

(2) *Helping practices, activities initiated by or under the leadership of the deacon*. For the nurse or the social worker, this aspect would have the label of interventions.[28] Here, we study the actual practices and doings, actions that presumably relate to theory and theoretical models of *diakonia* in some way.

---

[25] E.g. O.H. Angell and A.S. Selbekk, *Kirke og helse. Kartlegging av diakonalt helsearbeid innen Den norske kirke* (Oslo: Diakonhjemmet høgskole, 2005).

[26] H. Stifoss-Hanssen, *Tilstandsrapport for Den norske kirke 2010* (KIFO rapport, No. 1, 2010).

[27] V. DeMarinis, *Pastoral care, existential health, and existential epidemiology. A Swedish post-modern case study* (Stockholm: Verbum, 2003); H. Stifoss-Hanssen and L.J. Danbolt, 'Om å stå oppreist etter katastrofen – ritualer og resiliens etter 22 juli', in *Omsorg – Nordisk tidsskrift for palliativ medisin*, No. 1, 2014.

[28] See above in this chapter on nurse-client interaction, practical operations in the work.

Unlike point 1 above, we are here interested in the characteristics of the specific activity or set of activities – like the deacon M. Torp Træthaug, who has described and analyzed how she performed pastoral care partly through the medium of Facebook in specific critical situations, and the deacon A.M. Sverdrup, who has described and analyzed how she applied the psychodrama-method in pastoral care, assisting persons to deal with spiritual and existential challenges.[29] In such studies, there will be a focus on how diaconal interventions are carried out, how they are experienced by deacons, volunteers or clients, and on whether the goals of the activity seem to be attained.

It should be tried out to accumulate accounts of a range of such studies, in order to get closer to an empirically based picture of diaconal practice, in order to say something about what characterises this practice. Seen together with point 1 above, it will also open up the possibility of identifying areas of diaconal challenges that are not covered or not studied.

(3) *Innovative practices, interventions that go beyond what is usually done by diakonia.* Transcending limits for what is normally done and expected by the church and the deacon is an inherent obligation for both. Sensitivity to human needs is central to *diakonia*, and research activities can help support such sensitivity put into practice, by helping develop strategies and by attending to such practices with studies and evaluations that can enhance them. By definition, innovation implies taking risks; examination by researchers can limit the damage of failures and point to functional choices. The European development project cluster called INNOSERV, including a range of innovative social practices, exemplifies this kind of focus.[30] A different example is the provision of health care for illegal refugees to Norway.[31] We may also point to demographic developments in some western populations as an example, the fact that the proportion of elderly persons in those societies is increasing quite strongly. This phenomenon is given much attention by public authorities, but nevertheless, this is a field where there is room for crossing borders – partly because working with old people is low-status work in our society, but also because the demographic change is going to be so significant that innovation on several levels is needed if care is not going to deteriorate in welfare states. This is a challenge to the whole of society, but the church and its deacons are called to present innovative alternatives as far as the resources of the faith communities permit. It is reasonable to imagine that the innovative potential of Christian social practice and of the churches has to do with their

---

[29] M.T. Trethaug, 'Diakoni på Facebook. Hvordan kan bruk av Facebook være med og gi ungdom plass i sørgerommet?', in *Tidsskrift for sjelesorg*, No. 2, 2013; A.M. Sverdrup, 'Håpshandling i et utvidet sjelesorgrom. Psykodrama som sjelesorg', in *Tidsskrift for sjelesorg*, No. 4, 2013.

[30] Diakonhjemmet University College participated, see www.inno-serv.eu/

[31] Sturla Stålsett, 'Asylbarn og menneskeverd: Etiske refleksjoner med utgangspunkt i erfaringer fra helsesenteret for papirløse migranter', in *Etikk i praksis/Nordic Journal of Applied Ethics*, No. 2, 2012.

distinctive character – with their focus on marginalised persons, and their willingness to promote values like unselfishness, non-profit social coherence and meaning.

These roughly sketched research directives are meant to present a picture of the scientific field, having said nothing about methods or methodology. It is obvious that such a broad research programme will have to include all imaginable empirical methods. Research questions will have to determine the method. The area presents research challenges of all kinds, from the prevalence of measurable phenomena, to the character of a single case, and the relationship between them.

Diaconal Science

Going back to Nordstokke's metaphor of the three tracks, let me remind the reader that this article is an attempt at specifying the third track, the 'praxeological' track. The whole of diaconal science will need to be composed of all tracks, or if you will, of theory and practice. The aim here is to argue that empirical research methods are needed to include practice into the models of diaconal science in a way that is methodical. It is an attempt to take the idea of the theory-practice link a step further, trying to answer the questions: which practice, how, and in what way? In the end, we want to create conditions that allow for churches and deacons to initiate the best possible actions and make the best possible decisions.

Bibliography

Angell, O.H., and A.S. Selbekk, *Kirke og helse. Kartlegging av diakonalt helsearbeid innen Den norske kirke* (Oslo: Diakonhjemmet høgskole, 2005).

Bevans, S.B., *Models of contextual theology* (New York: Orbis, 1992).

Browning, D., *A fundamental practical theology* (Minneapolis, MN: Fortress, 1991).

DeMarinis, V., *Pastoral care, existential health, and existential epidemiology. A Swedish post-modern case study* (Stockholm: Verbum, 2003).

Eiesland, N., *The disabled God. Toward a liberatory theology of disability* (Nashville, TN: Abingdon Press, 1994).

Engel, C., *Svenska kyrkans sociala arbete – föt vem och varför?* (Ersta Sköndal/Uppsala Universitet, PhD dissertation, 2006).

Kirkevold, M., *Vitenskap for praksis?* (Oslo: Gyldendal akademisk, 2002).

Nordstokke, K., *Liberating Diakonia* (Trondheim: Tapir akademisk, 2011a).

Nordstokke, K., Reflections on the theology of *diakonia*, in *Diakonian Tutkimus*, No. 2 (2011b).

Nygaard, M.R., 'Diakoners profesjonsvilkår i Den norske kirke', in *Halvårsskrift for Praktisk Teologi*, No. 2 (2011).

Nygaard, M.R., and G. Afdal, Deacons' professional practice as knowledge creation – taking 'see-judge-act' a step further, in *Prismet*, No. 2 (2013).

Salomonsen, J., 'Fra hedendom til kristendom – eller er vi fortsatt "hedningekristne"? En argumentativ revy over nyere norrøn religionsforskning og dens utfordringer til teologien', in *Norsk teologisk tidsskrift,* No. 3 (2003).

Stifoss-Hanssen, H., *Tilstandsrapport for Den norske kirke 2010*. KIFO rapport, No. 1 (2010).

Stifoss-Hanssen, H., and L.J. Danbolt, 'Om å stå oppreist etter katastrofen – ritualer og resiliens etter 22 juli', in *Omsorg – Nordisk tidsskrift for palliativ medisin,* No. 1 (2014).

Stålsett, S., *The crucified and the Crucified. A study in the liberation Christology of Jon Sobrino* (New York/Oxford: Peter Lang (2003).

Stålsett, S., 'Asylbarn og menneskeverd: Etiske refleksjoner med utgangspunkt i erfaringer fra helsesenteret for papirløse migranter', in *Etikk i praksis/Nordic Journal of Applied Ethics*, No. 2 (2012).

Sverdrup, A.M., Håpshandling i et utvidet sjelesorgrom. Psykodrama som sjelesorg, in *Tidsskrift for sjelesorg*, No. 4 (2013).

Trethaug, M.T., 'Diakoni på Facebook. Hvordan kan bruk av Facebook være med og gi ungdom plass i sørgerommet?' in *Tidsskrift for sjelesorg*, No. 2 (2013).

Ven J. van der, *Practical theology: An empirical approach* (Kampen: Pharos, 1993).

West, G., *Biblical Hermeneutics of Liberation – modes of reading the Bible in the South African context* (Pietermaritzburg/New York: Cluster/Orbis, 1995).

The Development of Diakonia as Faith-Based Professional Practice

Olav Fanuelsen

Introduction

This chapter will focus on the development of and the relationship between *diakonia*, faith and professional practice. Traditionally *diakonia* has been looked upon as a faith-based practice or activity. The link between faith and life is one of the cornerstones of Christian theology and can be described in a variety of ways. For Paul the apostle, "The only thing that counts is faith expressing itself through love" (Galatians 5:6).

Today one can experience tensions between the traditional view of faith and modern scientific and professional values, tensions which also influence the relationship between faith and *diakonia* as professional practice. The *diakonia* of the church has this challenge in common with many kinds of church-affiliated institutions which have a faith-based foundation for their work. The formulation; 'Bridging the Gap: Connecting Christian Faith and Professional Practice in a Pluralistic Society' was launched as a main topic for leaders of higher education a couple of years ago.[1] Through plenary addresses and discussions, the challenges were discussed, and the audience sought for both theological and academic models to bridge the gap between the faith base and the secular worldview which is dominant in academic institutions.

The goal of this chapter is to contribute to this discussion and eventually come up with some views which can be used in a further exploration. What we will have in focus are three aspects. The first is the question of the relationship between *diakonia* and faith. Questions are asked: is it necessary to have a faith to do *diakonia*? Modern diaconal institutions have many loyal staff members who don't define themselves as active believers. Nevertheless they support the diaconal values and visions from a more value-based position. But the question arises sooner or later: what do faith-based help and faith-based professional practice mean? Or as the German theologian Anika Albert formulates it: is it at

---

[1] *Bridging the Gap: Connecting Christian Faith and Professional Practice* (Sioux Center, IA: Dordt College Press, 2011).

all possible to describe a difference between general human help and faith-based help?[2]

The next aspect is the relationship between faith and professional practice. It may be acute in different situations, but in general all who have a faith and want to live a faith-based life sooner or later raise the question: what does it mean to meet people in difficult situations and to discuss complicated ethical questions based on my faith? Even more, is it expected to give an answer, when the institution itself is faith-based? How should professional work be designed to answer this challenge? As Albert asks: how do help and care appear in a theological perspective?[3]

The third aspect is the relationship between *diakonia* and professional practice. The question is not whether *diakonia* is a practical activity or practice per se. The question is to what extent *diakonia*, as a part of the mission of the Christian church, shapes a professional practice which in a particular way is influenced by the basic aspects of the Christian faith, and makes it distinct to professional practice in general. It is also a question of how the link between faith and professional practice can be understood in a diaconal setting, and how the link between faith and *diakonia* has changed through the history of the church.

The context here is a Nordic Lutheran understanding of *diakonia* as "the caring ministry of the Church. It is the Gospel in action and is expressed through loving your neighbour, creating inclusive communities, caring for creation and struggling for justice", as it is expressed in the Plan for Diakonia in Church of Norway,[4] although we also bear in mind other definitions of *diakonia*, as they are expressed in other church traditions.[5]

The context is furthermore professional practice as it finds expression in different caring professions. Traditionally *diakonia* in the Lutheran tradition has been nursing and social work, but includes other professions like teachers, while some academic professions have carried out a caring ministry. Deacons as ministers have, in addition to their social or health profession, also a knowledge base from theology and tools from different parts of practical theology. This mixture and integration of theory and practice, and cross-professional knowledge base and skills are challenging, because of the different scientific paradigms involved. The question here is also how to make professional practice consistent and distinct.

It should also be mentioned that the topic is not quite identical with the discussion that has been going on for decades about faith and science, or faith

---

[2] Albert, *Helfen als Gabe*, 15.

[3] Albert, *Helfen Als Gabe*, 244ff.

[4] Kirkerådet, *Church of Norway Plan for Diakonia* (Oslo: Church of Norway, National Council, 2008).

[5] The relationship between the Lutheran and Anglican tradition is described in the report of the Lutheran World Federation, 'To Love and Serve the Lord. Diakonia in the Life of the Church', the Anglican-Lutheran International Commission (ALIC III) (2012).

and knowledge in higher education.[6] Because the focus is the diaconal perspective, which at least in principal is per se a faith-based perspective, the more general challenge concerning faith and knowledge is not the principal question, although it will be mentioned as important here too.

We will start the exploration with a description and discussion of the links between *diakonia* and faith, partly from a historical point of view, before we turn to some reflections on the concept of 'faith-based'. Later, we turn to the question of understanding professional practice, and finally we will outline some models for *diakonia* for faith-based professional practice, which can be used for further discussion.

Diakonia and the Faith

The concept of *diakonia* and the ministry and mission of *diakonia* can be discussed and worked out from a variety of perspectives. One of them is the basic links between faith and *diakonia*. The concept of *diakonia* in the New Testament is also used with a variety of meanings along a scale from a quite general understanding to a more distinct description of the content of *diakonia*. We will not here deal with the big discussion about *diakonia* and its relation to the ancient sources, as started by John Collins and others.[7] We will focus mainly on *diakonia* as it is described in Matthew 25, and where the links between faith and *diakonia* is described in the context of the Last Judgement. In the dialogue with the righteous it says: "They also will answer, Lord, when did we ever see you hungry or thirsty or a stranger or needing clothes or sick or in prison, and did not help you?" (Matthew 25:44). From the Greek text this can be translated as: "To do *diakonia* towards you." Probably a text like this inspired Christians and churches in the 19th and 20th centuries to define their charity as *diakonia*. In this chapter we will do the same.

From a historical point of view, it is worth mentioning that love of one's neighbour was not unique to the Christian church. In many cultures and religions one could find a moral tradition which regulated human interrelations. Kvalbein, with references to Bolkestein, mentions old Egyptian culture as an example, where care for the poor in society was defined and regulated. To help the hungry, the thirsty and the naked was an ideal and an obligation. The most important social virtue was justice. The strong should help the weak.[8] Some of the same tendencies one finds in Jewish tradition. The similarities are so

---

[6] Douglas Sloan, *Faith and Knowledge: Mainline Protestantism and American Higher Education*, 1st ed (Louisville, KY: Westminster John Knox Press, 1994).

[7] John N. Collins, *Diakonia: Re-interpreting the Ancient Resources* (New York: OUP, 1990).

[8] Hans Kvalbein, *Filantropi Og Diakoni Omsorg for Medmennesker I De Antikke Kulturer Og I Det Nye Testamente* (Oslo: Luther forlag, 1976), 37f.

distinct that we may talk about an oriental pattern. God is the protector of the weak, and justice is more or less the same as charity against the helpless.[9]

The socio-ethical principles in the New Testament are in general a reflection of the Jewish and oriental pattern. The interpretation is however different. Jesus underlines two new aspects of the faith which became decisive for the Christian life. The first one is the radical expansion of the concept of charity in a universal dimension. There are no borders for charity. The second is the principle of serving and sacrificing oneself for others. The point is not to achieve honour and recognition among people or profit before God, but to be a servant, to have a servant attitude and spread God's love to people.[10]

The *diakonia* of the Early Church can be described as a 'communion' *diakonia*. Faith had a very strong *koinonia* dimension: the fellowship was important in faith and life.[11] The church had an elliptically structured fellowship with two centres: the Eucharist and the *diakonia*. They are closely interrelated.[12] The *diakonia* of the word and sacrament, and the *diakonia* of the table were kept together (Act 6:1ff).

The relationship between faith and deeds was one of the main concerns of the Lutheran Reformation; but the importance of good deeds for salvation was meanwhile rejected. What happened during the Reformation was that responsibility for charity work in former church institutions and parishes was transferred from the church to the worldly and civil regime and authorities. The main argument for that was that God reigned over both the spiritual and civil regimes.[13] One could say that what today we would call *diakonia* continued as a faith-based responsibility but under a new organisation. It was not characterised as a secular regime or a secular activity. The role of the church in the civil organisation was distinct and it was a religiously homogeneous society, where everybody belonged to the church.

A change occurred during the Pietistic movement in the last part of the 17th and in the 18th centuries. Pietism, from the Latin *pietas*: piety, introduced a new angle on faith which regulated many parts of life. A small church or fellowship, a *societas*, was created within the framework of the larger church, an *ecclesiola in ecclesia*. The Pietists looked upon themselves as the true believers and the true church, the church of baptised believers.[14] The influence on what we today would define as *diakonia* was significant, with all kinds of

[9] Kvalbein, *Filantropi Og Diakoni*, 46.

[10] Kvalbein, *Filantropi Og Diakoni*, 63.

[11] Sven-Erik Brodd and Diakonistiftelsen Samariterhemmet, *The Theology of Diaconia*, Samariterhemmets Skriftserie (Uppsala: Diakonistiftelsen Samariterhemmet, 1999), 5.

[12] Sven-Erik Brodd and Diakonistiftelsen Samariterhemmet. *The Theology of Diaconia*, 12.

[13] Sven-Erik Brodd and Diakonistiftelsen Samariterhemmet. *The Theology of Diaconia*, 16.

[14] Sven-Erik Brodd and Diakonistiftelsen Samariterhemmet. *The Theology of Diaconia*, 17.

institutions and efforts emerging to help needy people, and within the educational system as well. Faith was transformed into action.

Since the 19th century the pioneers in the Lutheran tradition like Johann Hinrich Wichern (1808-81), Theodor Fliedner (1800-64) and Wilhelm Löhe (1808-72) defined *diakonia* based on the 'social' categories as we already have mentioned, and this is the tradition we know today. They started to train nurses, social workers and teachers to take care of all kinds of social and individual needs. They were pioneers, at least in Lutheran countries. It was a distinct faith-based tradition although the relationship with the church institution could be informal. And it was a continual challenge for *diakonia* accepted by the official church. In the last part of the century, new initiatives came into being, based on a more humanistic foundation or as a result of the emerging welfare state.

The pioneers claimed generally that *diakonia* belonged to the whole church and that it was the responsibility of each member of the congregation and of the whole *koinonia*. *Diakonia* appears as the individual person's love for his/her neighbour and as a professional practice done by deacons, deaconesses or others, belonging to a ministry. Whether professional or general, *diakonia* is in its very nature faith-based.

The general development in church and society has since that time influenced the practice and formation of diaconal work. Professional practice itself has substantially changed since the time of the pioneers for several reasons, such as the general secularisation and differentiation in modern society and the growth of the secular welfare state as an alternative to the charity work of the religious segment of civil society. Last but not least, there has also been a growing scientific development within the caring professions which has changed the relationship between personal attitudes and the knowledge base for action. The role of faith has continually been challenged as the only motivational factor for professional practice. The integration of *diakonia* into the welfare state system raises the question: on what basis should diaconal work survive as a faith-based activity and what role should it play?

The fact is that modern professional practice has deeply affected the *diakonia* of the church and its institutions. With reference to the German situation, Merz describes the change that gradually took place from the 1960s in diaconal institutions. To resolve a situation with lack of internal, traditionally trained staff, new groups of professionals were employed with alternative motivation, values and professional standards, and placed within the old diaconal culture. Professionalism without faith was placed in the centre of professional practice and adopted without any substantial critique.[15]

---

15 Rainer Merz, *Diakonische Professionalität: Zur Wissenschaftlichen Rekonstruktion des Beruflichen Selbstkonzeptes von Diakoninnen Und Diakonen. Eine Berufsbiographische Studie*, Vol. Band 33 (Heidelberg: Universitätsverlag Winter, 2006), 35.

It seems that during the past generation the profile has changed from being a faith-based orientation towards a more value-based orientation with a focus on general values capable of being accepted by a variety of staff members. The role of faith has changed from a position where faith was the basis of a profession, to a situation where faith has become a tool to solve specific spiritual needs in a caring situation, one instrument among many. Earlier professional practice was defined and looked upon as an important instrument of *diakonia*. Now it seems that faith and *diakonia* have become assets or tools in a limited sector of professional practice, namely, the sector which is working with the spiritual needs of patients and clients.

This development has introduced a good many tensions and uncertainties for the *diakonia* of the church, and there have been many attempts to resolve the situation. On the one hand, *diakonia* needs a professional practice of a high standard in order to fulfil its work. On the other hand, not all staff members are believers and the question comes up: can one carry out *diakonia* without a belief? Generally there are a number of unsolved questions concerning faith and professionalism; what is the relationship between faith and knowledge, etc?

What we have here described is discussed by Eurodiaconia, an umbrella organisation for a variety of diaconal agencies and organisations in Europe. In 2008 the organisation focused systematically on faith in social care. Eurodiaconia claims that:

> Our personal identity will always be determined and assembled by both internal and external components, such as history, the contemporary environment and personal convictions. In order to obtain and reflect a strong identity, it is of great importance that we first and foremost recognise and distinguish the different components which have influenced and still do influence the composition of our identity as a whole. In order to let others know who we are and what we stand for, we need to know these things about ourselves first.[16]

When *diakonia* takes place in institutions and organisations, the institutional framework means a great deal but so also does personal identity.

Diakonia in a parish will probably have a more focused faith perspective than *diakonia* in a complicated institution with hundreds of staff members from a variety of backgrounds. Nevertheless, professionally trained deacons also use tools and knowledge from general professional training in their daily work, and the question is to what extent they also manage to make their practice distinctly faith-based, or manages to 'talk the walk' – as Eurodiaconia expresses it.

Confronted with these challenges, we can briefly say that there are three preliminary models concerning faith and *diakonia*, which could be fruitful to focus on in further discussion.

---

[16] Eurodiaconia, *Diaconal Identity: Faith in Social Care. A Reflection from Eurodiaconia* (Brussels: Eurodiaconia 2010).

The first model is based on the individual's personal faith and calling. This is generally the model from the Pietistic epoch where the emphasis is on the Christian motivation and calling. The theological foundation is in Christology where Jesus as person becomes the model for the right way to serve, and personal salvation which not only sets the person free from sin, but also frees him/her to serve. The Lutheran perspective on Christian freedom here is basic.

Another model concerning faith and *diakonia* places more emphasis on the faith heritage of the institution. It is characteristic for many diaconal institutions today that general values are developed from the faith base. They are made available for everybody who is working there. The theological foundation may be a creation theology which underlines the ability of everyone to do well (Romans 2:14). From a theological point of view, this may be interpreted as part of general revelation. Everybody has the ability to do good.

As an alternative to these two models, a third way of linking faith and *diakonia* would to focus more on the phenomenon of professional practice itself and discuss it in relation to different interpretations of faith. This implies turning in a more epistemological direction, and reducing the importance of a purely soteriological perspective, resulting in the privatisation of the faith base. It will also be an alternative to a model which emphasises only the heritage and the framework where faith in daily life plays only a small role. From a theological point of view, human experience based on a general revelation have to be interpreted in the perspective of the more special revelation as it is given us in the Gospel.

The answers depend partly on one's understanding of faith itself, but also on the role of faith in relation to *diakonia* and how we understand professional practice. Is it faith-based, when the organisation has a faith-based foundation, or is it faith-based when my personal motivation and inner attitudes are faith-based? We will in the next part explore some of the different dimensions of faith and what it means when something is 'faith-based'.

Faith and 'Faith-Based' – Different Dimensions

Faith is a widely used concept. It is used in daily language, in philosophy and in theology. Within a theological framework, as will be the context of *diakonia*, faith is one of the ultimate concepts and it represents the centre of reality. In a Christian theological setting, faith has both an epistemological and soteriological aspect. It defines how things about God may be known, and also how salvation may be attained.[17]

Thomas Aquinas (1225-74) could be the reference point for the epistemological perspective. He adopts a strongly intellectualistic approach to faith, something midway between knowledge (*scientia*) and opinion. The

[17] Alister E. McGrath, *Christian Theology: An Introduction*, 3rd ed (Oxford: Blackwell, 2001), 238.

relationship between faith and knowledge is for him of great importance. In a 'scientia' perspective, truth is accepted by the human intellect either because it is self-evidently correct, or because I am convinced about it by logical arguments which appeal to every rational mind. In the case of faith, on the other hand, the evidence is not sufficient to convince the human intellect to accept it. Faith accepts as true the articles of the Christian faith as summarised in the creeds, even if they cannot be demonstrated to be so beyond any doubt, on the basis of evidence available. Aquinas insists upon the rationality of the Christian faith and that the content of the Christian faith can be consistent with human reason.[18]

Martin Luther (1483-1546), on the other hand, through the doctrine of justification by faith, made faith the cornerstone of his theology and spirituality. Luther's description of faith has three components: faith has a personal rather than a historical reference, faith concerns trust in the promises of God, and faith unites believers to Christ.[19] Faith is not simply historical knowledge: it must have a basic element of believing and trusting. Christ was born for us personally, and has accomplished for us the work of salvation. It includes an element of trust which unites believers to Christ.

Aquinas and Luther emphasise different aspects of the understanding of faith. Aquinas relates it to questions of evidence while Luther relates it more to the personal trustworthiness of God.

We will reflect both perspectives in relation to *diakonia* in the following, but we will also bear in mind that there is a difference between faith in a 'pure' scientific perspective and tradition, and faith in a theological perspective.

Since the time of the Enlightenment there has been a tradition of looking at faith as something like 'a lower form of knowledge', partial knowledge, with a degree of uncertainty, based on either lack of evidence, or evidence which is inadequate to convince fully. Kant (1724-1804) looked at faith as subjectively adequate but objectively inadequate.[20]

When we ask what it means that an activity is faith-based, it seems that both aspects of the understanding of faith are relevant. To act in faith, in good faith, and to act based on the knowledge of faith, could be reflected and interpreted both from a position where faith is defined as some sort of evidence and from a position were faith is looked upon as a merely personal 'project'. The personal aspect of faith has often dominated.

This understanding may also be adequate within the framework of *diakonia*. A ministry or practice can be founded on knowledge and reflection, and on a personal engagement as well. To take into account both the epistemological and soteriological aspects, that *diakonia* as the caring ministry of the church, the Gospel in action, builds on faith as knowledge as well as faith as a personal

---

[18] McGrath, *Christian Theology*, 238.

[19] McGrath, *Christian Theology*, 239.

[20] McGrath, *Christian Theology*, 238.

commitment, will give a more balanced possibility of finding the authentic *diakonia*.

To define what 'faith-based' means must include therefore our basic understanding of faith in a Christian theological setting.

The position of faith and the meaning of faith are not only a challenge within a diaconal and Christian horizon, but also from a more professional point of view in general. Many nurses and social workers have a personal Christian faith, and they want to look upon their profession and work as a Christian calling and based on faith. The role of religion in welfare work has changed during the last decades. While the 1970s can be characterised by a neutral tendency in society in general as well as in professional work, we observe today some sort of a revival of the importance of religion. The post-modern way of reflecting opens up a more individualistic perspective, and a more holistic anthropology includes religious needs in the care of suffering people. How the social worker conceives the relationship between faith and professional practice depends on his/her way of understanding the faith. One would presume that it has something to do with confessional questions, spiritual formation and traditions.

From a social work point of view, Furness and Gilligan point out two different faith-based approaches to social work, namely, a fundamentalist/ exclusive view and a more liberal/open one.[21]

A fundamentalist/exclusive approach claims that faith is fundamental for life in general, and not only for spiritual salvation. The acceptance of faith is seen as the essential component in being able to move from a difficult life situation to a better life. Faith is seen as an integral part of practice and will be fundamental in the repertoire of the social worker in his practice.

On the other hand, a faith-based agency adopting a more liberal and open concept of faith will present a different attitude to faith, where faith is seen as a motivation for action and not necessarily an essential part of that action. Practitioners may experience that their calling and faith require them to act and to do a professional job to those in need, but they will do so without integrating aspects of faith directly in the social work process.

For *diakonia* as the caring ministry of the church, neither the fundamentalist nor the liberal/open model seems sufficient. The weakness of a pure fundamentalist approach is that the question of scientifically based knowledge becomes very unclear. Professional practice can easily be transformed into solely bringing the faith to others, and not working on the social and psychodynamic underlying problems.

A purely liberal/open approach will focus on the person's inner motivation and personal attitudes, and avoid fundamental questions of anthropology and worldview, or the more doctrinal part of the faith. It has some of the same

[21] Sheila Furness and Philip Gilligan, *Religion, Belief and Social Work: Making a Difference* (Bristol: Policy Press, 2010), 151.

attitudes as the former Pietistic tradition, which also focused on personal faith, and the link between faith and practice. But the Pietistic movement built many institutions and did much work which was characterised by a faith identity, which they combined with new and modern pedagogical, educational and social reflection to reach their goals.

The understanding of faith as knowledge about human beings and one's worldview seems to be one of the important questions for *diakonia*, when *diakonia* wants to elaborate an adequate and distinct professional practice. It is not merely the question of faith as a personal matter reserved for inner life and motivation, where one focuses on spiritual needs, but to reflect and mirror the knowledge of faith in the encounter with questions of health, welfare strategies and care.

Professional Practice

It is also important to explore the understanding of professional practice itself, and generally ask how it would be possible to have a faith-based professional practice.

The main position today is that practice and professionalism should be evidence-based and research-based. To what extent may we integrate faith, as knowledge, in a position like that?[22]

One of the challenges is that professional praxis represents a huge variety but has some similarities. All forms of praxis generally have a knowledge base which is in varying degrees research-based. They promote certain attitudes and an ethical codex, and they have some basic skills which are important for the implementation of their professional tasks. We are here dealing with the knowledge base of *diakonia* which consists of the welfare professions which are relevant for the *diakonia* of the church, like nursing and social work, and the knowledge base of theology and *diakonia* science. The question is how the different parts of this knowledge base can be linked with each other. They represent different realities and scientifically different paradigms, but it is nevertheless important to find models for bridging the gaps between them, because they are in fact the foundation of an integrated practice, which takes place within the context of parishes and in church-based institutions and organisations. Deacons fulfil professional diaconal practice. They are trained as social workers or nurses, and have additional training in theology and in different branches of practical theology. The knowledge base of the deacon or the diaconal worker is heterogeneous. That means that it consists of elements from different scientific and knowledge areas. How could it be understood as a homogeneous foundation for practice?

---

22 Furness and Gilligan, *Religion, Belief and Social Work*, 4ff.

To explore this challenge a bit further, we will use Harald Grimen's presentation of profession and knowledge, to focus on and describe knowledge in professions.[23]

Grimen raises the important question: where do the knowledge elements of a profession come from?[24] The answer must be that for *diakonia*, they come from both a historico-hermeneutical tradition and a practical knowledge base. In this case it seems quite obvious that for the profession of *diakonia*, it is impossible to talk about a theoretical integration. The different parts of the knowledge base are too divergent. Grimen meanwhile defines links like this as a *practical synthesis*. The point is that different knowledge bases are combined because that is what is necessary to fulfil a set of described tasks. That is more important than trying to find a theoretical link between them. It is in the character of the task which prescribes the relationship between elements of relevant knowledge.[25] In training for the diaconal professions and in the *diakonia* practice itself, the model should be to create a constructive discussion and links between the different knowledge areas. If faith is just a personal concern and not identified also as knowledge, this challenge may be difficult.

But although the knowledge elements of *diakonia* are heterogeneous, the question remains how the different elements are linked with each other. This is not just a philosophical question but, with reference to the theological basis of *diakonia*, is also a normative one. The question includes another more basic one: how does theology look at other categories of knowledge?

From a theological point of view, the answers may differ. The two models given by Furness and Gilmore illustrate at least two different solutions. The first one, the fundamentalist or exclusive model, will give faith absolute priority as knowledge, over more empirical facts. The other, the liberal/open model, looks at faith as a personal motivation for action, but not as the fundamental part of that action.

A middle position would be to look at science, reasoning and professional reflection as part of general revelation, also given by God. Human experiences have meanwhile to be interpreted on the basis of the Gospel, the special revelation, as a continuous hermeneutical process. This process of interpretation of the human condition as it can be empirically described, on the basis of the knowledge of faith, will then impact the helping process, which is faith-based. It does not mean that empirical facts are set aside, but that they are complemented by a faith perspective. Alberts also reminds us that Kierkegaard claims that the difference cannot be described on a purely theological basis, but in dialogue with other sciences.[26]

---

[23] Harald Grimen, 'Profesjon Og Kunnskap' (Oslo: Universitetsforl., 2008).
[24] Grimen, 'Profesjon Og Kunnskap', 72.
[25] Grimen, 'Profesjon Og Kunnskap', 84.
[26] Albert, *Helfen Als Gabe*, 5.

The concept of faith and how faith is conceived of and understood, and the understanding of a heterogeneous professional practice, are in other words important if the relationship between faith and professional practice is to be relevantly explained. To be faith-based does not mean that everything should be placed under faith, but be reflected in dialogue.

Discussion of, and Models for, a Faith-Based Professional Practice

We have above discussed the three main concepts *diakonia*, faith-based and professional practice, and the links between them, and we have discussed the statement: what does it mean to say that *diakonia* is a faith-based professional practice? We have also explored the questions from the introduction: is it necessary to have a Christian faith to do *diakonia*? What does it mean to have a professional practice based on faith? And at last, how does *diakonia* eventually shape an alternative professional practice? Is it possible to pull the pieces together and to create answers or arguments which are consistent to give a more distinct description?

Based on the literature and resources we have mentioned, it seems that there are challenges and dilemmas in relation to all three concepts and questions, if we want to practise a *diakonia* which is more distinctly faith-based, and at the same time, of a high professional standard.

To the question whether faith is necessary to do *diakonia*, the answer is more than simply yes or no. It seems important to start a discussion on the dilemmas by placing more emphasis on the epistemological understanding of faith as knowledge. As we have mentioned, the Christian faith represents a type of knowledge about man and the human condition which is important, if not fundamental, and must be recognised as knowledge, to balance the epistemological and soteriological perspective of faith. It is not a matter of reducing the personal perspective, but of having a concept of faith which makes it possible to carry on a dialogue between faith as knowledge and all other kinds of knowledge which are relevant for *diakonia* through professional practice. What should characterise diaconal professionalism, among other things, is the ability to reflect in a dialogue how the different parts of knowledge relate to each other. The goal is to shape a more holistic care, based on what Grimen calls a practical synthesis between the different categories of knowledge.

Secondly, to the question of a faith-based professional practice, it's important for *diakonia* – which has been the victim of a shift in paradigm, as Merz comments, where the faith has been replaced with professionalism – to work more deeply on the identity of professional practice and to let professional practice reflect the knowledge of faith as an integral part. Which part of Christian knowledge is the most relevant must also be further discussed.

Finally, to the last question, professional practice exists both outside and inside diaconal mission and ministry, but today there are still many schools of higher education which train nurses and social workers based on the old diaconal traditions. Their foundation is faith-based, but what does it mean in relation to what we have said so far? To start a process towards a more distinct profile could perhaps be to start with an evaluation of the curriculum, to integrate knowledge-based elements about the faith, which makes it possible to start a dialogue between faith and profession. It seems that neither the 'person-oriented' nor the 'organisational model' as mentioned above, are sufficient. In addition, the qualifications of the staff must be adequate.

An 'individualistic' approach will reserve faith for personal motivation, and carry out professional practice based on general professional criteria. Inner motivation and Christian calling are important, but it can be difficult to 'talk the walk', and to explain more specifically what faith means and to see to what extent it makes a difference. To transform a faith base to a more general interest for spiritual needs, when they occur in a client relation, are not unimportant. It may even be the first step in deeper reflection on the relationship between faith and professional work.

An 'organisational' approach will emphasise that the faith base first and foremost is shown by the organisational structure, like the description in by-laws, and in different spiritual activities conducted by chaplains and other dedicated staff members. It may also be the model for people who cannot personally accept the faith base, but still want to support the values of the organisation.

The last approach, what we perhaps could define as a 'practical synthesis' approach, will analyze and discuss the different knowledge bases of professional practice, do an interpretation, and try to shape a practice which is more holistically founded. It will imply a better way of 'bridging the gap' between faith and professional practice in *diakonia* today.

Bibliography

Albert, Anika Christina, *Helfen Als Gabe Und Gegenseitigkeit Perspektiven Einer Theologie Des Helfens Im Interdisziplinären Diskurs*, Veröffentlichungen Des Diakoniewissenschaftlichen Instituts an Der Universität Heidelberg (Heidelberg: Winter, 2010).

Bridging the Gap: Connecting Christian Faith and Professional Practice (Sioux Center, IA: Dordt College Press, 2011).

Brodd, Sven-Erik, and Diakonistiftelsen Samariterhemmet, *The Theology of Diaconia*, Samariterhemmets Skriftserie (Uppsala: Diakonistiftelsen Samariterhemmet, 1999).

Collins, John N., *Diakonia Re-interpreting the Ancient Resources* (New York: OUP, 1990).

Diaconal Identity – Faith in Social Care: A Reflection from Eurodiaconia (Brussels: Eurodiaconia, 2010).

Furness, Sheila, and Philip Gilligan, *Religion, Belief and Social Work: Making a Difference* (Bristol: Policy Press, 2010).

Grimen, Harald, 'Profesjon Og Kunnskap', s. 71-86 (Oslo: Universitetsforl., 2008).

Kirkerådet, *Church of Norway Plan for Diakonia* (Oslo: Church of Norway, National

Council, 2009).

Kvalbein, Hans, *Filantropi Og Diakoni Omsorg for Medmennesker I De Antikke Kulturer Og I Det Nye Testamente* (Oslo: Luther forlag, 1976).

Lutheran World Federation, 'To Love and Serve the Lord. *Diakonia* in the Life of the Church', The Anglican-Lutheran International Commission (ed) (ALIC III), 2012.

McGrath, Alister E., *Christian Theology: An Introduction*. 3rd ed. (Oxford: Blackwells, 2001).

Merz, Rainer, *Diakonische Professionalität: Zur Wissenschaftlichen Rekonstruktion Des Beruflichen Selbstkonzeptes Von Diakoninnen Und Diakonen. Eine Berufsbiographische Studie*. Vol. Band 33 (Heidelberg: Universitätsverlag Winter, 2006).

Sloan, Douglas, *Faith and Knowledge: Mainline Protestantism and American Higher Education,* 1st ed. (Louisville, KY: Westminster John Knox Press, 1994).

Equipping for Service: Diakonia and Capacity-Building

Knud Jørgensen

The normal Greek word for leadership (*hodegos*) is in the New Testament and used when Jesus refers to guides and worldly leaders (Matthew 23:1-24 where he talks about 'blind guides'). The New Testament leadership model stands in stark contrast with the Hellenistic model. Instead, the word *diakonia* is used to describe leadership in the Christian community. In that way *diakonia* becomes the key concept for leadership in the Early Church. The words with the root *diak-* are found 98 times in the New Testament, and *diakonia* and *diakonos* are in most cases related to what we would call leadership and management. In this way, Paul calls himself a *diakonos* of the Gospel (Ephesians 3:7). And a primary task of the servant leader is, according to Paul, to *equip others for service*. This is the core of Ephesians 4:11-16 where Paul describes the service/*diakonia* of all God's people:

- Leadership is a gift and a task from God.
- There are different forms of service = leadership functions: apostles, prophets, evangelists, shepherds, teachers – a fivefold leadership. And one may add the deacon, based on other biblical texts where *diakonos* appears together with other leaders. The pastor is one among other functions. The NT knows nothing of a one-man ministry. There was always a plurality of leadership.
- The function of leadership is to prepare God's people for the work of Christian service (*ergon diakonias*). All God's people are called and gifted for ministry. This is what is meant by the Protestant teaching about 'the priesthood of all believers': not only do all Christians have direct access to God without the mediation of a priest; they also share together the responsibility of ministry. The primary function of the leader is to equip them for this ministry.
- Where this dynamic understanding of service is lacking, God's people will consist of immature people who easily fall prey to the cunning and craftiness of evil men – as happens when priority is not given to the main task of Christian leadership.
- The end purpose of this process is that "the whole body grows and builds itself up through love" (Ephesians 4:16). Paul is here using the word *oikodome* which means both the act of building and the actual building.

Equipping for service designates the biblical understanding of this building process; in other words, *capacity-building*. Capacity-building is therefore the primary task of servant leaders, and is at the very heart of *diakonia* and diaconal leadership.

In the first section of this paper, I shall look at capacity-building as part of organisational development in a rapidly changing society. I shall employ a Latin American model to illustrate the complexity of capacity-building, and a model from leadership development to illustrate the holistic nature of being equipped for service.

In the second section, my point of departure is to apply this theological reflection on *diakonia* on what sort of capacities and gifts are called for in various contexts. Capacity-building for *diakonia* is not a separate entity; different contexts will require specific capacities and capabilities – theological, practical, political, networking, redressing imbalances of power, etc. There is a variety of forms of *diakonia* and therefore also a variety of areas to be covered by capacity-building.

In the third section, the focus is on equipping in its practical sense at various levels. Knowledge of worldviews, values and the role of religion is here important, together with the basic recognition that, at all levels in all cultures and contexts, communities and humans have wisdom, gifts and abilities. Learning in *diakonia* applies to all levels of the church to enable and empower people to see *diakonia* as something they know and own and in which they participate. Here a renewal of the Protestant concept of *the priesthood of all believers* will go a long way in helping us live out God's call in the tasks of everyday life. This approach is based on an understanding of *diakonia* as part of the permanent character of the people of God. Finally, I expand on the need for developing a relevant leadership and on the challenge to include *diakonia* in the curriculum of theological education.

Equipping for service is more than training social workers and more than discovering one's spiritual gifts. We need both and therefore need people with *double qualifications* – with professional and theological competencies. Leaders in church and diaconal institutions need a vast array of competencies, including professional leadership tools.

What is Capacity-Building?

In 2009 the Lutheran World Federation (LWF) published a book on *Serving the Whole Person. The Practice and Understanding of Diakonia within the Lutheran Communion.*[1] The book reviews how *diakonia* is understood and practised within churches in various parts of the world. There are different models, needs and examples, illustrating that *diakonia* is a contextual ministry of churches. *Diakonia* in Norway takes on a shape that is different from

[1] Nordstokke (ed), *Serving the Whole Person.*

diakonia in South Africa or Latin America. In Norway, *diakonia* is the caring ministry of the church; in South Africa the focus is more on prophetic *diakonia*; and in Latin America, liberating *diakonia* through the sequence 'action – reflection – action' plays a central role in the *diakonia* of the churches.

At the same time, the LWF review shows that churches in different parts of the world have one thing in common and share a common concern: the need for training, for human resources, for capacity-building at various levels of churches, from grassroots *diakonia* to professional *diakonia*, and to political and prophetic *diakonia*.

Capacity-building and *capacity development* have been used since the 1990s within the field of human development. The United Nations Development Program (UNDP) defines capacity-building as "the process through which individuals, organisations and societies obtain, strengthen and maintain the capabilities to set and achieve their own development objectives over time".[2] This definition is also applicable to capacity-building within churches and within the ministry of *diakonia*. Within this context, the aim is also to develop goals and objectives to enhance professional quality and the impact of service, with the important addition: *based on Christian faith and participation in God's mission.*

Capacity-building belongs within a larger context where it finds its place as a component in *organisational development.*[3] One way of viewing organisational development is through the *abilities approach*. Here capacity-building encompasses four dimensions (see Figure 1): Ability to be, ability to relate, ability to do, and ability to organise. These abilities are not listed in any hierarchical manner; they simply indicate the four areas and abilities to be considered when working on organisational development. The last ability focuses specifically on human resources: the capability to recruit, train, compensate and keep people with good skills. But the other three abilities of an organisation also require development of capacity, e.g. development of leadership under 'ability to be', development of relational skills under 'ability to relate', and development of making an organisation sustainable under 'ability to do'. Deacons, voluntary workers and other persons within a holistic ministry are part of the larger organisational framework and therefore need to be able to 'read' an organisation and be equipped to change it.

---

[2] UNDP Practice Note: Capacity Development (undated), 4.

[3] Stein-Erik Kruse, *How to Assess NGO Capacity. A Resource Book on Organisational* Assessment (Oslo: Bistandsnemnda, undated), 18f. The diagram is borrowed from Kruse. For a critical view on 'organisational development', see Ola Segnestam Larsson, *Standardizing Civil Society. Interpreting organizational development in the tension between instrumentalism and expressivism (*Sweden: Santeus Academic Press, 2011).

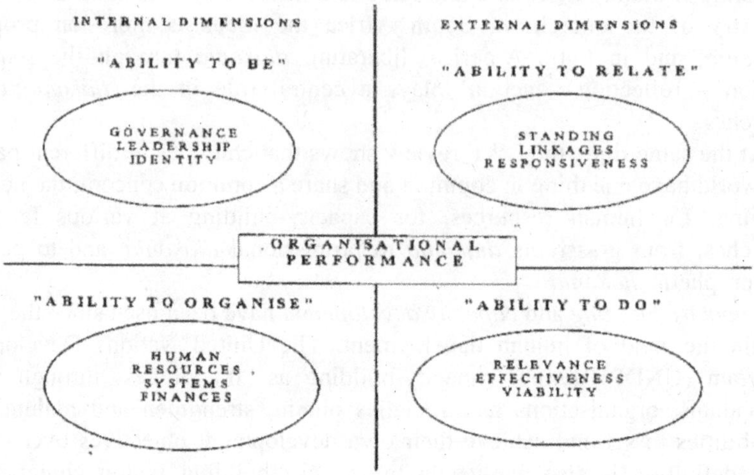

Figure 1

The importance of capacity-building should not only be viewed from an organisational perspective, but also against the backdrop of rapidly changing global and local realities in society, economics and the pursuit of human dignity. *Change* is at the core of globalisation, for better and for worse. Churches therefore must review their practices in the public arena (proclamation, *diakonia*, and advocacy) as institutions and organisations. An essential part of this is to develop skills in leadership, accountability and discernment (*see-judge-act*).

Lutheran churches in Latin America have developed a model with three interwoven threads and three cross-cutting supports (Figure 2).[4] *Mobilisation of resources* includes both human and spiritual resources; *integrated management* means that care for, overseeing and managing property and projects are essential within a diaconal understanding of capacity development; while *development of gifts* includes talents, time, charisma and skills used in mission and *diakonia*. The model further shows three cross-cutting supports: *cognitive development* of knowledge (learn, know, study, etc.); *theological reflection* guiding the processes and our understanding of gifts and resources; *spirituality* that allows us to discover, experience and express God's grace.

This model is holistic in the sense that it brings together several perspectives and disciplines – social science, theology, and cognitive and organisational

[4] Gustavo Driau, 'Human and Institutional Capacity Development: an approach in perspective of sustainability' (April 2012), quoted from LWF Department for Mission and Development, *Growing Together in Capacity for Holistic Mission. A Theological Framework for LWF Communion Learning* (Geneva: Lutheran World Federation, 2013), 5-6.

development. *Diakonia* will in this way need what traditionally has been called a 'double qualification' – the interaction between theological formation and professional education (e.g. in social work).[5] Inspired by the Latin American theology of liberation, Nordstokke further suggests that one of the focal points of a new diaconal praxis is training for an alternative lifestyle:

> This is especially relevant having in mind 'the society of consumption' and its negative environmental consequences ... The social and ecological costs of this lifestyle are enormous and its effects jeopardise the well-being of others in other parts of the world ... But do we know an alternative lifestyle? This is a challenge to the church and its witness on justice, peace and the integrity of creation.[6]

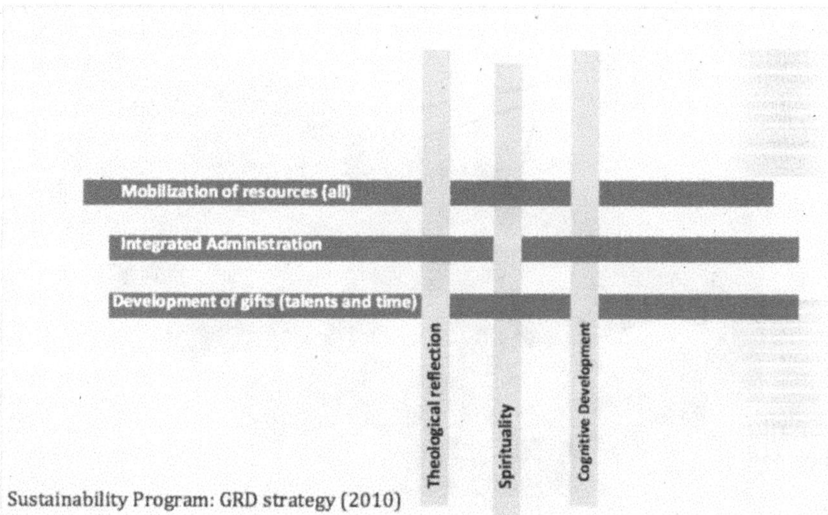

Figure 2

Furthermore, meaningful capacity-building requires that learning be viewed as the interchange between student/disciple/apprentice and their surroundings. That means it takes place through the active participation of the student; it is what he/she does that the student learns, and not what the teacher does. The aim of learning is therefore to order experiences and events where the student is stimulated to such an interchange. And the aim of the interchange (learning) is to enable the student to live and function within his/her context and culture.

[5] Nordstokke, *Liberating Diakonia*, 97.
[6] Nordstokke, *Liberating Diakonia*, 99.

Training is more focused than learning; it has to do with a learning process which provides the different skills needed in a certain context.[7] For more life-related learning to take place, the apprentice should have the opportunity to practise the behaviour to be learned, and the learning experiences must correspond with the level and abilities of the apprentice and the context in which he/she will be functioning.

Capacity-building of Christian leadership may be built on a model adapted from Theological Education by Extension. It is called Holland's Two-Track Analogy (Figure 3).[8] Its purpose is to emphasise balance and dynamic (e.g. dynamic interchange) in leadership training.

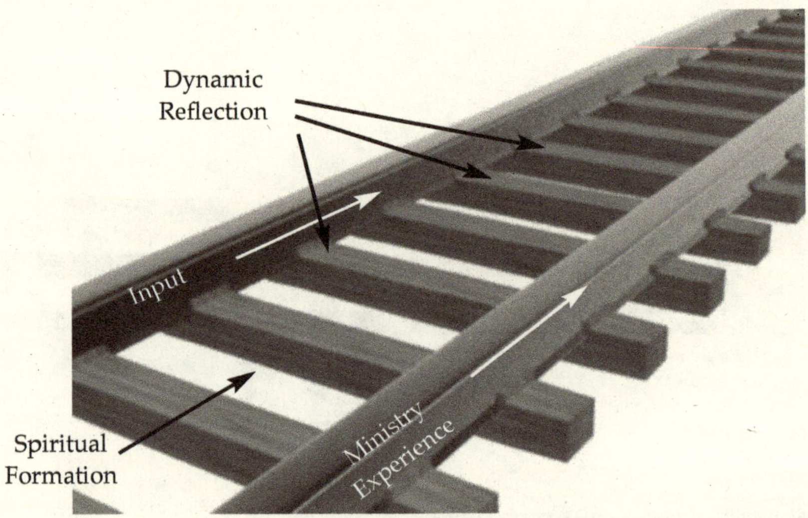

Fi ' 3

- Track one – Input: teaching of cognitive and affective skills, knowledge and attitudes.
- Track two – In-ministry experience: practical experience in actual service: deacon, nurse, social worker, teacher, etc. What the student brings along from his/her job and life.
- The sleepers (or ties) signify dynamic reflection: a twofold process where the student relates input relevantly to experience and spiritual formation, and where the student draws out from experience ideas

[7] A broader treatment of this is to be found in Knud Jørgensen, *Equipping for Service. Christian Leadership in Church and Society* (Oxford: Regnum, 2012), 121ff.

[8] Fredric L. Holland, *Theological Education in Context and Change* (Pasadena, CA: Fuller Theological Seminary, 1978).

which influence input and spiritual formation; in other words, there is a dynamic 'conversation' between the three components.

- The foundation for the railway tracks: spiritual formation: This concept is used in Roman Catholic seminary training and encompasses prayer, meditation, worship, scripture reading and spiritual growth. In this manner, spiritual formation functions as the foundation for input, dynamic reflection and in-ministry experience. The aim here is the development of the trainee as a whole person.

Learning here depends on whether one applies ideas and knowledge on life and service, and vice versa – whether one's service determines which knowledge, ideas and skills one is looking for. Learning takes place in the interchange between knowledge and life. And people learn more from life than from knowledge and ideas.

Capacity-Building and the Understanding of *Diakonia*

The understanding of *diakonia* will determine the focus of capacity-building. The Church of Norway defines *diakonia* as the caring ministry of the church: "It is the Gospel in action and is expressed through loving your neighbour, creating inclusive communities, caring for creation and struggling for justice." In a manner of speaking, this definition is a recipe for what sort of learning is required: care (health, counselling), conscientisation (loving one's neighbour), the teaching of congregations (the priesthood of all believers), and developing the ability to be involved in international *diakonia*.

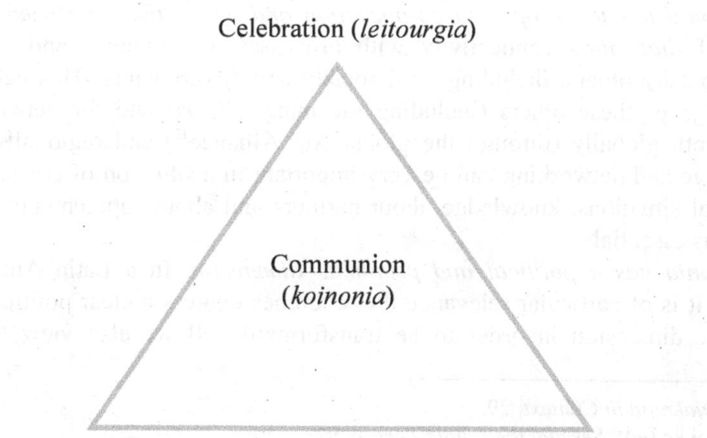

Figure 4

In the LWF study document, *Diakonia in Context,* there is a graphic illustration (Figure 4) of the three dimensions of celebration, proclamation and service.[9] The triangle underscores the understanding that these three dimensions are interrelated in such a way that each one is rooted in the other two, and could not exist without them. One might here place the Pauline *oikodome* (building) in the centre as the activity or function of building up the whole, i.e. as capacity-building of the *koinonia*. Capacity-building for *diakonia* as a *separate entity* will miss the point that all the dimensions of 'being church' must be part of learning and education.

The same need for a broad canvas is illustrated when looking at some of the key dimensions of a contemporary understanding of *diakonia*. Churches in Latin American list the following issues that are currently being discussed in the region:[10]

Diakonia in the context of neo-liberal globalisation: requires knowledge of such negative phenomena as market regulation, reduction of the state's role in ensuring rights, decline in quality of human relationships, and the value of human beings. *Diakonia* must respond to this 'erosion'.

Diakonia as an integral part of the church's mission: *Diakonia* is not an optional expression of 'being church'. If so, how may one clarify 'how *diakonia*, as part of the church's mission and holistic mission, is not an instrument of alienation and proselytism'?[11] How to make Christians and congregations view themselves as diaconal as part of their very being? Conscientisation, but also running courses at various levels and offering illustrations of what a serving community could be like, may be called for.

Diakonia has to be open to co-operation and interaction: We need to be aware of *diakonia*'s connectivity with processes, programmes and actions carried out by others, including civil society and governments. This calls for knowledge of these others (including the many NGOs) and for networking skills. Both globally (through the global Act Alliance[12]) and regionally, this knowledge and networking can be very important in a situation of crisis. Even in normal situations, knowledge about partners and about supplementing one another is essential.

Diakonia has a political and prophetic dimension: In a Latin American context, it is of particular relevance that churches express a clear political and prophetic dimension in order to be transformative. If we also view this in

---

[9] LWF, *Diakonia in Context*, 29.

[10] Nordstokke (ed), *Serving the Whole Person*, 92f.

[11] Nordstokke (ed), *Serving the Whole Person,* 92f.

[12] ACT Alliance is a coalition of more than 140 churches and affiliated organisations working together in over 140 countries to create positive and sustainable change in the lives of poor and marginalised people regardless of their religion, politics, gender, sexual orientation, race or nationality in keeping with the highest international codes and standards. Members are associated with the World Council of Churches or the Lutheran World Federation. http://www.actalliance.org/about .

relation to building citizenship, three main elements become important: advocacy, education and mobilisation. Together they enhance a process of transformation with many dimensions: overcoming attitudes of inferiority and fatalism, building knowledge and skills to participate in organised activities, and empowerment that allows people to create their own options. *Diakonia in Context* asserts that "It has been discovered that building citizenship is fundamental for strengthening democratic competence in society".[13]

In the Latin American listing of issues, one of the key challenges for the region is capacities:

> There is a dire need for capacity-building in the area of diaconal involvement, particularly for advocacy training programs in relation to human rights. Theological training is also needed, including in the area of inter-religious and ecumenical capacity. Finally, methodological training in participatory evaluation and monitoring … is required.[14]

A slightly similar listing of key issues that have developed and gained a widespread position over the last decade includes:

- The *holistic* dimension of *diakonia.*
- The *political* dimension of *diakonia.*
- The *ecumenical* dimension of *diakonia.*
- The *human* dimension of *diakonia.*

This more general listing will in different contexts require specific capacities and capabilities – theological, practical, political, networking, imbalances of power, etc.[15]

A Lutheran understanding of *diakonia* emphasises the holistic nature of mission and of 'being church': *diakonia* is a core component of the gospel itself, and is thus central to what it means to be the church. *Diakonia* is not "an option but an essential part of discipleship. Therefore all Christians are called through baptism to live out *diakonia* through what they do and how they live in the world. It begins as unconditional service to the neighbour in need and leads inevitably to social change and transformation"[16] – a broad perspective on *diakonia* which in turn requires a broad perspective on capacity-building; maybe so broad that the specific components and perspectives of a concrete plan for building capacity can become blurred.

The Lutheran document on *Mission in Context* is more specific when it describes the various forms in which *diakonia* may be expressed: international relief and development work, diaconal institutions, advocacy for peace, justice

[13] LWF, *Diakonia in Context*, 61.

[14] Martin Junge, 'Diakonia in the Latin American LWF Member Churches – Common Threads', in Nordstokke (ed), *Serving the Whole Person,* 94.

[15] Nordstokke, 'Introduction', in Nordstokke (ed), *Serving the Whole Person,* 13.

[16] LWF, *Mission in Context. Transformation, Reconciliation, Empowerment* (Geneva: Lutheran World Federation, 2004), 37.

and integrity of creation, congregational diaconal work, and social ministries.[17] Here is once again a fairly long and specific recipe for capacity-building, indicating the variety of forms of *diakonia* and therefore also the variety of areas to be covered by capacity-building. One could say that *diakonia* has become a way of living (like dialogue) rather than simply 'the good deeds of the Samaritan'. *Diakonia* marks the life of the Christian congregation, helping it overcome ethnic, social and gender differences (Galatians 3:28).[18] Along this 'way of living' (discipleship) one may then distinguish between a general *diakonia*, the diaconate (or priesthood) of all believers, and a specialised *diakonia* – distinguish but not separate as we have seen it happen in the global North, but also in the global South when the overflow of 'ODA funds' has stifled congregational *diakonia*.

As plans for capacity-building are developed, two additional perspectives should be reflected:

- The Australian scholar John N. Collins has an alternative understanding of *diakonia*. Rather than charitable or humble service, it describes a task or a mission for a person to be an envoy and spokesperson. The deacon is a 'go-between' entrusted with an important message, a mediator on behalf of someone in authority and with a vital task.[19] This reinterpretation of the biblical meaning of *diakonia* opens up new perspectives when we develop a theology of *diakonia* and plan capacity-building:

> (*Diakonia's*) biblical background presents it as bold action that announces good news for the poor. Secondly, *diakonia* cannot be limited to professional work; it belongs to the mandate given by the triune God to the church as an integral part of its mission.[20]

  This reinterpretation of *diakonia* and the function of the deacon (professional as well as lay) has implications for how and for what we equip people. 'The go-between function' requires the ability to be an advocate and mediator, to listen at the margins (as 'the bishop's ear') and report back to the centre about the toll and burdens of the marginalised.[21]

- 'Empowerment' is a common concept in the world of development, leadership, gender, *diakonia* and other arenas. It designates making others able and capable by giving them of our own power or of power in

[17] LWF, *Mission in Context*, 37.

[18] Kjell Nordstokke, 'The Study of Diakonia as Academic Discipline', in Simon Chow, Dieter Mitternacht and Nicholas Tai, *Exploring Bible, Church and Life. Essays in Celebration of the 100th Anniversary of Lutheran Theological Seminary* (Hong Kong: Lutheran Theological Seminary, 2013), 479.

[19] Collins, *Diakonia: Re-interpreting the Ancient Sources*, 194.

[20] Nordstokke, 'The Study of Diakonia as Academic Discipline', 481.

[21] See also Knud Jørgensen, *Equipping for Service,* 70ff.

society and church. In the two Lutheran documents on mission and *diakonia*, 'empowerment' is listed together with 'reconciliation' and 'transformation', thereby indicating the link between the three – and, by the same token, rejecting such expressions of power as coercion, the use of force, and manipulation. Positively understood, power has to do with legitimate authority, competence authority, and personal authority. An understanding of power is crucial for leadership and for the understanding and praxis of *diakonia*.[22] In Scripture, empowerment refers to the biblical understanding of creation where Yahweh 'empowers' human beings with capacities, abilities and the stewardship of his creation. At Pentecost the apostles and Jesus' followers were transformed and empowered by the Holy Spirit. In the same manner God continues to empower people, especially those who have little power in themselves. In the context of *diakonia*, empowerment is often the shifting of power with the aim of redressing the imbalances of power in a society governed by oppressive power and caught in the poverty trap. In Latin America diaconal workers therefore add a parallel concept to empowerment, namely, 'dignification'.[23] In that perspective, "diaconal work aims at empowering people to participate in processes of social change. The skill to achieve this goal must be an integral part of diaconal training and professional competence".[24] At the same time as *diakonia* seeks to respond to needs and to defend human rights, it must seek to "build and empower (action spaces, networks, citizenship, community life, inclusive communities)".[25] Just as a new interpretation of *diakonia* has been discovered, in the same way a new interpretation of power is needed – also to remind us that every baptised individual is empowered for *diakonia* and therefore representing a large reservoir of skills and experiences that can be shared in service and work. In this way 'empowerment' becomes a core value and method in capacity-building for *diakonia*.

Equipping at Various Levels and in Various Ways

Basic assumptions

Diaconal actions find different expressions, including individual *diakonia*, congregational *diakonia*, organised *diakonia*, institutionalised *diakonia*, and international *diakonia*. In the same way, there are various diaconal agencies,

[22] Jørgensen, *Equipping for Service*, 36.

[23] LWF, *Diakonia in Context,* 46; see also John Friedman who understands poverty as lack of access to social power and therefore human development as expanding access to social power, in Bryant Myers, *Walking with the Poor. Principles and Practices of Transformational Development* (Maryknoll, NY: Orbis, 2000), 69, 99.

[24] LWF, *Diakonia in Context,* 71.

[25] Nordstokke, *Serving the Whole Person,* 109.

including volunteers, professional workers, and people who belong to diaconal orders of ministry (deaconesses and deacons). The local models of diaconal work and diaconal agencies differ widely from church to church, from country to country and from continent to continent. Capacity-building for *diakonia* will therefore also differ. The local toolbox and its ingredients will, however, always reflect the basic assumptions and the basic theology of *diakonia*, as outlined above. We interpret biblical texts to give meaning in our local context and in relation to the particular needs in that context. In a similar manner we interpret *diakonia* in our context, emphasising those perspectives that are of particular importance. In order to do so, a solid understanding of not only *diakonia*, but of the local context, local culture, and local society, is needed.

Added to this is the importance of understanding the faith-based dimension of social action and, by the same token, the interconnectedness between religion and development.[26] All of this has to do with worldview and value systems. A solid understanding of these overriding perspectives as they appear in local dress is a must at any level of diaconal service.[27] "Diaconal development workers should be well trained to understand the role of religion, both its strength and weaknesses, and also to mobilise religious mindsets and values for transformation toward a more just and sustainable society."[28]

Stewardship and accountability are of particular relevance and importance since both these are so closely intertwined with *diakonia* and *oikonomia*; the Greek work for steward is *oikonomos*. *Oikonomos* is another of the biblical concepts of leadership. *Oikonomia* could be translated as management. The task of biblical stewardship has to do with being guardians of the Good News (2 Timothy 1:14) and with the responsibility of managing God's people (Luke 12:42-43). This calls for administration and order, resources must be in place, planning must take place, and goals must be set.

There is a need to bring learning into *diakonia* at all levels of the church to enable and empower people to see *diakonia* as something they know, they own, and in which they participate. If *diakonia* to be part of ecclesiology – in other words, to be part of the genes/identity and the praxis of the local people of God – a renewal of the Protestant concept of 'the priesthood of all believers' will go a long way towards helping Christians live out God's call in the tasks of everyday life. *Diakonia* is, in the biblical perspective, part of the permanent character of the people of God. Every member of the congregation is called to

---

[26] LWF, *Diakonia in Context,* 76.

[27] See on this Bryant Myers, *Walking with the Poor.*

[28] LWF, *Diakonia in Context,* 76. Recent Scandinavian publications on the interrelationship between religion and development include Mogens Mogensen (ed), *Religion og udvikling* (Copenhagen: Dansk Missionsråd, 2012); Asle F. Jøssang and Arne Olav Øyhus (eds), *Religionens rolle i bistand og utvikling* (Kristiansand: Portal forlag, 2012); Oslosenteret (ed), *Innblikk i forholdet mellom Religion og utvikling. En rapport for prosjektet religion og utvikling 2011-2012* (Oslo: The Oslo Center and the Norwegian Ministry of Foreign Affairs, 2012).

use his or her charisma (human and spiritual) in the service of others. Every member is part of the ministry of *diakonia.* Within congregations, there will then emerge specific groups doing diaconal work, e.g. women, Sunday school, youth, visitation, counselling and intercession. *Diakonia is not an appendix to being the church, but the Gospel in action*, i.e. *diakonia* participates in the proclamation of the Gospel; it is the bridge between Sunday morning in church and how believers live out their lives the rest of the week. It is usually also in the context of the local church that the role and leadership of women and youth should be affirmed and recognised in the planning and implementation of diaconal processes. Such recognition is an essential part of capacity-building: empowering entails giving trust to and thereby equipping people for service.

At all levels leadership is essential – leaders who equip others to serve. At various levels women, far more than men, have responded to the call to carry out diaconal work. Maybe that is a strong indicator of their role in leadership in this field? The traditional model of male leaders in institutions for deaconesses (in the 19th and 20th centuries) is not recommended. Leadership in church and society is a broad concern with many components which cannot be covered here; suffice it to say that the basic biblical and social perspectives on leadership need to be harvested also for diaconal leadership. Of particular importance is transformational leadership. This is today one of the popular approaches to leadership. Since the 1990s it has been part of the so-called 'New Leadership' paradigm. A fairly well-known perspective was developed by J.M. Kouzes and B.Z. Posner with their focus on 'how to get extraordinary things done in organisations'. Transformational leadership includes the components of what is called situational leadership (with a focus on the interrelation between leader-follower-situation), but takes them a step further by looking at leadership as a process that changes and transforms people. It is concerned with emotions, values, ethics, standards, and long-term goals. It includes assessing followers' motives, satisfying their needs, and treating them as full human beings. Transformational leadership moves followers to accomplish more than what is usually expected of them. It is a process that often incorporates charismatic and visionary leadership. 'Charisma' is here used in a secular context to describe a special gift that certain individuals possess which gives them the capacity to do extraordinary things. In the same manner, diaconal leadership is a ministry of transformation, also in the biblical sense; the diaconal leader/deacon is a church leader especially engaged in empowering and animating those at the periphery to active participation in the life of faith, hope and love. If this is the sort of leadership needed, then adequate steps in terms of both training and empowering such leaders must be taken.

International context

Basic to all kinds of *diakonia* at every level in every culture and context is the recognition that all communities and all persons have wisdom, gifts and abilities. A consultation in Addis Ababa in 2008 called attention to the fact that there are experiences and skills, structures and networks at the local level which should be acknowledged:

> This calls for an attitude that embraces a 'culture of listening' to what is on the ground and builds on it in all forms of diaconal praxis. This is especially valid for actors within international *diakonia.* Such a culture of listening sees and places *diakonia* within the context of societal culture, and uses language, approaches, methods and systems that belong to the people and that they understand.[29]

Professionals and professional skills are highly needed in *diakonia*, particularly the organised and institutionalised *diakonia*, but they should be combined with local insight, competence and expertise. The specialised ministries of *diakonia* (health, social work, counselling, development) require specific education. At the same time, it is an urgent task to translate and convey *local knowledge* of partners and networks (e.g. in the global South) into the dialogue with agencies and organisations in the North (e.g. Norwegian Church Aid and NORAD). Specialised ministries may contribute to such capacity-building among local partners, including the very concrete task of writing up projects and applications.

As regards international *diakonia*, the following should be added:

- Opportunities should be created for learning from each other, both regionally and globally.
- Local resources and opportunities should be identified before requesting international support.
- Leaders at local level should be trained for advocacy tasks in *diakonia* so that they are able to challenge government when required.
- Staff involved in international *diakonia* needs ongoing formation about the global ecumenical movement.[30]

Theological seminaries

The recommendation to include *diakonia* in the curriculum of theological seminaries has been voiced particularly by churches in the global South. Prior to that, churches ask that a common theological understanding of training for *diakonia* be developed. What has been said above has tried to outline such an understanding: the theology of *diakonia* should be developed, and churches need to continue to deepen their theological reflection on the meaning of *diakonia*. As regards theological seminaries, a consultation in 2005 in Bangkok challenged theological seminaries to:

- Strengthen diaconal education in all levels of the churches and introduce *diakonia* studies in the seminaries.
- Produce relevant biblical and theological foundation for praxis.

---

[29] Nordstokke (ed), *Serving the Whole Person,* 25f.

[30] Nordstokke (ed), *Serving the Whole Person,* 27.

- Strengthen diaconal understanding leading to the publication of books and other reading materials in the area of *diakonia*, preferably in local languages.[31]

Most seminaries and theological faculties have not included *diakonia* in their study programmes. A very few seminaries in the global North have initiated degrees in *diakonia* (e.g. in Norway). Together with colleagues from Diakonova and Diakonhjemmet University College, I have been involved in developing and establishing a Master of Arts in *Diakonia* at the Lutheran Theological Seminary in Hong Kong. The goals of the programme are:

- equipping students in Hong Kong and from the East Asian and Mekong region for diaconal service in church and society;
- providing insights into and understanding the content and task of *diakonia*;
- helping the students to develop diaconal attitudes and identity as a basis for service in church and society;
- facilitate students in developing the ability for teaching *diakonia* to others;
- equipping the students for leadership roles in diaconal projects and institutions.

Diakonia is, however, rather a new discipline, and seminaries may therefore be uncertain about how to organise it as an academic discipline. This issue was discussed in 2012 by a working group convened by the World Council of Churches. The aim was not to develop a fixed curriculum, but to identify the key components of such a curriculum (see Figure 5): Theology, social analysis, scientific approaches or methodology, and competencies (personal and professional).

> The two first elements point out the interdisciplinary nature of *diakonia*; diaconal action requires both knowledge of basic theological issues and the ability to analyze the social, political, economic, and cultural context. The third element refers to how this study is made, for instance, of linking theory and praxis, of discovering 'silent' knowledge, and of using hermeneutics of suspicion. The last element related to the development of professional competence, of leadership and management skills, and also of the identity as diaconal worker.[32]

Conclusion

In the introduction I referred to the fivefold ministry of diaconal leadership in Ephesians 4. I have above tried to unpack the aim and purpose of this leadership, namely, to equip others for service. But this requires that there be a fivefold *professional* leadership – a leadership which exhibits the charismas

[31] Nordstokke (ed), *Serving the Whole Person*, 57.

[32] Nordstokke, 'The Study of Diakonia as Academic Discipline', 483.

(spiritual gifts) of the New Testament and which as a team co-operates and co-ordinates. This professionalism requires that we acknowledge that there be different types of leaders at various levels, both within society and church.[33]

Ecumenical Diakonia Curriculum: A Working Framework				
Theology	Social Sciences	Scientific Approaches / Methods - how to study diakonia?	Competencies - skills - what is the professional outcome?	Transversals - Guiding Principles
Diakonia as a subject: dimensions, horizons, traditions, definitions of diakonia	Identifying Community	linking theory and practices	Leadership Skills	Inclusiveness /Inclusivity
Basic Theological Issues	Local Languages, cultures. The rootedness within the community/ among the peoples	cultural traditions and perspectives on teaching and learning	Management Skills	Interdisciplinary approach
Christian Education	History	interdisciplinary approaches	Counselling	Gender
Biblical Foundation	Multiculturalism	Bottom up - inductive & Top down - deductive	Organisational Sustainability	Persons with disabilities
Ethics	Systematic reflection of social, political, economic and cultural contexts	Dialectic Approach	Dia-praxis	minority groups
History of diakonia (ecumenical/ecclesial)	Analysis of theological, ecclesial and inter-religous context	Extracurricular activities that model community and help shape character	Transformational Leadership	
Spirituality	Organisational Analysis	Personal Development	Character Formation	
Hermeneutics			Prophetic diakonia - advocacy	
Theological Foundation			research skills	
Need for Introduction, some of the values coming from the Colombo document. Introduction to the concept of diakonia as a subject	Critical introduction that expresses the intentions and also the target groups, i.e. the marginalised groups	The more disiplined way of studying diakonia. A process of academic accreditation and recognition.	The international. Inter-faith and ecumneical character of the study/training/formation that is conducted.	
What would be the learning environment that helps to build character and mold transformational leadership?				

Figure 5

[33] See Knud Jørgensen, *Equipping for Service,* 11ff.

The range of leadership will encompass everyone from Sunday school teachers all the way to bishops and general secretaries. There is a need for Sunday school teachers, but without the professionals (deacons, pastors, managers, health workers, etc.), there will be no capacity-building for Sunday school teachers. It is therefore quite essential that the professionals are also equipped in the field of *diakonia*.

Mission is witness (*marturia*). Diaconal action is one of the dimensions of this witness. The diaconal witness comes in many shapes and forms – in a rainbow of imaginative ways to live out the Gospel locally and globally. For a local congregation it is foundational to live out *diakonia* and to proclaim the Gospel through *diakonia*. For this to continue to happen, the church must be equipped for service at all levels. The ingredients in this equipping for service will include professional expertise and empowerment of volunteers. Every baptised individual is empowered for *diakonia*, representing a large reservoir of skills and experiences to be called into life as we meet the diversity of challenges from the margins and the centre. Equipping for *diakonia* as a process of transformation, reconciliation and empowerment need not be a burden but rather an opportunity to set free the talents and abilities of humans created in the image of God.

Bibliography

Brattgård, Helge, *God's Stewards – a theological study of the principles and practices of stewardship* (Minneapolis, MN: Augsburg, 1963).

Bryman, A., *Charisma and Leadership in Organizations* (London: Sage, 1992).

Collins, John N., *Diakonia: Re-interpreting the Ancient Sources* (New York/Oxford: OUP, 1990).

Driau, Gustavo, 'Human and Institutional Capacity Development: an approach in perspective of sustainability' (April 2012), quoted from LWF Department for Mission and Development, *Growing Together in Capacity for Holistic Mission. A Theological Framework for LWF Communion Learning* (Geneva: Lutheran World Federation, 2013).

Fredric L. Holland, *Theological Education in Context and Change* (Pasadena, CA: Fuller Theological Seminary, 1978).

Junge, Martin, 'Diakonia in the Latin American LWF Member Churches – Common Threads', in Kjell Nordstokke (ed), *Serving the Whole Person. The Practice and Understanding of Diakonia within the Lutheran Communion* (Minneapolis, MN: Lutheran University Press, 2009).

Jørgensen, Knud, *Equipping for Service. Christian Leadership in Church and Society* (Oxford: Regnum, 2012).

Kouzes, J.M. and B.Z. Posner, *The Leadership Challenge* (3rd edn) (San Francisco, CA: Jossey-Bass, 1987).

Kruse, Stein-Erik, *How to Assess NGO Capacity. A Resource Book on Organisational Assessment* (Oslo: Bistandsnemnda, undated).

Larsson Ola, Segnestam, *Standardizing Civil Society. Interpreting organisational development in the tension between instrumentalism and expressivism* (Sweden: Santeus Academic Press, 2011).

Lutheran World Federation, *Mission in Context. Transformation, Reconciliation, Empowerment* (Geneva: Lutheran World Federation, 2004).

Lutheran World Federation, *Diakonia in Context: Transformation, Reconciliation, Empowerment. An LWF Contribution to the Understanding and Practice of Diakonia* (Geneva: LWF, 2009).

Nordstokke, Kjell (ed), *Serving the Whole Person. The Practice and Understanding of Diakonia within the Lutheran Communion* (Minneapolis, MN: Lutheran University Press, 2009).

Myers, Bryant, *Walking with the Poor. Principles and Practices of Transformational Development* (Maryknoll, NY: Orbis, 2000).

Nordstokke, Kjell, *Liberating Diakonia* (Oslo: Tapir akademisk forlag, 2011).

Nordstokke, Kjell, 'The Study of *Diakonia* as Academic Discipline', in Simon Chow, Dieter Mitternacht and Nicholas Tai, *Exploring Bible, Church and Life. Essays in Celebration of the 100th Anniversary of Lutheran Theological Seminary* (Hong Kong: Lutheran Theological Seminary, 2013).

Northouse, Peter G., *Leadership. Theory and Practice* (Los Angeles, CA: Sage, 2010).

UNDP Practice Note: *Capacity Development* (undated).

Aadland, Einar (ed), *Ledelse i diakonale virksomheter* (Oslo: Akademika forlag, 2012).

Empowering Diakonia:
A Perspective From the World Council of Churches

Carlos E. Ham

Introduction

Focusing on a methodology that I have called the *Five Dimensions of Empowering Diakonia*, the article will address theoretical and practical tools for *diakonia* as Christian social practice. From the perspective of the World Council of Churches, the article will unpack the visional, normative, need-oriented, contextual and transformative dimensions of this methodology in order to explore and construct the concept and practice of the *Empowering Diakonia* model. The article will also analyze how empowerment lifts the natural gifts and dignity of human beings, taking place in mutuality, in partnership, and in a spirit of power-sharing. From the standpoint of the Judæo-Christian tradition, it will explore empowerment as a process of reaching out to 'the other' with the love of the triune God; it is therefore intrinsically linked with *diakonia*, which affirms the power-service in Christ's way, towards transformative justice, as part of God's mission.

Definition of Concepts

Diakonia *in the World Council of Churches*

The ecumenical movement in general and the World Council of Churches (WCC)[1] in particular have dealt profusely both with the notions and practices of *diakonia* and empowerment down the years. In 1938, its first General Secretary, Willem Adolf Visser 't Hooft, made his acceptance of the position conditional upon the readiness of the Council to become active in the field of

[1] The WCC was founded in 1948 and brings together 345 churches, denominations and church fellowships in more than 110 countries and territories throughout the world, representing over 500 million Christians. It includes most of the world's Orthodox churches, as well as Anglican, Baptist, Lutheran, Methodist, Reformed, United and Independent churches. More information on the WCC website: www.oikoumene.org/en/about-us

service, "for there could be no healthy Ecumenical fellowship without practical solidarity," he said.[2]

The WCC's constitution acknowledges: "The primary purpose of the fellowship of churches in the World Council of Churches is to call one another to visible unity in one faith and in one eucharistic fellowship … through witness and service to the world … In seeking *koinonia* in faith and life, witness and service, the churches through the Council will … express their commitment to *diakonia* in serving human need …"[3] Therefore, for the WCC there has been a concern, not only to bring the churches together, in order to reach the goal of visible unity, but also to deal holistically with these issues of witness and service so critical for their life and ministry in today's world.

Numerous documents of the ecumenical movement recognise the fact that this diaconal mission is rooted in the Holy Scriptures; the concept of *diakonia*, as we understand it today, has been developed by the church mainly in the past 200 years, but its roots, images, understanding and motivation go back to Scripture and the Early Church. The diaconal ministry of the churches has grown and developed further, up to our own day.

In the flow of our understanding of *diakonia* within the WCC, it has been underlined that it reaches out to all persons, particularly the impoverished, the "least of these" (Matthew 25:40) and oppressed, to comfort them and also to confront the root causes of injustice. Because the *missio Dei* (God's mission)[4] is holistic, *diakonia* is also deeply interrelated with *kerygma* (proclamation of the Word), *didache* (teaching), *leitourgia* (worship) and *martyria* (witness), which lead to *koinonia* (community). *Koinonia* is the result and ultimate goal of these functions or activities, which mark the presence of the church in the world. *Diakonia*, therefore, is not an end in itself, but rather an instrument used by God, together with others, to build an inclusive and just community, an *oikos* (household) in which the entire creation is included, enjoying the fullness of life intended for all.[5]

---

[2] Kenneth Slack, *Hope in the Desert* (Geneva: WCC Publications, 1986), 9.

[3] WCC, *Constitution and Rules of the World Council of Churches*, 2006. Article III, 1.

[4] David Bosch, *Transforming Mission. Paradigm Shifts in Theology of Mission*, 16th. edn (New York: Orbis, 2001), 587. David Bosch points out that it was in the 1952 Willingen Conference of the International Mission Council where the idea (not the exact term) *missio Dei* surfaced clearly. "Mission was understood as being derived from the very nature of God," he stressed.

[5] David Gill, *Gathered for Life. Official Report, VI Assembly of the WCC, Vancouver, Canada, 1983* (Geneva, 1983), 197. This thought is based on the report of the WCC general secretary at the time, Philip Potter, to its VI Assembly, held in Vancouver, Canada, in 1983. He said: "The ecumenical movement is, therefore, the means by which the churches which form the house, the *oikos* of God, are seeking so to live and witness before all peoples that the whole *oikoumene* may become the *oikos* of God through the crucified and risen Christ in the power of the life-giving Spirit." Philip Alford Potter, born on 19 August 1921 in Roseau, Dominica, West Indies, was a Methodist pastor and the third General Secretary of the World Council of Churches, serving during 1972-84

In the ecumenical movement we have observed three phases or models of *diakonia*. These phases will show sometimes conflicting signs or moments of tension, along with and at the same time, trends complementing each other. These phases or models, which will be explained below, are the charity, the reciprocity and the transformative models.

(a) *The charity model*. This is the 'inter-church aid' period, characterised quite prominently by the transfer of funds in a rather vertical, top-down way, to support diaconal projects and persons in need. To a great extent, people were seen as *objects* of the aid, coming from the most powerful churches and church-related organisations, primarily from the global North. *Diakonia* was defined in this period as the 'responsible service of the gospel by deeds and by words performed by Christians in response to the needs of people'.[6] This charity model runs from the early 20th century up until the beginning of the 1980s, and its effect was aid.

(b) *The reciprocity model*. This phase is represented by the *Ecumenical Sharing of Resources* process, which was developed in the 1980s, primarily by the 1986 Global Consultation on Inter-Church Aid, Refugee and World Service, *Diakonia 2000. Called to be Neighbours*, held in Larnaca (Cyprus), and the 1987 El Escorial (Spain) Consultation on *Koinonia*. During this period we start to observe a paradigm shift, mostly as a result of the presence and influence of voices and ministries from the churches in the global South. Here we begin to see emerging the notions and practices of empowerment in relation to *diakonia*.

In this model, which runs up to the first decade of the 21st century, in a more intentional and collective way there is an assessment of the needs, the challenges and the problems, also on a more horizontal level. E.g. the participants at the Larnaca consultation underscored in their final Declaration: "... Our *diakonia* now and for the future must be based on mutual trust and genuine sharing. We recognise that people and churches on all continents have needs and that our *diakonia* must reach out to all those who suffer."[7] Also at the El Escorial consultation there was an intentional attempt to overcome the false dichotomy between mission and service. Its report acknowledges: "... All activities of the Christian community in evangelism, *diakonia*, the struggle for human dignity, healing, peace and justice belong together in the one mission of

---

(quoted on February 2014): www.oikoumene.org/en/about-us/organizational-structure/general-secretary/since-1948

[6] Teresa Joan White, "Diakonia", in *Dictionary of the Ecumenical Movement*, ed. by Nicholas Lossky et al, 2nd. edn (Geneva: WCC Publications, 2002) www.oikoumene.org, 305.

[7] Klaus Poser, *Diakonia 2000 – Called to Be Neighbors*. Official Report of the WCC World Consultation on Inter-Church Aid, Refugee and World Service, Larnaca, Cyprus, November 1986 (Geneva: World Council of Churches, 1987), 125.

God."[8] Nevertheless, we observe in this period that the *we-they* mentality is still quite prominent, while at the same time there is a stronger emphasis on resources other than financial, e.g. human, that are expected to be shared. The effect of this trend is moving towards change.

(c) *The transformative model*. The process leading to the 2012 Conference on *Theological Perspectives on Diakonia in the Twenty-First Century*, held in Colombo, Sri Lanka (this will be mentioned in more detail later) marks this period that we call transformative. There is a stronger influx in relation to the notion of the practice of *diakonia* from the different WCC-related mission networks, and not least from those quite often excluded by society and even by the churches. This further worked towards achieving inclusiveness and integration of the different diaconal efforts, a stronger relationship *to-each-other*; done by those from the periphery, by those on the margins (disabled, women, indigenous people, afro-descendants, impoverished), empowered to change society in a *bottom-up* approach, in an inductive manner. The effect of this model is transformation. Further down, I shall analyze *Five Dimensions of Empowering Diakonia*, taking into consideration the *Theological Perspectives on Diakonia* produced at this Colombo conference.

Empowerment in relation to diakonia *in the ecumenical movement*

Empowerment and *diakonia* are integral parts of 'being church'. Empowerment goes back to the Biblical notion of the *imago Dei*. In Genesis 1:26, we read "Then God said, 'Let us make humankind in our image, according to our likeness ...'", i.e. the fact that each and every human being is created in God's image implies that they are empowered with abilities and gifts to do God's will. The Holy Spirit plays an empowering role. The Old Testament mentions the *ruah*, the breath of God, which gives life (Isaiah 42:5).

In the gospels, Jesus empowers his disciples and followers, "giving them authority over unclean spirits, to cast them out, and to cure every disease and every sickness" (Matthew 10:1). The New Testament also refers to the experience and promise of Pentecost where the disciples are empowered to be Jesus' witnesses worldwide (Acts 2:1-13). Paul says that God sends "the Spirit of the Son" to the followers of Jesus (Galatians 4:6).

The history of the ecumenical movement in the 20th century shows the multiple resources, particularly financial, that have been invested and allocated for diaconal work. Today, many churches and specialised ministries in the global North no longer have the means to support their partners in the global South. This scenario also affects the way the WCC accompanies the diaconal work, moving from being a *grant-giving* organisation to one which creates

[8] Hubert van Beek, *Sharing Life in a World Community. Official Report of the WCC World Consultation on Koinonia, El Escorial, Spain, 1987* (Geneva: WCC Publications, 1989), 45.

more space to sustain and encourage the empowerment of the churches in their reflections and actions on *diakonia*.

In my view, this notion of empowerment is a dynamic process that enables and inspires, that enhances people's skills and self-confidence; it is a movement by which persons are liberated, to take back and develop the power within, in order to *unlock* their immense potential and to boost their skills, self-confidence and self-assertion. This process aims at promoting collective resistance, challenge and mobilisation against basic power relationships and systemic forces that impoverish and exclude the vulnerable. It is a development towards positive change in the situations where they live, by creating justice, inclusiveness and participation towards transformation and fullness of life.

From the perspective of our Judæo-Christian tradition, empowerment takes place in mutuality, in partnership, in a spirit of power-sharing, a process of reaching out to the other with the love of the triune God and is, therefore, intrinsically linked with *diakonia*. Nowadays many local churches are being empowered for diaconal work as a result of their ecclesial condition[9] and of being urged on by the needs of the people. Empowerment and *diakonia* are integral parts of being a missional church; people are emerging *self-empowered* for action, becoming subjects of their own destiny, and beyond being simply objects of aid and charity.

The Empowering Diakonia *model*

In the booklet *Diakonia: Creating Harmony, Seeking Justice and Practising Compassion. A Study on Ecumenical Efforts in Diakonia and Justice*, published by the WCC, we find this quote: "Empowerment is at the heart of diaconal and justice-seeking activities and can be seen as an overarching characteristic or goal of much of the work of the churches and church-related organisations. Empowerment activities in a Christian framework address the dignity of humanity and reveal to each person and group their inherent gifts and abilities so that they may actively work towards transformation."[10]

Considering the relevance of this interconnectedness of *diakonia* and empowerment, I would like to propose an *Empowering Diakonia* model, with a dual function. *Diakonia* is empowering (adjective) for those who are being

---

[9] It is interesting to observe how many local churches are in fact empowered for diaconal work inspired by their own community wisdom (indigenous knowledge and experience related to day-to-day living, occupations and culture passed on from generation to generation, in areas like agriculture, industrial work and handicraft, herbal doctors, management of natural resources and environment, community's business and fund-raising, art and folk drama, local language and literature, etc.). In addition, local congregations are empowered by their ecclesial nature and Christian faith (living mystical values and experiences of community, solidarity, dignity, spirituality, theological reflections).

[10] WCC, *Diakonia: Creating Harmony, Seeking Justice and Practising Compassion* (WCC: Geneva, 2005), 7.

served, and at the same time I want to affirm the forces or actions which actually help to empower (verb) *diakonia*. In other words, (1) *diakonia* empowers, on the one hand, and (2) *diakonia* may be empowered, on the other. In both senses, *diakonia* stands as the principal word.

I will argue therefore, that the *Empowering Diakonia* model is one of the most effective ways for diaconal ministry today, since it is a comprehensive way of thinking, binding together both empowerment and *diakonia* in a system that can provide a fresh and meaningful vision for the diaconal endeavour. It is a concept and practice of *diakonia* that is both empowering and empowered.

The Five Dimensions of Empowering Diakonia

In order to structure or design this model, I am suggesting *Five Dimensions of Empowering Diakonia* as a useful conceptual *toolbox* for diagnosis and evaluation. I am building my conceptual platform based on the book *A Fundamental Practical Theology. Descriptive and Strategic Proposals*, written by Don S. Browning.[11] Here the author refers to what he calls "the validity claims of a fundamental practical theology .... These five validity claims or levels of meaning reflect the five levels or dimensions of all forms of practical thinking or practical reason, whether explicitly religious or avowedly secular".[12]

Consequently, I am implying a similar logic and structure for my *Five Dimensions* which include the following: visional, normative, need-oriented, contextual and transformative; and as we will see, they are interdisciplinary and interrelated. Here is the explanation of each one of these:

(a) *Visional* – referring to the ability to envision future reality so as to consider prophetic action with imagination and wisdom. The vision is our motivation, our engine, our ideological foundation, the all-embracing goal of our action, like the view of utopia, what "causes us to advance".[13] According to

---

[11] Don S. Browning (1934-2010), an ordained minister of the Christian Church (Disciples of Christ) in the USA, was a long-time professor and theologian at the University of Chicago Divinity School who brought 'Ivory Tower' theological theory down to earth by bridging the study of religious thought with social sciences, in fields including psychology and law, specifically in the way theological ethics may employ sociology, psychology, and the social scientific study of religion. In this way Browning was one of the architects of Practical Theology. His ideas, descriptions and strategies were laid out in the book, *A Fundamental Practical Theology*, one of his most widely known volumes, which was published for the first time in 1991.

[12] Don S. Browning, *A Fundamental Practical Theology. Descriptive and Strategic Proposals* (Minneapolis: Augsburg Fortress Press, 1996), 71.

[13] This quote is from Eduardo Galeano (b. 1940), a Uruguayan journalist, writer and novelist, who expressed: "Utopia lies at the horizon. When I draw nearer by two steps, it retreats two steps. If I proceed ten steps forward, it swiftly slips ten steps ahead. No matter how far I go, I can never reach it. What, then, is the purpose of utopia? It is to cause us to advance" (quoted in January 2014): www.goodreads.com/quotes/33846-

our Judæo-Christian tradition this is crucial since "where there is no vision, the people perish" (Proverbs 29:18). A diaconal vision is inspired and empowered by God the Father, the Son and the Holy Spirit. We are seeking a diaconal vision, which relates to our theological reflection, to our spiritual-mystical understanding and to our liturgical practices, towards a critical analysis of reality and action, an imagination of what is possible. But it is also an empowering vision that affirms the fact that "a different world is possible".[14] Therefore, the vision is seeking empowerment and, at the same time, empowers for diaconal action.

(b) *Normative* – relating to or deriving from a standard or norm, particularly of behaviour, which therefore has ethical connotations. It is a commanding point of reference, which provides meaning for the actions of a particular group. It is expressed in our core values, principles and standards of comportment, in our judgement of what is important in life. In our particular Judæo-Christian tradition, it is rooted in the authority of the Biblical text, in accordance with the Word of God, and at the same time it reflects professional effectiveness. As diaconal engagement is not an option, but part of the essence of 'being church', it is normative, essential for its mission, and therefore a faith-based empowered service.

(c) *Need-oriented* – pointing to material and spiritual necessities or circumstances requiring some course of action, particularly for humankind, focusing on the causes (asking not only what the needs are, but also why they are present in the first place) and on the consequences of such needs. Thus, this is yet another scope that requires the churches' social intervention, in order to comfort people in need, but also to confront holistically and prophetically the powers that destroy the web of life. At the same time, the needs identify processes of empowerment that are necessary, feasible and self-realisable. Following the ministry of Jesus Christ, who was moved by the needs of the people (Matthew 14:14; Mark 6:34; John 11:33), when we see the needs of others, our values are activated, from a perspective of solidarity, as if to say, "This cannot go on like this; something must be done." Therefore, this need-oriented dimension does not mean that the consequence is pitying people. We are motivated and challenged by the reality of people when their dignity is being neglected, our values are being challenged in order to improve this situation.

(d) *Contextual* – considering a theology and a praxis that are contextual; guided and informed by our vision, but also by the social-political-economic-ecological context in which the churches are serving. Therefore, diaconal involvement is concerned with the community, society in general and the environment as well. Service is not pursued in abstraction but is fully

---

utopia-lies-at-the-horizon-when-i-draw-nearer-by

[14] 2001 Letter from Porto Alegre: *A Different World is Possible* (quoted in January 2011): www.commondreams.org/views01/0129-05.htm

empowered and focused creatively on the surrounding reality and challenges in today's world. What we see activates our values and we have to reflect upon it in a wider context to apply other sciences and understanding, to avoid being narrow-minded, which points to the importance of the multidisciplinary approach. That would be the action, the moment when *diakonia* really happens, since we don't stop with the analysis, but we seek for an empowered action that regenerates the lives of people.

(e) *Transformative* – lifting a diaconal vision that urges and empowers us to address the needs of people and of the whole creation, both locally and globally, which will be effective through concrete prophetic actions towards transformative justice. In situations of injustice, action is required, a diaconal pro-action which is transformative, asking what difference it makes. It is a matter of not just charity, or feeding people, but also of enabling empowerment within ourselves and others for transformation.

A Practical Application of the *Five Dimensions of Empowering Diakonia*

Three programmes of the WCC – Solidarity and *Diakonia*, Just and Inclusive Communities and Mission and Evangelism – organised in the 2012 *Conference on Theology of Diakonia for the 21st Century*, held 6-12 June in Colombo, Sri Lanka. Fifty participants involved in various diaconal initiatives in about 25 countries attended the meeting. As mentioned above, this conference held in Colombo marks the third period in the ecumenical movement, in relation to *diakonia*, that we have identified as the transformative model.

The Colombo conference had a clear purpose and actually achieved integration of the different ecumenical efforts to serve people in need, bringing voices from the periphery of the churches and society (indigenous people, persons living with disabilities, Afro-descendants and other marginalised people), but also people representing their respective mission networks and those traditionally considered *objects* of diaconal efforts and projects. The event itself was an empowering experience, moving, as described in the introduction to this chapter, in a *bottom-up* approach, in an inductive manner.

"As an expression of its commitment to justice, human dignity and liberation, the WCC, since its inception, has been a reliable partner of discriminated and excluded people – racial and ethnic minorities, those with disabilities, indigenous peoples, Dalits and others – in their struggles. For decades, it has facilitated shared reflection and analysis, advocacy and communication among them. It has supported their efforts at local, national and international levels, encouraging churches and societies to be more just, responsive and inclusive".[15] This event held in Colombo was yet another

---

[15] This is quoted from the 2013 WCC programme on *Towards Just and Inclusive Communities*, one of the co-organisers of the event: www.oikoumene.org/en/what-we-do/just-and-inclusive-communities

example of this emphasis and inclusiveness, interrelating it more intentionally and explicitly with *diakonia* and mission, as three inseparable components, or pillars and actions carried out jointly by the churches and the ecumenical movement in general.

In order to explore new understandings and practices of *diakonia*, three vantage points were identified and considered at the conference: (1) the shift of the centre of gravity of world Christianity to the global South and also the locale where struggles for justice are many; (2) the experience, perspectives and visions of the marginalised and those yearning for justice; and (3) the view of *diakonia* as essential to the nature and mission of the church.

In the following pages, I will apply briefly the methodology of the *Five Dimensions of Empowering Diakonia* to examine the Colombo conference, and more specifically its theological statement.[16] This will help us to illustrate this new paradigm of transformative *diakonia* while, at the same time, give meaning to the concept of *Empowering Diakonia* in the way I have articulated above.

The visional dimension

In this dimension I include elements that point to our motivation and ideological foundation, which encourage our goal of action. The more explicit references to empowerment as well as theological reflection, liturgy and spirituality, or a combination of them, are incorporated here. In this regard, I must say, there were at least two explicitly critical components that contributed to this dimension, both taken from the name of the event itself. One, the theological, since there was an intentional focus on *Theology of Diakonia*, and the other, forward-looking, while, as stressed earlier, the vision requires a component of future, and the conference had in mind *the 21st Century*, at its beginning. The following are my guiding terms and concepts, taken from Colombo, for the analysis of this section.

The conference acknowledged the importance of spirituality (e.g. *Liturgy after the liturgy*) as an empowering source for *diakonia* and links it with what in the ecumenical movement is understood as *prophetic diakonia.*[17] Another significant component to construct our *Vision of Colombo* is the commitment to the "allegiance to the God of life" that empowers us to defeat the "death-dealing powers of Empire" and to transform the world towards the values of the kingdom.[18]

---

[16] This statement: Theological Perspectives on Diakonia in 21st Century can be found in the following link: http://www.oikoumene.org/en/resources/documents/wcc-programmes/unity-mission-evangelism-and-spirituality/just-and-inclusive-communities/theological-perspectives-on-diakonia-in-21st-century

[17] WCC, *Theological Perspectives on Diakonia,* 105, para 4.

[18] WCC, *Theological Perspectives on Diakonia*, 105, para 4. The term *Empire* here is used as defined in the *Accra Confession*, by the former World Alliance of Reformed Churches (today the World Communion of Reformed Churches), which points out "As

In Colombo there was recognition of *non-conventional* forms of practicing *diakonia* like those experienced by people living at the margins. It was stressed, "*Diakonia* of the marginalised ... is crucial for the church's engagement in realising God's *oikoumene,* the alternative vision of the world".[19] Hence the importance of an inclusive diaconal engagement, since "Marginalised people, through their yearnings for life with dignity and justice and through their participation in movements, are offering alternative visions of a world free of forces that deny justice, dignity and life for many "[20] This again is a relevant example of the relationship between empowerment and *diakonia*, where the direct involvement of marginalised people is fundamental for diaconal engagement.

The normative dimension

This dimension is expressed in our core values, principles and standards, which are rooted in the authority of the Bible; therefore some Biblical texts quoted at the Colombo meeting will be listed under this dimension. References to the multidisciplinary approach of diaconal action, as well as its interconnectedness with God's mission, are also included in this section.

On the latter, the Colombo statement begins by expressing, under the portion named *Church, Mission and Diakonia*, that "God's mission is about the realisation of God's vision for the world, a world in which 'God rejoices ... where the aggressors are transformed so that all shall live in peace' (Isaiah 65:17-25) ... This mission of God is dynamic and inclusive of all people and forces that uphold the sanctity and integrity of God's creation".[21] The document claims a foundational ecclesiology that purposely interrelates service with God's mission. It states: "The Church, as a community called into being through baptism and led by the Holy Spirit, participates in this mission through its very being, proclamation and service. Commonly understood as service, *diakonia* is a way of living out faith and hope as a community, witnessing to what God has done in Jesus Christ."[22] This quote urges the church to be a serving community, pursuing a witnessing service, by assisting, caring for and supporting people in need, as a response to God's mission.

---

seekers of truth and justice and looking through the eyes of powerless and suffering people, we see that the current world (dis)order is rooted in an extremely complex and immoral economic system defended by empire. In using the term 'empire', we mean the coming together of economic, cultural, political and military power that constitutes a system of domination led by powerful nations to protect and defend their own interests". WARC, *The Accra Confession. Covenanting for Justice in the Economy and the Earth. World Alliance of Reformed Churches* (Geneva, 2004), 3, para 11.

[19] WCC, *Theological Perspectives on Diakonia,* 107, para 13.

[20] WCC, *Theological Perspectives on Diakonia*, 108, para 15.

[21] WCC, *Theological Perspectives on Diakonia*, 104, para 1.

[22] WCC, *Theological Perspectives on Diakonia*, 105, para 2.

The last section of the document called *Diakonia for Transformation* begins with this short, but very meaningful and normative, quote from Micah 6:8: *"To do justice and to love kindness"*, mentioning two key elements related to the diaconal endeavour, namely, to comfort the people in need – motivated by 'love kindness' – while at the same time, confronting the root causes of injustice, precisely by 'doing justice'.

And the document ends quoting two other Biblical texts, namely, Romans 12:2, pointing to a diaconal action that "not merely resists and confronts evil, but also proposes alternatives to the ways in which human beings relate with one another and with nature", through transformation. The other text is taken from Matthew 5:13-14, where Jesus calls his disciples to be "salt of the earth, the light, and the leaven of the world". This text is quoted to explain how his followers are called "to be agents of change and transformation", while just after, there is an explicit reference to "empowerment by the Holy Spirit".[23] Likewise today, Christian communities are equally empowered through their own daily means (in the sense explained in footnote 9), which obliges and urges to resist the neo-liberal unjust system and to work towards a transformed world.

The need-oriented dimension

The participants at the conference mentioned the need to focus on the following challenges to be taken into account in this reflection towards action for *diakonia* in the 21st century. These were, among others, the institutionalisation of injustice, particularly in the present regime of neo-liberal economic globalisation; the reality of climate change and its impact; wars and conflicts and the consequent destruction, trauma and broken relationships; the fragmentation of communities due to aggressive assertion of religious and ethnic identities. Also the dispossession and displacement of vulnerable people; the violence against many sections of society, especially of women, children, people with disabilities and the aged; malnutrition, disease and the HIV and Aids pandemic.[24] Participants at the conference mentioned the need not only to analyze these challenges critically, but also to find solutions in a proactive and prophetic manner.

The Colombo statement mentions not only the role of the churches in addressing the needs of the people, but also acknowledges the important function of other related organisations, empowering through capacity-building. It says, "Some of the larger institutional expressions of *diakonia* must be affirmed for their role in enabling human resource development, meeting human need in crisis situations, and for advancing the causes of justice and

[23] WCC, *Theological Perspectives on Diakonia,* 111, para. 22.
[24] WCC, *Theological Perspectives on Diakonia,* Introduction.

economic development of vulnerable people …".[25] Consequently, there is a need to engage creatively in a multidisciplinary approach for diaconal action.

"For many, *diakonia* is a Christian response to people in need and situations of crisis, and is characterised by actions of reaching out to them from locations of power and privilege with resources and infrastructure. Such an understanding has often resulted in viewing those in need as objects or recipients of *diakonia*. … Some forms of *diakonia* have been pursued without attitudes of respect, awareness of the potential or a spirit of partnership with local communities."[26] So the statement calls for the needs of people to be addressed, not in a paternalistic way, but with the active participation of the marginalised, discussing together not only their needs, but the causes as well as the solutions.

The contextual dimension

From the perspective of the *oikoumene*, the Colombo document understands each and every context where diaconal action takes place, both as a reason and also as an instrument for unity. It notes the following: "Every Christian community in every geo-political and socio-economic context is called to be a diaconal community, witnessing to God's transforming grace through acts of service that hold forth the promise of God's reign. It heals relationships, and nurtures partnerships for the sake of God's good creation."[27] The unique role of the WCC is precisely bringing together the rich expressions of these various contexts in order to continue addressing the challenges locally, but from a global standpoint. This provides not only inspiration – since the participants say, "We are not alone in this struggle!" – but also the experience and practical solutions to tackle the issues more creatively and effectively.

This way of working also generates partnerships and networks. The document points out, "As a response in faith to the hope of the coming reign of God, the signs of which are present in all experiences of hope amidst turmoil, in actions that heal and nurture people and relationships, in struggles that seek justice and affirm truth, *diakonia* has to be dynamic, contextual, and versatile. It must affect partnerships, not only at the level of global or larger church structures, but also among congregations, special ministries, and networks of people committed to values of justice, peace and human dignity at local, regional and national levels."[28]

This partnership also includes working in collaboration with other sciences, by which the church can understand better the causes and consequences of the exclusion of people due to ethnic reasons, or in relation to people living with

[25] WCC, *Theological Perspectives on Diakonia*, 105, para 6.
[26] WCC, *Theological Perspectives on Diakonia*, 106, para 8.
[27] WCC, *Theological Perspectives on Diakonia*, 105, para 5.
[28] WCC, *Theological Perspectives on Diakonia*, 105-06, para 7.

disabilities, and also to work on capacity-building to further empower the marginalised and excluded.

The transformative dimension

The last section of the Colombo statement is called *Diakonia for transformation*, pointing both to the third phase of *diakonia* in the ecumenical movement, and to the fifth and last *Dimension of Empowering Diakonia*. Again, the *Transformative Dimension* refers to a *diakonia* that "will be effective through concrete prophetic actions towards social transformation and justice". The document signals, "*Diakonia* ... is service that makes the celebration of life possible for all. It is faith-effecting change, transforming people and situations so that God's reign may be real in the lives of all people, in every here and now."[29]

This 'faith-effecting change' points to a re-conversion to the God of Life who has opted preferentially for the poor, the exploited, the victims of injustice and exclusion. This re-conversion seeks not only a 'celebration of life for all', but also the necessary empowerment for 'transformation of peoples and situations' towards the values of God's kingdom. This is indeed, a distinctive feature of our Judæo-Christian spirituality that motivates for action, compared with other human efforts that aim at social transformation.

The document makes a sharp distinction between *diakonia* as charity aiming at "binding the wounds of the victims or doing acts of compassion" and transforming *diakonia*.[30] It also defines diaconal transformation by establishing a difference between "resisting and confronting evil" on the one hand and "proposing alternatives to the ways in which human beings relate with one another and with nature" on the other. And the sentence concludes, "To that extent, *diakonia* is transformative."[31]

Conclusion

In conclusion, considering the findings of the Colombo consultation, we reaffirm the importance of the *Empowering Diakonia* model that lifts spirituality and a vision founded on the allegiance to the God of life that empowers to defeat the unjust powers and to transform the world towards the values of God's kingdom. The church of Jesus Christ is urged to fulfil God's mission, to be a united and inclusive diaconal community, empowered by the Holy Spirit with life-affirming values, to exercise the power of service over the power of domination. It addresses the needs of the people at the margins with their own participation, as subjects, since they experience the power of God manifested in their daily struggle and lives.

---

[29] WCC, *Theological Perspectives on Diakonia*, 108, para 16.
[30] WCC, *Theological Perspectives on Diakonia*, 108, para 18.
[31] WCC, *Theological Perspectives on Diakonia*, 109, para 22.

Empowering Diakonia also takes into serious consideration the context, both local and global, where diaconal engagement is being exercised, particularly in solidarity with those excluded, victims of unjust situations; seeking re-conversion and effecting change that is grounded and inspired in a spirituality of transformation. Therefore, following the footsteps of Jesus Christ, the church today is empowered for a prophetic diaconal action that resists the power of the Empire and transforms society by proposing and living alternative values and visions towards justice and peace.

Bibliography

Bosch, David, *Transforming Mission. Paradigm Shifts in Theology of Mission* (16th ed), (Maryknoll, NY: Orbis, 2001).

Browning, Don S., *A Fundamental Practical Theology. Descriptive and Strategic Proposals* (Minneapolis, MN: Augsburg Fortress Press, 1996).

Gill, David, *Gathered for Life. Official Report, VI Assembly of the WCC, Vancouver, Canada, 1983* (Geneva: WCC, 1983).

Poser, Klaus, *Diakonia 2000 – Called to Be Neighbours. Official Report of the WCC World Consultation on Inter-Church Aid, Refugee and World Service, Larnaca, Cyprus, November 1986* (Geneva: WCC, 1987).

Slack, Kenneth, *Hope in the Desert* (Geneva: WCC, 1986).

Van Beek, Hubert, *Sharing Life in a World Community. Official Report of the WCC World Consultation on Koinonia, El Escorial, Spain, 1987* (Geneva: WCC, 1989).

WARC, *The Accra Confession. Covenanting for Justice in the Economy and the Earth. World Alliance of Reformed Churches* (Geneva: WCC, 2004).

WCC, *Constitution and Rules of the World Council of Churches*, 2006.

WCC, *Diakonia: Creating Harmony, Seeking Justice and Practising Compassion.* Edited by Diakonia and Solidarity Team (Geneva: WCC, 2005).

White, Teresa Joan, '*Diakonia*', in *Dictionary of the Ecumenical Movement*, Nicholas Lossky et al (eds), (2nd. ed), (Geneva: WCC, 2002).

Part 2

Social Perspectives

Diakonia as Rights-Based Practice

Hans Morten Haugen

Human rights express the main content of a life in dignity, and human rights derive from the inherent dignity of the human person, as specified in the preambles to the two human rights covenants, on civil and political rights (ICCPR), and on economic, social and cultural rights (ICESCR). Human rights and human dignity are increasingly integrated into the strategies of diaconal agencies.

The three questions that this article seeks to answer and that structure the article are: what are the actual implications of viewing diaconal work as rights-based? How and where is rights-based diaconal work promoted? What are the main limitations in a rights-based approach? Norwegian Church Aid (NCA) will be used as an example. This chapter is based on the presumption that diaconal organisations working in the realm of international development are generally the most advanced in rights-based practice. The data material consists of strategic documents and reports from NCA; NCA is owned by twelve Norwegian Protestant churches and organisations, and presents itself as ecumenical, diaconal and humanitarian.[1]

As a theoretical approach, the moral philosophy developed by Pogge providing a framework for assessing global institutions' contributions to global injustice will be used. This is both because justice is so central for diaconal organisations working in the realm of international development,[2] and because Pogge applies human rights as the basis for his assessments.

Conceptual and Theoretical Framework

Diakonia, irrespective of whether it is primarily compassion-based or rights-based, must be undertaken in a non-discriminatory manner, starting from the premise that all human beings irrespective of their abilities and conduct have the same dignity. *Diakonia* should direct particular attention to those in most need – seeking to achieve substantive equality, and seeking to hold political authorities accountable for their failure to act in an adequate manner, and for

[1] NCA, *Global Strategy 2011-2015* (Oslo: NCA 2011), 12.

[2] Aprodev [Association of World Council of Churches related Development Organizations in Europe] *Rights-based development from a faith-based perspective* (Brussels: Aprodev 2008), 8-9.

their harmful acts. While respect for the existing laws is a general requirement for both individuals and companies, individual and collective conscience can imply that disobeying the law may be necessary in certain circumstances – and there is no provision in any human rights treaty that justifies restrictions in freedom of conscience. Moreover, *diakonia* must be undertaken with the purpose of fostering empowerment of individuals, households and communities, by promoting participation, which in turn must be facilitated by transparency. Such transparency, providing access to relevant information on a proposed project, enhances the quality of any decision-making process.

Dignity, non-discrimination, accountability, rule of law, transparency, participation and empowerment can also be referred to as *human rights principles*, understood as basic norms specifying minimum standards of conduct. It has been confirmed by the United Nations (UN) specialised agencies that human rights principles are integral to a rights-based approach to development.[3] To be effective, these human rights principles must always be seen in conjunction with substantive human rights.

Is there any difference between a rights-based approach and a human rights-based approach? First, the wider notion of rights as found in local custom – which do recognise rights, but not necessarily in a human rights-compatible manner – can be included. In many traditional communities women might be denied equal rights with men in terms of decision-making. This is covered by International Labour Organisation's (ILO) Convention 169 concerning Indigenous and Tribal Peoples in Independent Countries, Article 8.2:

> These peoples shall have the right to retain their own customs and institutions, where these are not incompatible with fundamental rights defined by the national legal system and with internationally recognised human rights. Procedures shall be established, whenever necessary, to resolve conflicts which may arise in the application of this principle.

In other words, while traditional customs and institutions shall be respected and promoted, human rights take precedence over customary rights if there is a conflict between the two.

Second, the wider notion of the term 'rights' is frequently used in the Bible, always in the context of acting in accordance with what is right and righteous, which is specified as a duty in both the Old and the New Testaments. This ancient concept of rights which gave rise to the natural law tradition also influences contemporary diaconal thinking. The current era, where positive law prevails over natural law, might lead to the misunderstanding that human rights have come into existence by being included in international conventions. This is not correct; human rights exist irrespective of states' efforts, but by recognising human rights in international conventions, states can specify the

[3] UN Development Group, *The Human Rights Based Approach to Development Cooperation: Towards a Common Understanding Among UN Agencies*, 2003.

obligations that are derived from these rights, while many states actively restrict human rights activities within their borders.[4]

An additional explanation for why the term 'rights' is applied in some contexts and not the term 'human rights' is the fact that organisations working for human rights are subject to more severe restrictions in certain countries. Hence, the term 'human rights' is avoided for strategic reasons, but at least for the NCA, the term 'rights' refers essentially to internationally recognised human rights.[5]

NCA and other church-related development organisations are tools established by churches for international *diakonia*. Both these and other specialised diaconal organisations and institutions based in secular societies believe that, if the recruitment universe is restricted to Christian believers, there is a rather limited universe to recruit from. Can any practice undertaken in good faith by a non-Christian person working for a diaconal employer be said to constitute *diakonia*? The brief answer to this question is yes, as this practice or conduct is done within the context of a diaconal institution or organisation. The diaconal character of any diaconal institution or organisation does not depend on the faith of the individual employee. The leadership, however, must be Christian, and the board must ensure that this is emphasised when leaders are recruited. This cannot be said to represent discrimination against non-believers. It is then up to the leadership to ensure that all staff gain adequate knowledge of what it means to be an employee in a diaconal institution.[6]

The same reasoning applies when assessing whether a concrete practice is adequately rights-based or not. An employee working for a diaconal organisation is working within a human rights-based approach if such a working method is what the diaconal organisation strives to achieve – and its practice is in accordance with the requirements of this approach. Hence, a human rights-based approach must apply a certain method.

When seeking to understand the operations of any organisation, it is important to be aware that there may be discrepancies between desired practices and actual practices. There might also be discrepancies between expressed values, on the one hand, and values that influence the working of the organisation and the actual conduct of its employees, on the other hand. Hence, what is written in a diaconal organisation's official documents might not adequately represent the realities of the work undertaken on the ground by or with the funding from the diaconal organisation.

---

[4] ACT Alliance, *Shrinking political space of civil society action* (Geneva: Act Alliance, 2011).
[5] NCA, 'Global Strategy', 33.
[6] Eurodiaconia, *Diaconal Identity*, 19-20.

Inspiration from Moral Philosophy Promoting Global Justice?

As Christians we are encouraged to present arguments in ways that have appeal across faith boundaries. This section will apply current moral philosophy to assess if it can give both inspiration and be a practical tool for promoting global justice.

More specifically, we will analyze one tradition within moral philosophy which applies substantive human rights as the benchmark, to assess the current international economic system, focusing on how institutions maintain global injustice and holding everyone able to influence these institutions to account. Thomas Pogge is the central philosopher in this tradition.

Thomas Pogge writes within the liberal tradition of Rawls,[7] and his more recent writings have an emphasis on negative obligations of avoiding harm rather than positive obligations of engaging in redistribution.[8] He argues that this is not because he denies the existence of positive duties, but because emphasising negative duties enables Pogge to reach those persons who deny the positive duties.[9] Since his thinking has developed, a more recent contribution is our primary source.[10]

The main argument of Pogge is that each and everyone in the wealthy nations – with the exception of children and persons who are mentally ill – is responsible for violating the human rights of everyone in poor nations who does not have secure access to crucial goods like safe medicines, food or clean water. Hence, by not seeking to influence their own authorities to exercise influence over the institutions so that they change their policies, those living in developed countries are involved in human rights violations affecting at least one billion people. He then lists six policy realms where international institutions act – or do not act – in a manner which foreseeably produces massive human rights violations. First, exploitation of natural resources, which might benefit small élites, but not the poor. Second, demanding debt payment, even if the debts were incurred by dictators and against the wishes and interests

[7] For a concise analysis of both Rawls and Pogge and other global justice theories, see Malcolm Langford and Mac Darrow, 'Moral Theory, International Law and Global Justice', in Malcolm Langford et al (eds), *Global Justice, State Duties. The extraterritorial scope of economic, social and cultural rights in international law* (Cambridge and New York: CUP, 2013), 428.

[8] Thomas Pogge, 'Are We Violating the Human Rights of the World's Poor?', in *Yale Human Rights and Development Law Journal* 14:2 (2011), 1-33; 'The Role of International Law in Reproducing Mass Poverty', in Samantha Besson and John Tasioulas (eds), *The Philosophy of International Law* (Oxford and New York: OUP, 2010), 417-36; 'Responses to the Critics', in Allison Jaggar (ed), *Thomas Pogge and His Critics* (Cambridge: Polity, 2010), 175-250; *World Poverty and Human Rights: Cosmopolitan Responsibilities and Reforms* (2nd edn) (Cambridge: Polity 2008); *Freedom from Poverty as a Human Right: Who owes what to the very poor?* (Oxford and New York: OUP, 2007).

[9] Pogge, 'Responses', 200.

[10] Pogge, 'Are We Violating?'.

of the people (illegitimate debt). Third, providing safe havens for money stolen from the public (embezzled funds). Fourth, allowing companies to manipulate their company structures and prices when transferring funds to nations with low or no taxes (tax havens). Fifth, continuing (and increasing) greenhouse gas emissions, which harm most those that bear the least responsibility for climate change. Sixth, upholding a trading regime that allows subsidies and export credits in rich countries, but that allows neither protectionist measures against the resulting dumping in poor countries, nor measures for assisting poor countries.[11] Pogge has also proposed various ways that life-saving medicines can be made affordable to persons in developing countries.[12] All these issues have been addressed by the NCA through publications and campaigns.

While most – including the present author – agree on the problems described above, Pogge's line of argument is nevertheless open to fundamental criticism. A central premise is that he establishes individual accountability for the conduct of international institutions anywhere in the world. This is a link that extends accountability beyond normal understanding, based on the actual conduct of participants. Individuals can neither be expected to be able to understand all foreign policy issues, nor be able to direct the policies of their governments to the extent that will affect the conduct of international institutions.[13]

Moreover, Pogge himself is not consistent in the central terms – sometimes writing that international institutions produce 'massive human rights deficits';[14] but also that these institutions contribute to these human rights deficits.[15] There is a difference between producing something and contributing to something. Terrible life conditions were also a fact of the past, and not all such conditions can be explained by the conduct of unjust international institutions. It should, however, be emphasised that living in dire conditions today is worse than before, because those suffering are increasingly exposed to others' wealth. Also the term 'large crime against humanity'[16] is objectionable, as Pogge does not refer to the international definition of what constitutes such crimes.[17]

---

[11] Pogge, 'Are We Violating?', 29-30.

[12] Pogge, *World Poverty*, 222-61.

[13] Søren Flinch Midtgaard, 'On Thomas Pogge's Theory of Global Justice. Why We Are Not Collectively Responsible for the Global Distribution of Benefits and Burdens between Individuals', in *SATS, Nordic Journal of Philosophy* 13:2 (2012), 207-22.

[14] Pogge, 'Are We Violating?', 1, 20.

[15] Pogge, 'Are We Violating?', 22.

[16] Pogge, 'Are We Violating?', 18-19.

[17] UN, *Rome Statute of the International Criminal Court*, 2187 U.N.T.S. 90 (1998), which specifies what constitutes crimes against humanity. See, however, ICC 2011, Article 7.1 (b), Element 1, note 9, which specifies that 'extermination' encompasses 'conditions of life', including deprivation of food; also ICC 2011, Article 6 (c), Element 4, note 4 (conditions of life in the context of genocide). Moreover, Article 8 (xxv) specifies starvation as one category of war crime.

Pogge's argument is that, just as it was wrong to argue for 'ethical slavery', as the only response to slavery was abolition, it is wrong to argue for ethical codes for international institutions. He calls for the elimination of institutional injustice not by eradicating the institutions, but by reforming them,[18] but he also notes that citizens of wealthy countries do *not* seem to be too concerned about influencing their authorities to take a different approach in international negotiations.[19] His challenges have earlier been directed to persons in developed countries to work for reforms in 'global institutions that cause widespread and severe poverty',[20] and for compensation for each individual's 'share of responsibility for this harm'.[21] In his more recent writings he stresses only compensation for one's country's responsibility,[22] resulting in a surprisingly small amount when calculating this compensation. Hence, when seeking to specify what each can do, the argument comes close to the positive duties elaborated by Peter Singer,[23] specifying how each of us is able to save lives of persons in other countries.

Pogge can be criticised for extending the accountability too far and for using legal terms imprecisely. His uncompromising approach is nevertheless appealing, and the fact that he explicitly links global justice with states' human rights obligations adds to this. For diaconal agencies working with a human rights basis, Pogge can be an inspiration.

Diakonia as Rights-Based: What Does it Imply?

The human rights principles listed in the introduction are also important principles in diaconal work. Eurodiaconia highlights one of these principles:

> Human rights … express what we mean by human dignity. God's will is … societies where … caring and loving our fellow man is expressed in human rights, and where the kingdom of God is expressed through our commitment to human rights. Human rights give hope to people when confronted with poverty, discrimination, marginalisation and destructive powers and structures …[24]

Human dignity can be upheld through care, love and work against discrimination, according to Eurodiaconia. This overriding principle must be relevant even in controversial theological issues. Even if there are theological

[18] Pogge, 'Are We Violating?', 20.
[19] Pogge, 'Are We Violating?', 31.
[20] Pogge, 'Responses', 210.
[21] Pogge, 'Responses', 210.
[22] Pogge, 'Are We Violating?', 32.
[23] Peter Singer, *The Life You Can Save: Acting Now to End World Poverty* (New York: Random House, 2009); see also Jeffrey Schaler (ed), *Peter Singer Under Fire: The Moral Iconoclast Faces His Critics* (Chicago, IL: Open Court Publishers, 2009), Part III.
[24] Eurodiaconia, *Diaconal Identity*, 14.

and doctrinal disagreements about whether to acknowledge homosexual relationships, from a diaconal and human rights perspective there is no doubt that we as Christians are called to confirm the dignity of persons who are homosexuals (the wider term applied is lesbians, gays, bisexuals and transpersons or LGBT), and actively oppose any harassment or discrimination against them. In other words, as stated initially in this chapter, human rights specify appropriate conduct.

NCA affirms in its Global Strategy 2011-15 the so-called integrated approach, consisting of three rights-based working methods: long-term development aid, emergency, and advocacy.[25] When analyzing how human rights challenge development organisations, Ghere underlines that human rights work necessitates advocacy,[26] and that a rights-based approach seeks to enable communities to better control the circumstances that impact the quality of life.[27]

Hence, all aspects of NCA's operative work are defined as being rights-based. In the context of development interventions, NCA says: "International human rights standards and conventions will guide design, monitoring and evaluation processes."[28] Within the United Nations there are standards and manuals for both long-term development co-ordination,[29] and for humanitarian relief work.[30] For the purposes of this article, the most interesting is not development programmes, but rather how NCA views its advocacy work, and what role is expected from its partners in such work. The reason is that advocacy is presumed to lead to wider and more long-term impacts as compared with other activities.[31] Rights-based advocacy will be elaborated in the section below; here I shall attempt to clarify relevant basic relationships and possible tensions between *diakonia* and human rights, and do this by elaborating on NCA's Global Strategy.

The five values that guide NCA's work are: the integrity of creation, human dignity, global justice, inclusive communities and compassion.[32] To assess the centrality of these values in diaconal thinking, they will be analyzed in relation to five elements that Eurodiaconia claims must be present if diaconal care

[25] NCA, 'Global Strategy', 13.

[26] Richard Ghere, *NGO Leadership and Human Rights* (Sterling, VA: Kumarian Press, 2013), 163.

[27] Ghere, 'NGO Leadership', 7.

[28] NCA, 'Global Strategy', 33.

[29] UN Development Group, *CCA/UNDAF Guidelines* (2009).

[30] UN Inter-Agency Standing Committee, *Human Rights Guidance Note for Humanitarian Coordinators* (2006).

[31] NORAD Civil Society Panel, *Tracking Impact. An exploratory study of the wider effects of Norwegian civil society support to countries in the South* (Oslo: NORAD, 2012), 30.

[32] NCA, 'Global Strategy', 12.

should 'truly be expressed'.[33] While Eurodiaconia's fifth element ('praise') is not included among NCA's values, Eurodiaconia's four other elements (creation, fellowship, justice and care) relate very well to NCA's values. Whether the omission of the element of praise implies that NCA's work cannot 'truly' express *diakonia* may to some extent be answered by assessing other parts of NCA's Statement of principles. The second paragraph of NCA's mission statement says that NCA shall 'manifest God's love in the world'.[34] This phrase does not equal praise in the traditional sense, but having a self-understanding that encompasses manifesting God's love, it should be considered compatible with Eurodiaconia's five elements of diaconal care.

As the working methods cannot be contrary to NCA's values, there must be a presumption that a rights-based working method is contributing positively to the observance of the values. This, however, cannot merely be presumed; it must be investigated. What is the relationship between human rights and a human rights-based approach, and each of NCA's five values? We shall review each of the values in the order they appear in NCA's Global Strategy.

Concerning *the integrity of creation*, there are several substantive human rights, the realisation of which depends on a healthy environment, like the human right to adequate food, water and housing, and to the highest attainable standard of health. Moreover, the right to self-determination of peoples and the right to take part in culture – which should be exercised in community with others – depend on adequate access to natural resources. NCA's 2011-15 strategy emphasise creation by prioritising climate justice, and the right to water and health.

With regard to *human dignity*, by definition there can be no human rights-based approaches that undermine human dignity. Human dignity has diverse meanings in different contexts, covering prohibitions of certain treatment, conditions for individual autonomy, conditions for maintaining cultures, and conditions for satisfaction of basic needs.[35] For a diaconal organisation working in international development, the latter is the central understanding.[36] NCA's 2011-15 strategy prioritises gender justice, particularly the participation and empowerment of women.

On *global justice*, human rights obligations for wealthy states do not imply massive transfer of resources to economically poor nations, even though

---

[33] Eurodiaconia, *Diaconal Identity*, 9.

[34] NCA, *Together for a just world. Norwegian Church Aid's Statement of principles* (Oslo: NCA 2008), 5.

[35] Andrew Clapham, *Human Rights Obligations of Non-State Actors* (Oxford and New York: OUP, 2006), 545-46; see also Christopher McCrudden, 'Human Dignity and Judicial Interpretation of Human Rights', in *European Journal of International Law* 19:4 (2008), 655-724, at 685-94.

[36] UN, A/CONF.157/23, Vienna Declaration and Programme of Action (1993), I, para 25; acknowledging that extreme poverty and social exclusion constitute a violation of human dignity.

Article 28 of the Universal Declaration of Human Rights reads: "Everyone is entitled to a social and international order in which the rights and freedoms set forth in this Declaration can be fully realised." The general obligations are specified in Article 2.1 of the ICESCR, saying that every national party "undertakes to take steps, individually and through international assistance and co-operation, especially economic and technical ..." When examining nations' implementation of the ICESCR, the Committee on Economic, Social and Cultural Rights calls for 0.7% of rich nations' gross national income (GNI) to be set aside for development assistance.[37] Global justice obligations under international law are therefore rather limited, but NCA's 2011-15 strategy prioritises economic justice, ranging from improving community livelihoods to reforming global trade, finance and aid systems.

Are human rights promoting *inclusive communities*? Not only individuals are rights-holders, but also families (ICCPR Article 23.1), minorities (ICCPR Article 27) and indigenous peoples (ICCPR/ICESCR Article 1). Human rights do promote inclusive communities and can be applied to challenge customary discriminatory practices.[38] Moreover, individuals should – if necessary – be allowed to disassociate themselves from the culture and the traditional norms they belong to. Hence, human rights claims might create tensions within traditional communities. The main rule is that human rights need human communities to be fully exercised. NCA's 2011-15 strategy prioritises the right to peace and security, with a particular emphasis on local communities and the role of women within such communities.

Finally, what is the relationship between *compassion* and human rights? The preamble to the ICCPR and ICESCR confirms that individual is 'having duties to other individuals and to the community to which he belongs ...' In this context, it is interesting to note that an initiative in 2003-05 to adopt a UN declaration on human responsibilities did not succeed.[39] Moreover, human rights can be restricted if this is necessary to protect others' rights and freedoms, as illustrated by the exceptional provisions on religion, assembly and association in ICCPR articles 18.3, 21 and 22.2, respectively. Hence, while love and compassion are somewhat beyond the scope of human rights, the responsible conduct of each individual in all relationships is central.

---

[37] This target was first agreed to in 1970; see UN, General Assembly Resolution 2626 (XXV), International Development Strategy for the Second United Nations Development Decade (1970), para 43.

[38] Colombia Constitutional Court Judgment T-603/05, Hilda Rocío Quistanchala Chacua et al v. Wilson Morales (9 June 2005); see also ILO (International Labour Organization), Application of Convention No. 169 by Domestic and International Courts in Latin America (Geneva: ILO, 2009), 98-99.

[39] Hans Morten Haugen, 'International Obligations and the Right to Food: Clarifying the Potentials and Limitations in Applying a Human Rights Approach when Facing Biofuels Expansion', in *Journal of Human Rights*, 11:3 (2012), 405-29, at 422 n. 3.

We see that some of the principles which express general diaconal approaches are more easily identified as falling within the realm of human rights than others, but *this review shows that there are no contradictions between human rights principles and diaconal principles.*

How and Where – and for Whom?

In long-term development and emergency responses, responsible conduct is crucial. Any humanitarian organisation, diaconal or not, should at least be familiar with, and preferably be certified in accordance with, the Humanitarian Accountability Partnership (HAP) Standard in Accountability and Quality Management which, for instance, specifies participation by communities and mechanisms for handling complaints.[40] The objective of any intervention should be to ensure that self-reliance of the beneficiaries is sought.[41] Accountability is defined as a process of "being held accountable by ... different stakeholders, and primarily those who are affected by the exercise of power".[42]

As a tool to influence those in power, NCA promotes human rights-based advocacy. NCA itself presents advocacy as consisting of three dimensions: dialogue (lobby and negotiation); confrontation (public debate, demonstrations or litigation); and mobilisation (awareness and movement-building).[43] In order to have effective advocacy, the building of a large constituency is important.

NCA also says that advocacy for social change must always be rights-based, rooted in the experiences of NCA and its partners, and addressing structural causes of poverty.[44]

While NCA has been part of a wide range of advocacy campaigns over the last two decades, including debt cancellation and fair trade, where the main efforts have been directed at Norwegian authorities, there are also examples of NCA's advocacy efforts being directed at authorities in partner countries and at companies. An example of the former is female genital circumcision (FGM) in Eritrea, where the campaign by the National Union of Eritrean Women was given as the explanation for the Eritrean FGM ban.[45] The NCA, in co-operation with the Eritrean Ministry of Health, produced the 2004 video 'Behind the

---

[40] HAP, *HAP Standard in Accountability and Quality Management* (Geneva: HAP 2010), 18-22; see also NCA, *Norwegian Church Aid's Accountability framework* (2012).

[41] UN Committee on Economic, Social and Cultural Rights, *E/C.12/1999/5, General Comment 12, The right to adequate food (Art. 11)* (2000), para 39.

[42] HAP, 'HAP Standard', 5.

[43] NCA, 'Global Strategy', 34.

[44] NCA, 'Global Strategy', 34; see also Eurodiaconia, *Diaconal Identity*, 14.

[45] *New Scientist*, Female genital mutilation banned in Eritrea (5 April 2007).

Curtains of Agony' that was reported to make 'a strong impression on the audience'.[46]

Regarding campaigns against companies, we choose the campaign against Tommy Hilfiger's treatment of employees – mostly exiled Burmese – in factories in Northern Thailand in 2003-04.[47] This campaign was evaluated over one full page in the NCA 2004 Annual Review. It found that the distance to Tommy Hilfiger's main office and the lack of a Norwegian decision-maker made it difficult to influence the company, but the fact that NCA was threatened with legal action, nevertheless leads NCA to conclude that "we were successful in moving a decision-maker".[48] According to NCA, overall working conditions in the factories in Northern Thailand were improved.

While projects are to be rooted in one's own or partners' experiences, it is somewhat difficult to identify why some experiences result in advocacy efforts, while other experiences are not resulting in similar efforts. Synergies achieved through co-operating with other church-based development organisations, like Christian Aid, might be relevant.

In summary, NCA's integrated approach, encompassing advocacy, development and emergency interventions, implies that NCA seeks to promote both policy change and social change. Moreover, there is a mutually reciprocal relationship between having a rights-based platform and devoting resources to advocacy efforts.

Limitations in a Rights-Based Approach?

Can human rights promote global justice, understood as a fair distribution of resources within and between countries? We saw above that the Universal Declaration of Human Rights sets out a more transformative vision as regards social justice compared with the ICESCR.

To clarify the relationship between international human rights obligations and global justice, there is a need to introduce three approaches. First, human rights violation can take place through acts of omission (failing to act) or acts of commission (acting in harmful ways). Second, there have been attempts to clarify nations' human rights obligations, by applying the standard typology of obligations, namely, *respect* – avoid interfering; *protect* – prevent others from interfering; and *fulfil* – facilitate and provide. Third, to engage in international

[46] NORAD, *Review of Female Genital Mutilation/Cutting (FGM/C) Projects in Eritrea, NORAD Collected Reviews 18/2007* (Oslo: NORAD, 2007), 15-16.

[47] This is not NCA's largest advocacy campaign against companies, however. The campaign against gold mining companies in Tanzania in 2007-09 was larger – and more comprehensively presented in Hans Morten Haugen, 'Community empowerment as rights-based practice: A particular diaconal approach?' (2014).

[48] NCA, Annual Review 2004 (2005), 17.

co-operation and provide international assistance is an obligation.[49] In 2011-12 human rights experts formulated the Maastricht Principles on Extraterritorial Obligations of States in the area of Economic, Social and Cultural Rights.

In the context of obligations to *respect*, paragraph 21 of the Maastricht Principles reads as follows:

> Nations must refrain from any conduct which:
> a) impairs the ability of another state or international organisation to comply with … obligations as regards economic, social and cultural rights; or
> b) aids, assists, directs, controls or coerces another state or international organisation to breach … obligations …

We see that six kinds of actions are identified (impair, aid, assist, direct, control and coerce). How are these kinds of acts relevant for organisations working with international *diakonia*? The integrated approach as specified by NCA seeks to address 'root causes of poverty and injustice by challenging those in power'.[50] Powerful states can act in a way that can obviously affect the abilities of other states and international organisations to work for the realisation of economic, social and cultural rights. Both NCA and its youth movement, Changemaker, are regularly seeking to challenge Norwegian authorities to change their policies.

On obligations to *protect* (prevent others' interference), the Maastricht Principles specifies that nations 'must take necessary measures to ensure that non-state agencies … do not nullify or impair the enjoyment of economic, social and cultural rights'.[51] Whether states are legally required to regulate the conduct of their NGOs operating in other countries is still subject to disagreement. While there is no human rights treaty that regulates conduct of NGOs abroad, host states can be found to have violated their human rights obligations by not regulating the conduct of any company which has been given a licence to operate.

There are human rights-embedded tools that can be applied in order to regulate the conduct of companies that affect the livelihoods of local communities. One of these are the "Guiding Principles on human rights impact assessments of trade and investment agreements",[52] which stipulate that human rights obligations trump obligations under so-called bilateral investment

---

[49] UN Committee on Economic, Social and Cultural Rights, *General Comment 3, The nature of states parties obligations (Art. 2, para. 1 of the Covenant)* (1990), paras 13 and 14.

[50] NCA, 'Global Strategy', 13.

[51] Maastricht Principles 2012, para 25.

[52] UN Special Rapporteur on the right to food, *Guiding principles on human rights impact assessments of trade and investment agreements A/HRC/19/59/Add.5, Appendix* (2011). No states voted against the resolution which welcomed the Special Rapporteur's report; UN Human Rights Council, *A/HRC/RES/19/7, The right to food* (2012), para 42.

agreements (BITs). Moreover, the Guiding Principles call for much broader participation in discussing the impact of BITs. The Guiding Principles are just one example of tools that NGOs and faith-based agencies like churches should be familiar with. Hence, while the issue of investment agreements might seem to be a peripheral concern of diaconal agencies, the consequences of harmful investments are overriding concerns for those working in and with the affected communities. Such concerns could promote the use of various human rights tools.

Weaknesses inherent in human rights become particularly visible when encountering economic agencies and economic agreements, as illustrated by three situations. First, the BITs are legally binding, with strong enforcement mechanisms. The human rights instruments described above (general comments, the Maastricht Principles, and the UN Guiding Principles on human rights impact assessments of trade and investment agreements), on the other hand, are all so-called 'soft law'. Second, the consequences if states have been found to violate a BIT might be substantial – compensating the company that brought the state before an arbitration tribunal that is mandated to solve conflicts arising under BITs.[53] Third, the capacity of the UN human rights treaty bodies, monitoring the implementation of the human rights treaties and allowed to receive individual complaints – from persons in states that have ratified additional protocols mandating such complaints – is limited.

In summary, therefore, international human rights provisions have a rather limited scope. It must be remembered, however, that it is not only what is formulated in the relevant treaties that matters, but also whether tools and principles derived from human rights treaties are actually applied. Such tools can be applied to hold states accountable to what they have themselves agreed – first in international negotiation processes and then through national ratification processes.

Conclusion

We have seen that the NCA's integrated approach, encompassing emergencies, development and advocacy, implies that NCA applies a rights-based approach also in countries where there a certain risk associated with such an approach. NCA's advocacy work is acknowledged, for instance, in the context of climate justice for the disadvantaged and vulnerable persons who will be most affected by the impacts of climate change.[54]

---

[53] Note that compensations have been ordered also by human rights bodies and tribunals under treaties that are not explicitly human rights treaties, but that are built upon human rights; see SADC [Southern African Development Community] Tribunal, *Mike Campbell et al. vs Republic of Zimbabwe, SADC (T) Case No. 2/2007* (2008) (finding jurisdiction in SADC Treaty Article 4c).

[54] Cowi, *Organizational Performance Review of the Norwegian Church Aid (NCA), NORAD Report 2/2011 Review* (Oslo: NORAD, 2011), 14-15.

While this chapter has primarily analyzed the experiences of a diaconal organisation working within the realm of international development, it is relevant to ask why other diaconal organisations working primarily within a domestic context seemingly are less inclined to talk about human rights – even if they frequently apply central human rights terms like accountability, participation and dignity. While the answer to the question might differ depending on which diaconal organisation is being studied, three explanations will be provided, relating to risks, competence and doubts.

On risks, the shrinking space in many countries is a growing concern.[55] The fact that advocacy work is believed to be the most controversial activity[56] can force diaconal organisations to avoid terms and approaches that might be risky.

On competence, the institutional architecture of international human rights is complex. Comprehending the human rights treaties represents one challenge, but being informed about the developments within each of these treaties is an even bigger challenge. The UN 'Common understanding' specifies as a 'necessary' element to a human rights-based approach the following: "Programming is informed by the recommendations of international human rights bodies and mechanisms."[57] In practice, many UN country programmes are *not* informed by these recommendations, even if they have their own experts and can ask for assistance from the UN High Commissioner for Human Rights. Hence, it is not surprising that diaconal organisations are uncertain concerning how to engage with a human rights-based approach.

On doubts, this refers to uncertainties about what a human rights-based approach adds to the overall work. This article has identified some crucial elements of this approach. First, there must be an adequate analysis of the relevant context, identifying the most vulnerable and marginalised, and those seeking to prevent changes from taking place. Second, there must be an understanding of capacities and other resources of both right-holders and duty-bearers. Third, participatory processes are important for achieving good outcomes. Fourth, human rights provide an objective standard upon which states and companies' conduct can be assessed – and criticised. Fifth, the human rights system has produced guidelines and tools that give additional assistance.

Finally, while it is true that the realisation of social human rights, like food, health and education, is costly, it is much more costly for a nation to have many persons who have reduced abilities to work due to hunger, or who are chronically sick or illiterate. Under such circumstances, socio-economic development and community cohesion will be most difficult to achieve.

---

[55] For an assessment by diaconal development organisations, see ACT Alliance, *Shrinking political space*.

[56] NORAD's Civil Society Panel, 'Tracking impacts', 46.

[57] UN Development Group, 'The Human Rights-Based Approach', 3.

Bibliography

ACT Alliance, *Shrinking political space of civil society action* (Geneva: ACT Alliance, 2011).

Aprodev [Association of World Council of Churches related Development Organisations in Europe], *Rights-based development from a faith-based perspective* (Brussels: Aprodev, 2008).

Clapham, Andrew, *Human Rights Obligations of Non-State Actors* (Oxford and New York: OUP, 2006).

Colombia Constitutional Court, *Judgment T-603/05, Hilda Rocío Quistanchala Chacua et al. v. Wilson Morales* (9 June 2005).

Cowi, *Organisational Performance Review of the Norwegian Church Aid (NCA), NORAD Report 2/2011 Review* (Oslo: NORAD, 2011).

Eurodiaconia, *Diaconal Identity: Faith in Social Care. A Reflection from Eurodiaconia* (Brussels: Eurodiaconia, 2010).

Flinch Midtgaard, Søren, 'On Thomas Pogge's Theory of Global Justice. Why We Are Not Collectively Responsible for the Global Distribution of Benefits and Burdens between Individuals', in *SATS, Nordic Journal of Philosophy* 13:2 (2012), 207-22.

Ghere, Richard, *NGO Leadership and Human Rights* (Sterling, VA: Kumarian Press, 2013).

HAP, *HAP Standard in Accountability and Quality Management* (Geneva: HAP, 2010).

Haugen, Hans Morten, 'Community empowerment as rights-based practice: A particular diaconal approach?' (unpublished paper; available via the author).

Haugen, Hans Morten, 'International Obligations and the Right to Food: Clarifying the Potentials and Limitations in Applying a Human Rights Approach when Facing Biofuels Expansion', in *Journal of Human Rights*, 11:3 (2012), 405-29.

International Criminal Court (ICC), *Elements of Crimes*, 2011; www.refworld.org/docid/4ff5dd7d2.html

ILO, *Application of Convention No. 169 by Domestic and International Courts in Latin America* (Geneva: ILO, 2009).

Jaggar, Allison, *Thomas Pogge and His Critics* (Cambridge: Polity, 2010).

Langford, Malcolm, and Mac Darrow, 'Moral Theory, International Law and Global Justice', in Malcolm Langford *et al* (eds), *Global Justice, State Duties. The extraterritorial scope of economic, social and cultural rights in international law* (Cambridge and New York: CUP, 2013, 419-44).

Maastricht Principles on Extraterritorial Obligations of States in the area of Economic, Social and Cultural Rights (2012).

McCrudden, Christopher, 'Human Dignity and Judicial Interpretation of Human Rights', in *European Journal of International Law* 19:4 (2008): 655-724.

NCA, *Norwegian Church Aid's Accountability framework*, 2012;
www.kirkensnodhjelp.no/en/About-NCA/About-NCA/Accountability-Commitments

NCA, *Global Strategy 2011-2015*. Oslo: NCA, 2011.

NCA, *Together for a just world. Norwegian Church Aid's Statement of principles* (Oslo: NCA, 2008).

NCA, *Annual Review 2004* (Oslo: NCA, 2005).

New Scientist, female genital mutilation banned in Eritrea, 2007;
www.newscientist.com/article/dn11543-female-genital-mutilation-banned-in-eritrea.html

NORAD, *Review of Female Genital Mutilation/Cutting (FGM/C) Projects in Eritrea NORAD Collected Reviews 18/2007* (Oslo: NORAD, 2007).

NORAD's Civil Society Panel, *Tracking Impact. An exploratory study of the wider effects of Norwegian civil society support to countries in the South* (Oslo: NORAD, 2012).

Pogge, Thomas, 'Are We Violating the Human Rights of the World's Poor?' in *Yale Human Rights and Development Law Journal*, 14:2 (2011), 1-33.

Pogge, Thomas, 'The Role of International Law in Reproducing Mass Poverty', in Samantha Besson and John Tasioulas (eds), *The Philosophy of International Law* (Oxford and New York: OUP, 2010, 417-36).

Pogge, Thomas, 'Responses to the Critics', in Allison Jaggar (ed), *Thomas Pogge and His Critics* (Cambridge: Polity, 2010, 175-250).

Pogge, Thomas, *World Poverty and Human Rights: Cosmopolitan Responsibilities and Reforms* (2nd edition) (Cambridge: Polity, 2008).

Pogge, Thomas (ed), *Freedom from Poverty as a Human Right: Who owes what to the very poor?* (Oxford and New York: OUP, 2007).

SADC Tribunal, *Mike Campbell et al. vs Republic of Zimbabwe, SADC (T) Case No. 2/2007* (2008).

Schaler, Jeffrey (ed), *Peter Singer Under Fire: The Moral Iconoclast Faces His Critics* (Chicago, IL: Open Court Publishers, 2009).

Singer, Peter, *The Life You Can Save: Acting Now to End World Poverty* (New York: Random House, 2009).

UN, *Rome Statute of the International Criminal Court*, 2187 U.N.T.S. 90, 1998.

UN, *A/CONF.157/23, Vienna Declaration and Programme of Action,* 1993.

UN, *General Assembly Resolution 2626 (XXV), International Development Strategy for the Second United Nations Development Decade*, 1970.

UN Committee on Economic, Social and Cultural Rights, *E/C.12/1999/5, General Comment 12, The right to adequate food (Art. 11)*, 2000.

UN Committee on Economic, Social and Cultural Rights, *General Comment 3, The nature of States parties' obligations (Art. 2, para. 1 of the Covenant)*, 1990.

UN Development Group, *CCA/UNDAF Guidelines*, 2009; www.undg.org/index.cfm?P=16

UN Development Group, *The Human Rights Based Approach to Development Co-operation: Towards a Common Understanding Among UN Agencies,* 2003; http://hrbaportal.org/the-human-rights-based-approach-to-development-co-operation-towards-a-common-understanding-among-un-agencies

UN Human Rights Council, *A/HRC/RES/19/7, The right to food*, 2012.

UN Inter-Agency Standing Committee, *Human Rights Guidance Note for Humanitarian Coordinators*, 2006; www.refworld.org/docid/4ae9ac8d0.html

Diaconial Work and Research about Diakonia in the Face of Welfare Mix and Religious Pluralism in Sweden and Germany

Annette Leis-Peters

Research about *diakonia* and Christian social practice has traditionally had a national focus with the exception of those projects that looked at international *diakonia* explicitly. There are some publications that juxtapose different contexts and conceptions of diaconal work, but only very few work with parallels between contexts in a more elaborate way. Diaconal work is, among other things, affected by the welfare system within which it is operating and by the way in which church-state relationships are organised. Due to different national and church contexts, *diakonia* and diaconal work can mean very different things in different places (if the *diakonia* terms are used at all). The differences affect the ways in which diaconal work is organised, conducted and perceived, what kind of research is done about it, and how research questions are posed. However, the internationalisation of all areas of life – and of research – makes it increasingly questionable to just focus on and relate to a limited national context. This might be an explanation of recent efforts to make the results of the national research about *diakonia* more accessible for an international audience.[1]

Bringing together different approaches has been discussed as a way of handling global trends such as the growing plurality of religion and welfare mix solutions.[2] As diaconal agencies in different contexts are facing similar social challenges, it is supposed that they can benefit from knowing about each other and about their respective strategies. But are diaconal practices converging internationally? Do similar social challenges really result in comparable strategies in diaconal work? And how is research mirroring these processes?

---

[1] Cf. http://www.v-r.de/en/magazine-0-0/diaconia_journal_for_the_study_of_christian_social_practice-500059/ and see www.diaconiaresearch.org

[2] Cf. Theodor Strohm, 'Diakonisch-soziale Arbeit im europäischen Einigungsprozeß. Schwerpunkte und vorrangige Aufgaben', in Theodor Strohm (ed), *Diakonie an der Schwelle zum neuen Jahrtausend. Ökumenische Beiträge zur weltweiten und interdisziplinären Verständigung* (Heidelberg: Universitätsverlag Winter, 2000), 517-38.

This article can only give some limited indications when trying to answer these questions by presenting and analysing key results from two projects with a comparative approach in which the author herself was involved. The article concentrates on two national contexts: one Swedish and the other German. From a global perspective, these two contexts seem to be quite close to one another as they are situated in the same part of the world with similar living conditions and religious traditions. However, both in welfare research and in state-church research, Sweden and Germany are discussed as prototypes of two different models which are currently undergoing change due to major developments such as religious pluralism and the growing welfare mix.

In the first part, some of the characteristics of the Swedish and the German contexts are introduced and compared with trends of religious pluralism and the growing welfare mix. The second part presents relevant findings from two comparable projects before some conclusions are drawn in the third part.

Understanding Two Different Contexts: Sweden and Germany

Germany and Sweden have in the course of the 20th century chosen different ways of organising both welfare[3] and relations between church and state, as sketched below:

Sweden

What makes the Swedish welfare state a prototype for the social democratic welfare regime is its ambition to take care of the social and health care needs of its citizens from the cradle to the grave. Every citizen is entitled to general and equal welfare services, no matter where in the country she or he might live.[4] Already in the 1920s the late prime minister Per Albin Hansson formulated the vision that the Swedish state should be a home for all people (*folkhemmet*) in which publicly provided welfare services would be a major feature. Swedish welfare politicians have been characterised as social engineers. For them the municipalities were the point of departure for establishing equal welfare and health care services all over the large country with its only about nine million inhabitants today.[5] No other network covered the country in the same way and was at the same time so easily accessible. Sweden experienced considerable economic growth even in the late 1940s when most of other European countries were still rebuilding after the Second World War. This meant also a boost for the welfare state which expanded rapidly until the oil crisis in the 1970s. This

---

[3] Gøsta Esping Andersen, *The Three Worlds of Welfare Capitalism* (Cambridge: Polity, 1990).

[4] Allan Cochrane, John Clarke and Sharon Gewirtz (eds), *Comparing Welfare States* (London: Sage 2001).

[5] Yvonne Hirdman, *Att lägga livet till rätta. Studier i svensk folkhemspolitik* (Stockholm: Carlsson, 2010); Thomas Etzemüller, *Die Romantik der Rationalität. Alva and Gunnar Myrdal. Social Engineering in Schweden* (Bielefeld: Transcript, 2010).

expansion of the welfare and health care services took place in the public sector, mainly in the municipalities.[6]

The development left out both church-based (welfare) organisations, such as diaconal institutions and parishes of the Lutheran majority church, the Church of Sweden, which was a state church until the year 2000. The state church was excluded from the realm of welfare service provision because the same tax money could not finance two competing welfare services (until the year 2000 there was no explicit church tax, but the church tax was a part of the general tax and thus 'invisible' to the individual citizen).[7]

When the Swedish state and the Church of Sweden changed relationships in 2000, a positive expectation assumed that parishes would make use of the new opportunity to offer welfare services on its own.[8] The Swedish welfare state which was strongly dominated by public providers opened gradually to private – both non-profit and for-profit – providers even in the 1990s. These changes were accompanied by a comprehensive political debate[9] and supported by EU regulations.[10] However, it was not the non-profit organisations (like diaconal institutions or parishes) that benefited from this development, but mainly the for-profit organisations. In 2011, about 15% of all welfare services in Sweden were provided by for-profit agencies while the share of non-profit organisations in welfare provision was still less than 2%.[11] Actually, parishes have been so inactive in the field of welfare provision that the Church of Sweden initiated an investigation before a church meeting in 2013 to find out if a central church welfare organisation at national level would help parishes become more active in the field of welfare provision.[12]

Not only the welfare state environment, but also the religious landscape has changed considerably during the past three decades. In the course of almost the entire 20th century the Church of Sweden had a membership rate of about 90% of the Swedish population. Between the 1980s and today the percentage of members of the Church of Sweden among the Swedish population sank from more than 90% to below 70% in 2013. This is only partly due to defections from the church. Sweden has also become an country of immigrants.

---

6 Sven Hort, *History, Policies and Institutions 1884-1988* (Social Policy, Welfare State and Civil Society in Sweden) (1, Lund: Arkiv, 2014).

7 Thomas Ekstrand, *Folkkyrkans gränser. En teologisk analys av övergången från statskyrka till fri folkkyra* (Stockholm: Verbum, 2001).

8 Anders Bäckström, *Svenska kyrkan som välfärdsaktör i en global kultur. En studie av religion och omsorg* (Stockholm: Verbum 2001).

9 Lars Trägårdh, 'The "civil society" debate in Sweden. The welfare state challenged', in: Lars Trägårdh (ed), *State and civil society in Northern Europe. The Swedish model reconsidered* (New York: Berghahn Books, 2007), 9-36.

10 SOU 2007:37, *Vård med omsorg. Möjligheter och hinder* (Stockholm: Fritze, 2007).

11 Ola Johansson, *Tjäna eller tjäna? Privatisering av vård, omsorg och skola. Vilka tar över?* (Stockholm: Famna: 2011).

12 Svenska kyrkan, *Att färdas väl. Hur Svenska kyrkan kan navigera i välfärden* (Svenska kyrkans utredningar 2013:3: Uppsala: Svenska kyrkan, 2013).

According to Swedish statistics, 15.1% of the Swedish population was born abroad in 2011, while it was only 8.6% in the late 1980s.[13] In the 1950s and 1960s immigrants came mostly as guest workers from neighbouring countries and Southern Europe. However, during the 1970s this kind of immigration started to decrease. Instead, the number of refugees and asylum seekers was increasing.[14] Growing immigration contributed also to greater religious diversity which it is difficult to assess since Swedish statistics do not register religion.[15]

Growing attention to the existence and plurality of religion in Swedish society comes at the same time as the majority church declines both with regard to membership numbers and importance in society generally. Nevertheless, the Church of Sweden has maintained its identity as 'the people's church' and still feels responsible for the whole Swedish population, and not only for its members. This explains why the Church of Sweden is the major player for inter-faith activities in Sweden.[16]

The Swedish context affects also how diaconal studies (or the science of *diakonia*) are perceived by other researchers. A good example of this is Jonas Alwall who evaluates diaconal studies from the perspective of his discipline, the sociology of religion. He concludes that diaconal studies are an interdisciplinary field of research that includes theology, social sciences and studies in care. Like other new and practice-related disciplines like social work studies, diaconal studies do not have their own theoretical presuppositions and methods, but borrow them from other disciplines. However, in contrast to studies like social work, diaconal studies have only a very limited field of practice. According to Alwall, diaconal practice consists mainly of what the approximately 1,000 deacons in Swedish parishes do. Against this background, he advises *diakonia* researchers to choose other, more established, disciplines as their point of departure.[17] Developing his argument, one could claim that diaconal studies cannot be (or become) an academic discipline in Sweden due to the fact that diaconal practice is so limited.

Germany

Compared with Sweden, diaconal work and diaconal agencies are much more visible and significant in Germany. The German welfare system is characterised as co-operative and conservative, and among the oldest in

---

[13] Statistics Sweden, *Sveriges framtida befolkning 2011-2006* (Stockholm: SCB, 2012).

[14] Statistics Sweden, *Finländerna fortfarande flest* (Stockholm: SCB, 2007).

[15] Daniel Andersson and Åke Sander (eds), *Det mångreligiösa Sverige. Ett landskap i förändring* (Lund: Studentlitteratur, 2009).

[16] Sven Halvardson, *Kanske alla har rätt – eller fel. Religionsmöten och syn på andra i mångreligiösa miljöer* (Skellefteå: Artos & Norma, 2012).

[17] Jonas Alwall, 'Diakoni som religionssociologiskt kunskapsområde', in Curt Dahlgren, Eva Hamberg and Thorleif Pettersson (eds), *Religion och sociologi. Ett fruktbart möte. Festskrift till Göran Gustafsson* (Lund: Teologiska institutionen, 2002), 57-77.

Europe. Its emergence can be seen as a direct reaction of the German emperor to growing protests of the workers' movement in the 1880s. In 1881 the emperor asserted that, while he wanted to repress the workers' movement, he aimed at improving the well-being of the workers. As a result, a system of insurances against life's major risks was established in the following decades. The logic of this insurance-based welfare system was not to give each and every German citizen the same rights to high-quality welfare services all over the country as in Sweden, but to protect the working individual (and his family) against existential risks according to his/her status and position in society.[18]

Religiously, it seems appropriate to think of Germany as a country of three components: Protestants, Roman Catholics along with a third group: those who are not affiliated with any faith community, who represent about a third of the German population of approximately 82 million inhabitants. In addition, other faith communities and Christian churches are growing in Germany, mostly due to immigration.[19] Among them Muslims are the fastest-growing group.[20]

Both political and religious developments provide an important background for understanding the importance of church-based welfare organisations in the German welfare system. The diaconal movement of the 19th century had a major impact, and resulted in the founding of many Protestant and Roman Catholic welfare organisations. These organisations managed to be included in the welfare planning processes of the first German democratic state, the Weimar Republic (1918-33). After the totalitarian Nazi regime and the Second World War, and after the fall of the Berlin Wall, welfare politicians picked up these traditions again and transferred them to the new welfare system.[21] Moreover, after the experience of two totalitarian systems during the 20th century (the Nazi regime 1933-45 and the Socialist regime in the Eastern part of Germany GDR 1949-89), it was unthinkable in Germany to give all power in the area of welfare into the hands of the state. Unlike in Sweden, the state was not seen a friend in Germany, but as a possible threat.[22]

The principle of subsidiarity that emerged from Roman Catholic social teaching became an important guideline for German welfare policy. This principle holds that help should be provided as close as possible to the individual in need, i.e. by family, neighbours and local organisations like parishes. Only if the immediate environment of a person in need does not

---

[18] Gøsta Esping Andersen, *The Three Worlds of Welfare Capitalism*.

[19] Detlef Pollack (ed), *Religiöser Pluralismus im Fokus quantitativer Religionsforschung* (Wiesbaden: VS Verlag für Sozialwissenschaft, 2012).

[20] Kerstin Rosenow-Williams, *Organizing Muslims and Integrating Islam in Germany. New Developments in the 21st Century* (Leiden: Brill, 2012).

[21] Jürgen Zerche and Ingrid Krieger (eds), *Vom sozialistischen Versorgungsstaat zum Sozialstaat Bundesrepublik. Ausbau oder Abbau der sozialen Lage in den neuen Bundesländern?* (Regensburg: Transfer, 1994).

[22] Adalbert Evers and Thomas Olk (eds), *Wohlfahrtspluralismus. Vom Wohlfahrtsstaat zur Wohlfahrtsgesellschaft* (Opladen: Westdeutscher Verlag, 1996).

manage to give appropriate help should the state involve itself.[23] This theoretical guideline was made a task-sharing practice in welfare provision. When the responsibility for new – publicly funded – welfare services was distributed, value-based welfare organisations had priority as long as they could demonstrate that they had the qualifications and staff to provide these services. The public sector would only become involved when no non-profit organisations were available. This gave all value-based welfare organisations in the German welfare system a unique and privileged position. Among them, church-based welfare organisations were, and are, by far the largest. While municipalities in Sweden became huge welfare providers during the boom of the welfare state between the 1950s and the 1970s, church-based welfare organisations grew massively during the same period in Germany and became huge welfare concerns.[24] Up till now they represent in some areas 30-50% of all services. In 2010 the Roman Catholic organisation Caritas[25] had 559,000 employees and 25,646 institutions and services, while the Protestant Diakonie had 452,592 employees and 27,083 institutions and services.[26]

All the employees of Caritas and Diakonie come under specific church employment law. In Germany, church employment law is exempt from general employment law.[27] Specific employment law gives church-based welfare providers a large space, an advantage in the competition with other providers. However, this model is losing legitimacy in society due to growing religious pluralism and secularisation. When actually fewer and fewer employees choose a church-based welfare organisation because of their faith, it may be asked why there should be any employment law exceptions for church-based agencies.[28] This is particularly challenging in the eastern, formerly socialist, part of Germany where only about 25-30% of the population have any religious affiliation.[29]

Value-based welfare providers in Germany are also challenged by public tendering and a growing welfare mix like the Swedish ones. In 1993, when

---

[23] Peter Hammerschmidt, *Wohlfahrtsverbände zwischen Subsidiaritätsprinzip und EU-Wettbewerbsrecht* (Kassel: Kassel University Press, 2003).

[24] Traugott Jähnichen (ed), *Caritas und Diakonie im 'goldenen Zeitalter' des bundesdeutschen Sozialstaats. Transformationen der konfessionellen Wohlfahrtsverbände in den 1960er Jahren* (Stuttgart: Kohlhammer, 2010).

[25] Deutscher Caritasverband, *Die katholischen sozialen Dienste und Einrichtungen der Caritas. Einrichtungsstatistik* (Freiburg: Deutscher Caritasverband, 2010).

[26] Diakonie Deutschland, *Einrichtungsstatistik zum 1. Januar 2010* (Berlin: Diakonie Deutschland, 2011).

[27] Axel von Campenhausen and Heinrich de Wall, *Staatskirchenrecht. Eine systematische Darstellung des Religionsverfassungsrecths in Deutschland und Europa. Ein Studienbuch* 2006 (München: Beck, 2006).

[28] Christian Albrecht (ed), *Wieviel Pluralität verträgt die Diakonie?* (Tübingen: Mohr Siebeck 2013).

[29] Heike Lubatsch, *Führung macht den Unterschied. Arbeitsbedingungen diakonischer Pflege im diakonischen Krankenhaus* (Berlin and Münster: LIT, 2012).

long-term care insurance was introduced, the priority of value-based welfare organisations was replaced by public procurement through tendering in which public, non-profit and for-profit providers competed with one another. Since then, church-based organisations have been pressured both with regard to economy and with regard to quality.[30]

The strong position of *diakonia* in the German welfare system generates also a specific climate for diaconal studies. The theologian Dierk Stranitzke uses the system theory of the German sociologist Niklas Luhmann to analyse the system of *diakonia* in society. *Diakonia* is, according to him, affected by other systems such as economy, pedagogics, social work and science. *Diakonia* can neither isolate itself totally from the influence of other systems, nor can it open up completely for other systems if it wants to maintain its own identity. He calls his model the 'openness and self-limitation of the diaconal system' and transfers it also to science. The science of *diakonia* emerges both from the interaction with and the delimitation from other academic disciplines. In contrast to the Swedish sociologist of religion, Alwall, Starnitzke has no doubt that there is a core that is specific to the science of *diakonia*. According to him, this core can be updated if research on *diakonia* is in touch with diaconal practice.[31]

Researching Diakonia in Two Different Contexts

In the passages above, the different contexts of diaconal work in Sweden and Germany have been presented. The second part of the article looks at two research projects in order to see some tendencies of how these contexts affect the character of the research and its results. The first research project is an individual PhD project while the second one is a European research project with a Swedish point of departure. Both the growing welfare mix and growing religious pluralism will be taken into consideration.

Comparing diaconal institutions in Sweden and Germany

One of the aims of the comparison of Swedish and German diaconal institutions presented in my dissertation was to gain understanding of the actual differences.[32] Though there are many parallels between diaconal work in Sweden and Germany, diaconal work has developed quite differently in the two countries. In the dissertation I had chosen two diaconal institutions for study because these examples clearly illustrated the parallels and differences in

30 Klaus Baumann, Johannes Eurich and Karsten Wolkenhauer (eds), *Konfessionelle Krankenhäuser. Strategien, Profile, Potenziale* (Stuttgart: Kohlhammer, 2013).

31 Dierk Starnitzke, *Diakonie als soziales System*.

32 The following section builds mainly on the work of Annette Leis, *Den kyrkliga diakonins roll inom ramen för två välfärdssystem. En jämförande fallstudie av två diakoniinstitutioner i Sverige och Tyskland* (Uppsala: Diakonivetenskapliga institutet, 2004).

development. Both diaconal institutions, the Samariterhemmet in Uppsala/Sweden and the Evangelisches Diakoniewerk in Schwäbisch Hall, were founded almost at the same time in the 1880s. The initiative for both of these came from a charismatic leader influenced by the revival movement. Both started with hospital work, by educating young women destined to become deaconesses in nursing, and by running a hospital in order to provide high-quality education in nursing. In both cases, running the hospital soon became the most important activity. However, the situation of both institutions today could not be more different. The Swedish institution has only about 150 employees and is no longer involved in hospital work (the former diaconal hospital building is rented out to the district that is carrying on hospital work there). The German institution has grown to a big diaconal company with about 2,300 employees, is the second largest employer in town and runs the hospital as the major activity, but also serves other fields of welfare and care such as services for people with disabilities or care for the elderly.

As a first step, the dissertation tried to follow all fields of activities in both diaconal institutions in a long-term perspective, i.e. from their foundation until the early 21st century. The fields of activity in both diaconal institutions covered the areas of hospital work, education, recreation homes, care of the elderly, and children's and youth work. In addition, Samariterhemmet worked with open services for people in need, and with research and development, while the Evangelisches Diakoniewerk furthermore offered services for disabled people. A long-term comparison illustrates that development of the German institution can be described as one of continuous growth, even though this also includes periods of crisis and decline. Evangelisches Diakoniewerk was in principle never compelled to give up services, but was always able to build on its earlier work. Compared with that, the development of Samariterhemmet was characterised much more by endings and new starts. Several fields of activity were tested, but not continued. Many of the endings were not decisions of the diaconal institution itself, but the result of coercion by public welfare planners and funders. In this respect, the development of the diaconal institutions mirrored their welfare context. While Swedish municipalities take over more and more welfare services (and replace church-based providers), German diaconal institutions benefit directly from the expansion of the welfare system.

In the dissertation, a closer look was taken at one of the core areas of both diaconal institutions: hospital work. In this area, crucial decisions were identified and decision-making processes were analysed with the help of an analysis of internal documents. Two decisions turned out to be crucial for further development in both cases, one in the 1960s and the early 1970s when the welfare systems were still expanding, and one in the 1990s when the integration of for-profit providers into the welfare system had started both in Sweden and in Germany.

The progress in medicine and medical advances made it necessary for Samariterhemmet to build a new hospital in the 1960s. The old hospital could no longer meet the demands of modern medicine. The new hospital was a huge project for the diaconal institution which it could afford only with the financial support of the district of Uppsala. However, receiving public funding also implied becoming a co-operative partner with the district. When the new hospital opened in 1967, the diaconal institution was no longer the only ruler but part of a board with representatives from both institutions. In this constellation of authority, it had for example to be discussed if a chapel was necessary in the hospital. That the chapel got a rather hidden location in the basement floor showed that the diaconal profile was no longer a self-evident guideline for hospital policy. The position of Samariterhemmet in the governance of the hospital was weakened even more when the national education agency decided in 1971 that Samariterhemmet could no longer run its nursing education. Until then, the diaconal profile of the hospital was at least upheld by those nurses who had been educated at the Samariterhemmet nursing school with its special diaconal profile. Without the nursing school, it was much harder to justify the diaconal institution running a hospital – and having a diaconal profile. On the governing board, Samariterhem felt less and less the owner of the hospital. In 1983, for the first time, a nurse educated at a secular nursing school became head of nursing at the hospital. The annual reports document a declining interest in the hospital with each passing year.

In 1991, the district of Uppsala asked Samariterhemmet if it wanted to run the hospital on its own again. This was a result of changed Swedish welfare policy that now emphasised a plurality of providers in welfare. One might have expected that this request would have resulted in a wide-ranging discussion with the diaconal institution being offered a huge opportunity. However, the question was hardly visible in the minutes of the board and was never considered as a real option. There seemed to be no interest in the diaconal institution taking on exclusive responsibility for the hospital again. Arguments that were used to turn down the suggestion were the lack of information about the financial arrangements of such a takeover. In addition, Samariterhemmet had developed a new understanding of its role in the welfare system. It saw itself in the first place no longer as a welfare provider but as a critical companion of the public welfare system. Placing itself outside the main responsibility for welfare service provision was regarded as the ideal position for carrying out this role by the diaconal institution. With such an outside perspective, the institution could observe the welfare service provision critically and help to find gaps and potential problems.

For the German diaconal institution, the changes in German hospital funding in 1972 became a considerable challenge for the co-operation hitherto existing with the public sector. Since the federal state was withdrawing from the funding of all investments in hospital infrastructure, the risk of running a hospital increased considerably. The board of Evangelisches Diakoniewerk decided to separate the hospital organisationally from the rest of the diaconal institution. This was a sensitive decision as it separated the Motherhouse (and the deaconesses) from what many of them saw as their life's work. The decision met considerable resistance from within the diaconal institution, but was never questioned by the leaders of it.

A similar challenge arose in the 1990s. Again, the hospital had to face a change in funding. This time, the whole hospital funding system was converted to case-based lump sums. The leadership of the hospital soon realised that the institution could not adapt to the new system in its organisational form. Moreover, the new funding system brought to light the problem that the old hospital building was not adequate for the demands of modern medicine. Against this background, the leadership of the diaconal institution initiated a process of increasing efficiency, both to adjust to the new funding system, but also in order to save money for building a new hospital. This resulted in huge protests from the employees who claimed that the new working procedures did not match the diaconal profile of the hospital. The most productive units were leading the protests. However, the leadership never considered reversing the decision. To survive as a hospital, it was essential to adapt to the new framework. The leadership of the diaconal institution could not imagine being anything other than a major local hospital. One of the motivations for this decision was that the leaders viewed the role of the diaconal institution in the welfare system as a critical companion of it, just as it was for Samariterhemmet. But in contrast to the Swedish institution, Evangelisches Diakoniewerk thought that the ideal position for remaining within the welfare system in a constructively critical way was to be a provider of welfare services itself. Only with this inside perspective did the leaders believe they would be able to understand and critically evaluate the problems and gaps of the welfare system. Interestingly, both the Swedish and the German diaconal institutions wanted to take on the same role in the welfare system, but identified different positions within the welfare system as the ideal point of departure for this role.

While the trend of religious pluralism is hardly apparent in the dissertation, the growing welfare mix heavily influences both diaconal institutions and their hospitals. While the Swedish diaconal institution offered to run the hospital on its own owing to the implementation of the welfare mix, the German one was forced to change its working practices in order to adapt to the new funding regime that was introduced to promote competition between health care providers. In both cases, decisions on future strategy are taken in the light of earlier experience in the welfare system. None of the diaconal institutions seriously considers changing its role within the welfare system.

Comparing the welfare role of majority churches in local communities

The second project that is used as an example is the European project 'Welfare and Religion in a European Perspective. A comparative study of the role of the churches as agents of welfare within the social economy'. The project was conducted between 2003 and 2006. It involved eight European countries (Norway, Sweden, Finland, UK, France, Germany, Italy and Greece), and aimed "to analyse the function of majority churches as social providers from a comparative perspective".[33] The project used a case study method, collected qualitative data and promised to come up with new knowledge about the attitudes of local public authorities, local church representatives and the local population about church-run welfare provision and advocacy in social issues.

This article focuses on the results of the Swedish and the German case studies.[34] The Swedish case study was located in Gävle, a town with about 70,000 inhabitants about 200 km north of Stockholm. In this study, the research team looked almost exclusively at activities and relationships that the parishes of the Lutheran majority church were involved in. Many of these activities were closely related to the core activities of the parish – such as alternative services, individual counselling or groups for children, young and elderly people. Some of the activities, such as day care centres for children, a youth centre and a hostel for homeless people, were financed by the municipality. However, these initiatives are only occasionally touched on in the Swedish case study. More attention is given to recent joint ventures between the majority church, the public sector and other organisations – such as emergency counselling, an emergency group for dealing with accidents, and a multicultural and multi-religious family centre.

The most interesting outcome of the Swedish case study was not what the majority church was actually doing, but what the researchers identified as seven areas of consensus regarding the welfare system and the role of the church within it, between representatives of the public authorities, the church and the population. There was agreement that the state was mainly responsible for the provision of basic welfare. Social commitment was considered to belong to the church's mission. But this did not mean that the church was expected to take over social services from the public authorities. Instead, all agreed that the church had a complementary role in welfare since it provided good value, along with a sense of meaning and belonging. All felt that relationships between public sector and church had changed positively, and they were more open to each other than they were just a few years ago. All also

---

[33] Institute for Diaconal and Social Studies (ed), *Welfare and Religion in a European Perspective. A comparative study of the churches as agents of welfare within the social economy. Project description* (Uppsala: Institute for Diaconal and Social Studies, 2003), 88.

[34] The following part builds mainly on the work of Ninna Edgardh and Per Pettersson, 'The Church of Sweden. A Church for All, Especially the Most Vulnerable', in Anders Bäckström, Grace Davie, Ninna Edgardh and Per Pettersson (eds), *Welfare and Religion in 21st Century Europe, Vol. 1: Configuring the Connections* (Farnham, UK: Ashgate, 2010, 39-56); and Annette Leis-Peters, 'The German Dilemma: Protestant Agents of Welfare in Reutlingen', in Anders Bäckström, Grace Davie, Ninna Edgardh and Per Pettersson (eds), *Welfare and Religion*, 95-112.

supported church participation in the public welfare debate as long as the church did not interfere with political party policy. All groups still also had a perception of the Church of Sweden as a 'people's church' available to the whole population and not just for its members. Finally, all three groups emphasised the importance of the value of equality between men and women.

Surprisingly, the tendencies of growing religious pluralism and more welfare mix are only to a small extent apparent in the results of the Swedish case study. There are some findings that could be developed from these perspectives – for example, the publicly funded activities of the Lutheran parishes or the multi-religious family centre that they run in co-operation with the municipality. However, since these aspects did not, overall, bulk large in the data, the researchers had no reason to emphasise them. This is an interesting outcome, bearing in mind that the research project itself related explicitly to the general trends of religious pluralism and the growing welfare mix in its background description.

The German case study took place in Reutlingen, a town with about 100,000 inhabitants 50 km south of Stuttgart. In contrast to the Swedish case study, there is both a diaconal institution with about 2,000 employees and publicly funded welfare services run by the parishes of the majority churches (such as kindergartens, a home care service, a youth centre, a family training centre and a counselling centre) present in the German case. Given the comparative design, it was difficult to focus on the specific challenges of these professional, publicly funded but church-run services within the framework of the European research project.

Instead, the case study concentrates on the role of the majority church in general in the local welfare system, and on more informal parish activities that could be related to the field of welfare since these aspects were more comparable with the findings of the other European case studies. What turned up in this material was a dilemma in which the majority church parishes in Reutlingen found themselves. On the one hand, they were experiencing decline. Their membership was falling and the parishes were experiencing increasing difficulties in finding the resources needed to maintain their activities and to preserve their buildings. In some city districts, with a high percentage of inhabitants with immigrant backgrounds and a low share of majority church members, church buildings had to be closed down.

However, it was not only the majority church that had to reduce overheads. The German welfare system was also in economic crisis and had to cut back. Actually, the study period of the European research project coincided with a comprehensive restructuring of the German welfare system. As a consequence, representatives of the public authorities, of the church and the population felt that more people were falling through the welfare system's safety net. In this situation, enormous expectations were directed at the church: When the state withdrew from some of its responsibilities in the field of welfare, it was presumed that the church would fill the gap. But from a parish perspective, the dilemma was that the majority church had hardly enough resources to maintain its own core services and buildings, and now it was expected to focus on welfare as well. In a way, the parishes were bound to disappoint expectations, either those of society – which expected more church participation in the field of welfare – or the expectations of church members – who wanted the church to maintain their core services and buildings.

The trends of religious pluralism and growing welfare mix appear more clearly in the German case study than in the Swedish one. The dilemma of the majority church parishes was one result of immigration, religious pluralism and secularisation. As a declining number of the population was affiliated to the majority church, the parishes had to prioritise and to adjust their infrastructure accordingly. In addition, both the diaconal institution at the case study location and the majority church parishes themselves ran professional, publicly funded welfare services. This meant that they both experienced changes in the welfare system such as a growing welfare mix. However, this line of research could not be followed in the case study due to the research question and the design of the European project.

Conclusion

As mentioned at the beginning of this article, its limited approach does not allow for any generalised conclusions. What is suggested below on the basis of the two studies presented is mainly intended to inspire further debate on these issues:

(1) The studies presented confirm what was claimed at the beginning of the article. There are different contexts of diaconal work, and these contexts have a strong impact on how diaconal work and diaconal research are shaped. It does actually matter if there is an inherent (ideologically motivated) interest in integrating church-based agencies into welfare provision (as in the German case) or not (as in the Swedish one). These preconditions affect the extent to which church-based organisations contribute as providers of welfare services, but also how they interpret their role in the whole system. When learning from best practice, it is important to take differences of context into consideration. Otherwise, while these practices might seem inspiring, they are hard to transfer to other contexts.

(2) One of the trends that this article had in mind is the growing welfare mix. However, this trend is much more visible in the German context. As *diakonia* in Germany co-operates closely with the public, it is not surprising that the welfare mix can be seen in the material. More surprising is it that the welfare mix shows up only to a very small extent in the Swedish material and is hardly responded to by the diaconal agencies. This suggests that the considerable changes in the Swedish welfare system and in church-state relationships have influenced the practice of diaconal agencies only marginally. Though the trends of religious pluralism and growing welfare mix have been

affecting both Swedish and German welfare systems for at least two decades, church-based organisations still seem to act as if they were placed in a flawless social democratic (in the Swedish case), respectively in a co-operative-conservative (in the German case) welfare system. Even more striking is that the trend of religious pluralism which is currently discussed in all kinds of arenas is not emerging as an important issue from these two studies at all. This might, however be related to the way in which these two research projects have been devised.

(3) The different contexts affect not only the way in which diaconal agencies involve themselves in the welfare system, but also how research about them comes across. The contexts influence both what kind of activities and what kind of agencies are highlighted in research. While professional church-based welfare providers such as diaconal institutions are a self-evident part of research about *diakonia* from a German perspective, Swedish studies start instead from parishes in general and deacons in particular. This difference could be used as an interesting topic for future research. Why not consider using the perspectives and research questions of one context actively to design a research project in another context or in a comparable project? The multiple contexts of *diakonia* definitely invite to exciting opportunities for research that, hopefully in return, may also influence diaconal practice.

References

Albrecht, Christian (ed.). *Wieviel Pluralität verträgt die Diakonie?[How much plurality can diakonia bear?]* Tübingen: Mohr Siebeck 2013.

Alwall, Jonas. 'Diakoni som religionssociologiskt kunskapsområde' [Diakonia as knowledge area in sociology of religion]. In Curt Dahlgren, Eva Hamberg and Thorleif Pettersson (eds), *Religion och sociologi. Ett fruktbart möte. Festskrift till Göran Gustafsson.* Lund: Teologiska institutionen, 2002, 57-77.

Andersson, Daniel and Sander, Åke (eds.), *Det mångreligiösa Sverige. Ett landskap i förändring [The multireligious Sweden. A landscape in change].* Lund: Studentlitteratur, 2009.

Baumann, Klaus, Eurich, Johannes and Wolkenhauer, Karsten (eds.). *Konfessionelle Krankenhäuser. Strategien, Profile, Potenziale [Faith-based hospitals. Strategies, profiles, potentials].* Stuttgart: Kohlhammer, 2013.

Bäckström, Anders. *Svenska kyrkan som välfärdsaktör i en global kultur. En studie av religion och omsorg [The Church of Sweden as an agent of welfare in a global culture. A study of religion and welfare].* Stockholm: Verbum 2001.

Campenhausen, von Axel and de Wall, Heinrich. *Staatskirchenrecht. Eine systematische Darstellung des Religionsverfassungsrecths in Deutschland und Europa. Ein Studienbuch [State Church Law. A systematic presentation of constitutional law in the area of religion in Germany and Europe. A record of study].* 2006. München: Beck, 2006.

Cochrane, Allan, Clarke, John & Gewirtz, Sharon (eds.). *Comparing Welfare States.* London: Sage 2001.

Deutscher Caritasverband. *Die katholischen sozialen Dienste und Einrichtungen der Caritas. Einrichtungsstatistik [The Catholic social services and institutions of Caritas. Institutional Statistics].* Freiburg: Deutscher Caritasverband, 2010.

Diakonie Deutschland. *Einrichtungsstatistik zum 1. Januar 2010 [Institutional Statistics on 1. Januayr 2010].* Berlin: Diakonie Deutschland, 2011.

Edgardh, Ninna and Pettersson, Per. 'The Church of Sweden. A Church for All, Especially the Most Vulnerable'. In: Anders Bäckström and Grace Davie with Ninna Edgardh and Per Pettersson (eds.), *Welfare and Religion in 21st Century Europe 1. Configuring the Connections.* Farnham: Ashgate, 2010, 39-56.

Ekstrand, Thomas. *Folkkyrkans gränser. En teologisk analys av övergången från statskyrka till fri folkkyrka [The limits of folk church. A theological analysis of the transition from state church to free folk church].* Stockholm: Verbum, 2001.

Esping Andersen, Gøsta. *The Three Worlds of Welfare Capitalism.* Cambridge: Polity, 1990.

Etzemüller, Thomas. *Die Romantik der Rationalität. Alva & Gunnar Myrdal. Social Engineering in Schweden [The romance of rationality. Alva & Gunnar Myrdal. Social Engineering in Sweden].* Bielefeld: Transcript, 2010.

Evers; Adalbert and Olk, Thomas (eds). *Wohlfahrtspluralismus. Vom Wohlfahrtsstaat zur Wohlfahrtsgesellschaft [Welfare pluralism. From welfare state to welfare society].* Opladen: Westdeutscher Verlag, 1996.

Halvardson, Sven. *Kanske alla har rätt – eller fel. Religionsmöten och syn på andra i mångreligiösa miljöer [Maybe everone is right – or wrong. Religious encounters and the view on others in multireligious environments].* Skellefteå: Artos & Norma, 2012.

Hammerschmidt, Peters. *Wohlfahrtsverbände zwischen Subsidiaritätsprinzip und EU-Wettbewerbsrecht [Welfare organisations between the principle of subsidiarity and the EU on competition].* Kassel: Kassel University Press, 2003.

Hirdman, Yvonne. *Att lägga livet till rätta. Studier i svensk folkhemspolitik [To arrange live. Studies in «folkhem» policy].* Stockholm: Carlsson, 2010.

Hort, Sven. *History, Policies and Institutions 1884-1988* (Social Policy, Welfare State and Civil Society in Sweden. 1, Lund: Arkiv, 2014).

Institute for Diaconal and Social Studies (ed.). *Welfare and Religion in a European Perspective. A comparative study of the churches as agents of welfare within the social economy. Project description.* Uppsala: Institute for Diaconal and Social Studies, 2003.

Jähnichen,Traugott (ed). *Caritas und Diakonie im „goldenen Zeitalter" des bundesdeutschen Sozialstaats. Transformationen der konfessionellen Wohlfahrtsverbände in den 1960er Jahren [Caritas and Diakonie in the „golden age" oft he social state of the Federal Republic of Germany. Transformations oft he faith-based welfare organisations in the 1960s].* Stuttgart: Kohlhammer, 2010.

Johansson, Ola. *Tjäna eller tjäna? Privatisering av vård, omsorg och skola. Vilka tar över? [To serve or to earn. Privatisation of nursing, care and school? Who is taking over?]* Stockholm: Famna; 2011.

Leis, Annette. *Den kyrkliga diakonins roll inom ramen för två välfärdssystem. En jämförande fallstudie av två diakoniinstitutioner i Sverige och Tyskland [Church social work in two different welfare systems. A comparative case study of two diaconal institutions in Sweden and Germany].* Uppsala: Diakonivetenskapliga institutet, 2004.

Leis-Peters, Annette. 'The German Dilemma: Protestant Agents of Welfare in Reutlingen'. In: Anders Bäckström and Grace Davie with Ninna Edgardh and Per Pettersson (eds.), *Welfare and Religion in 21st Century Europe 1. Configuring the*

Connections. Farnham: Ashgate, 2010, 95-112.

Lubatsch, Heike. *Führung macht den Unterschied. Arbeitsbedingungen diakonischer Pflege im diakonischen Krankenhaus [Leadership makes the difference. Working conditions of diaconal care in diaconal hospitals]*. Berlin and Münster: LIT, 2012.

Pollack, Detlef (ed.). *Religiöser Pluralismus im Fokus quantitativer Religionsforschung [Pluralism in the focus of quantitative religious studies]*. Wiesbaden: VS Verlag für Sozialwissenschaft, 2012.

Rosenow-Williams, Kerstin. *Organizing Muslims and Integrating Islam in Germany. New Developments in the 21st Century*. Leiden: Brill, 2012.

SOU 2007:37. *Vård med omsorg. Möjligheter och hinder [Nursing with care. Possiblities and hinders]*. Stockholm: Fritze, 2007.

Starnitzke, Dierk. *Diakonie als soziales System. Eine theologische Grundlegung diakonischer Praxis in Auseinandersetzung mit Niklas Luhmann [Diakonia as a social system. A theological foundation of diaconal practice in discussion with Niklas Luhmann]*. Stuttgart et. alt.: Kohlammer, 1996.

Statistics Sweden. *Finländerna fortfarande flest [The Finns are still most]*. Stockholm: SCB, 2007.

Statistics Sweden. *Sveriges framtida befolkning 2011-2060 [Swedens future population 2011-2060]*. Stockholm: SCB, 2012.

Svenska kyrkan. *Att färdas väl. Hur Svenska kyrkan kan navigera i välfärden [To fare well. How the Church of Sweden can navigate in welfare]*. Svenska kyrkans utredningar 2013:3, Uppsala: Svenska kyrkan, 2013.

Strohm, Theodor. 'Diakonisch-soziale Arbeit im europäischen Einigungsprozeß. Schwerpunkte und vorrangige Aufgaben' [Diaconal-social work in the European process of unification. Focus and prioritised tasks]. In: Theodor Strohm (ed.), *Diakonie an der Schwelle zum neuen Jahrtausend. Ökumenische Beiträge zur weltweiten und interdisziplinären Verständigung*. Heidelberg: Universitätsverlag Winter, 2000, 517-538.

Trägårdh, Lars. 'The "civil society" debate in Sweden. The welfare state challenged', in: Lars Trägårdh (ed), *State and civil society in Northern Europe. The Swedish model reconsidered*. New York: Berghahn Books, 2007, 9-36.

Zerche, Jürgen and Krieger, Ingrid (eds.). *Vom sozialistischen Versorgungsstaat zum Sozialstaat Bundesrepublik. Ausbau oder Abbau der sozialen Lage in den neuen Bundesländern? [From socialist maintainance state the social state of the Federal Republic of Germany. Construction and deconstruction of the social situation in the new federal states]*. Regensburg: Transfer, 1994.

Websites

Journal for the Study of Diaconia and Christian Social Practice: http://www.v-r.de/de/magazine-1/diaconia_journal_for_the_study_of_christian_social_practice-500059/

International Society for the Research and Study of Diaconia and Christian Social Practice: www.diaconiaresearch.org.

Diakonia, Hospitality and Welfare

Olav Helge Angell

In this article I will study three affiliated concepts, *diakonia*, hospitality and welfare (work). They relate to social practice that in many cases may be characterised by all three concepts. The concepts of *diakonia* and hospitality have a long history; welfare is a new concept (the term 'welfare state' first appeared in the Anglican bishop William Temple's book *Christianity and Social Order*).[1] I will relate the concepts to each other, and exemplify how they may be used and made topical in 'diaconal organisations'. By using examples from social practice in such organisations, I will demonstrate how social practice may have symbolic implications and political significance.

The Concept of *Diakonia*

Diakonia is fundamentally a theological concept 'that points to the very identity and mission of the Church'.[2] Nordstokke spells out the concept a little further: *diakonia* is oriented towards practice, meaning that *diakonia* involves "a call to action, as a response to challenges of human suffering, injustice and care for creation".[3] Much discussion has taken place to try to give the concept a more precise definition, which Nordstokke claims is not possible, not even on the basis of how the concept is used in the Greek language of the New Testament. Today's conception of or approach to *diakonia* is more fruitfully understood as shaped by how the church has tried to come to terms with the call to neighbourly love throughout its history.

From social science, Swatos has explored the dimensions of religion involved in the work of Max Weber and derived two basic dimensions, one regarding social relationships and another related to ethical considerations. Based on this analysis, he constructs what he calls a 'situational approach' to religion, in which three sets of considerations are included: that religions create

[1] William Temple, *Christianity and Social Order* (Harmondsworth, UK: Penguin, 1942).
[2] LWF, *Diakonia in Context,* 8.
[3] LWF, *Diakonia in Context,* 8.

action orientations, involve subjective experience, and consist of systems of discourse.[4]

The practical role of religion is an important part of many religious traditions, not least the so-called 'religions of the book', among them Christianity. In Christian theology, one way of viewing the Christian religion or the responsibility of the church is through the dimensions of *leiturgia*, *martyria*, *diakonia* and *koinonia*.[5] In a simplified manner, the first refers to the ritual dimension, the second to the witness dimension (that is, the belief system and the way it is shared among the believers and communicated in society), the third to the human service aspect of religion – the 'social service' role of the church, and the fourth to the social community aspect. These dimensions may be related to sociological distinctions as drawn by Weber.[6] The ritual, witness and community dimensions may be associated with the Weberian social relationship dimension. *Diakonia* is more difficult to relate to Swatos' analysis; like Weber, Swatos does not seem to include social actions in the form of social service in his framework. However, *diakonia* may be interpreted as referring to social relationships based on ethical considerations, and a form of action.[7] Thus in a social science context, *diakonia* may be conceived of as referring to moral action systems involving subjective experience, usually couched in a system of discourse. This does not imply that the actions or activities constituting *diakonia* in practical life necessarily distinguish themselves from other, non-church-based welfare activities. Most important here is their cultural embeddedness.

Various paradigms may be identified in the understanding of *diakonia*. Two such paradigms are a welfare-centred paradigm and a church-centred paradigm.[8] In the *welfare-centred paradigm, diakonia* is perceived primarily as social practice to help those in need, to put it simply and a bit superficially. The difference between secular welfare provision and church-based, religiously motivated social engagement is not significant within this paradigm. A definition along these lines, at an operational level, may be the following: "*Diakonia* is social activity within the framework of or linked with a Christian

---

[4] W.H. Swatos, Jr., 'Differentiating Experiences: The Virtue of Substantive Definitions', in A.L. Greil and D.G. Bromley (eds), *Defining Religion: Investigating the Boundaries between the Sacred and Secular* (Amsterdam: JAI Press, 2003), 39-53.

[5] G. Heitink, *Practical Theology: History, Theory, Action Domains: Manual for Practical Theology* (Grand Rapids, MI: Eerdmans, 1999).

[6] Swatos, 'Differentiating Experiences'.

[7] O.H. Angell, 'Sacred Welfare Agents in Secular Welfare Space: the Case of the Church of Norway in Drammen', in Anders Bäckström and Grace Davie (eds), *Welfare and Religion in 21st Century Europe, Vol. 1: Configuring the Connections* (Farnham, UK: Ashgate, 2010), 89-115.

[8] K.I. Johannessen, 'Diakontjenestens plassering i kirken [The placing of the diaconate in the church]', in K.I. Johannessen, K. Jordheim and K.K. Korslien (eds), *Diakoni: en kritisk lesebok* (Trondheim: Tapir akademisk forlag, 2009), 29-43, 31.

community or organisation."[9] In the *church-centred paradigm, diakonia* is perceived as one of the core elements of the mission of the church in the world.[10] It means that the worshipping congregation is the centre from which service for others takes its departure, and where the social community aspect is prominent, be it around the worship itself or in the life of the congregation more generally. These paradigms primarily serve an analytic purpose; in discourses on and in the work of the churches they may live side-by-side. The programme statement of *diakonia* in the current Plan for *diakonia* in the Church of Norway is wide, and may well be associated with both paradigms. In the previous version of the Plan, which preceded the current statement by twenty years, and which was more limited in scope, *diakonia* was conceived of as 'the church's care for fellow human beings and its development of community spirit, and as service particularly directed at people in need',[11] more in line with the welfare-centred paradigm.

In its practical role in society and its action orientations, 'the church', including what we may call 'church-based welfare organisations', may serve different functions. Drawing on theories of voluntary organisations, we may e.g. use US professor of social welfare Ralph Kramer's analysis of the functions of voluntary organisations in the welfare state to identify functions in society of the diaconal agency.[12] Kramer specifies four main types of organisational roles of voluntary agencies in the welfare state: the vanguard role, the improver or advocate role, the service provider role and the value guardian role. The vanguard is the pioneer, the innovator. Both diaconal and other voluntary organised agencies have traditionally been associated with this role or function in the context of welfare policy. The improver or advocate is the critic or watchdog vis-à-vis the state and its services. The value guardian role involves the ways by which "a voluntary agency (among other things) is expected to promote citizen participation, to develop leadership, and to protect the special interests of social, religious, cultural and other minority groups".[13] We may take this definition as a guideline without restricting the role the way Kramer does. The value guardian role is thus associated with the role of the 'critical voice'.[14] Participation in the public discourse refers to how the voice of the church-based agencies is made visible in the media. The church as an

---

[9] E. Blennberger and M.J. Hansson, 'Vad menas med diakoni? [What do we mean by diakonia?]', in E. Blennberger and M.J. Hansson (eds), *Diakoni: tolkning, historik, praktik* (Stockholm: Verbum, 2008), 13-27, 23.

[10] Heitink, *Practical Theology*; LWF, *Diakonia in Context.*

[11] Church of Norway, *Comprehensive Diaconal Programme for the Church of Norway* (Oslo: National Council for the Church of Norway, 1988), 9.

[12] R.M. Kramer, *Voluntary Agencies in the Welfare State* (Berkeley, CA: University of California Press, 1981).

[13] Kramer, *Voluntary Agencies*, 9.

[14] T. Lundström and F. Wijkström, *Från röst till service? [From voice to service?]* (Sköndal: Sköndalsinstitutet, 1995).

institution is by definition a guardian of (religious) values, and a policy document like the Plan for *diakonia* in the Church of Norway provides examples of some ways by which local agencies may take on a value guardian role as part of their diaconal mission.

Diakonia and Welfare

The welfare-centred paradigm demonstrates that *diakonia* may be associated with aspects of the concept of welfare and with welfare service. What is the relationship between *diakonia* and welfare? If we choose *diakonia* to refer to social relationships based on ethical considerations, and a form of action, to moral action systems involving subjective experience usually couched in a system of discourse, the question becomes whether *diakonia* and welfare (service) refer to the same or different moral action systems and discourses. The US/Norwegian theologian Roald Kverndal[15] claims that the difference between welfare (work) and *diakonia* – understood as practice/praxis – is the Christological dimension of the work of the church, e.g. as it is expressed in 2 Corinthians 5:14 ('For Christ's love compels us'), which gives the diaconate a special 'ecclesiological' identity as a 'particular way of being church'. Kverndal refers to the Finnish theologian Kaarlo Kalliala who says that to simply translate *diakonia* as 'church-based welfare work' or 'the church's welfare work' (in English language contexts *diakonia* is a rather new word) is as appalling as to call 'baptism' a 'church child wash'.[16] I find that statement and understanding too simple. First, it seems that Kverndal's understanding of *diakonia* is person-centred. In institution-based *diakonia*, the person-centred understanding has been the basis for a traditional way of grounding the diaconal character of the institution or organisation. Over time, as society has changed to become more secular and also religiously and culturally more diverse, those in charge in such institutions and organisations have felt a need to find new ways of grounding the diaconal character or identity of their work. One way of doing this has been to shift attention from the individual level to the organisational level. It means that it is usually not required by the individual member of staff providing the services to the users/clients/patients, that they identify with the theological or ideological foundation of the organisation, though such expectations may be directed at the top management. This is partly a consequence of the legal framework regulating employment in general (the Health and Safety at Work Act), and partly an effect of demands with regard to the level of (secular) professional competence required of the staff in welfare service organisations. It is reasonable to think that a shift from person-centred to organisation-centred *diakonia* changes the character of the

---

[15] R. Kverndal, *The Way of the Sea: The Changing Shape of Mission in the Seafaring World* (Pasadena, CA: William Carey Library, 2008), 237.

[16] Kverndal, *The Way of the Sea*, 237.

organisation, the moral action systems involving subjective experience, and the discourse.

In the Nordic countries, the vast majority of the diaconal organisations providing social or health care services are integrated in public welfare services schemes. The Danish sociologist Lars Qvortrup claims that some specific public welfare functions have historically been established on the basis of a decoupling of *diakonia* from the church:

> And when the diaconal health care and care work in the congregations do not develop within a religious plausibility structure any longer, it changes its self-understanding. The work is no longer charitable but professional in its justification.[17]

Qvortrup claims that this change in the moral action systems and the discourse will change the character of the social services – or social practice – of the organisations. One of the challenges facing the professional diaconal organisation in the field of health and social care services is therefore how to institutionalise the moral action systems of *diakonia*, as a dimension of the mission of the church, in the day-to-day life of the organisation.

For an understanding of the concept of welfare, let us take advantage of the research of another Finn, the sociologist Erik Allardt and his discussion of the concept.[18] Welfare is best understood as a multidimensional concept. The concept of 'need' is his starting-point, and he differentiates between three dimensions of welfare: a material or economic dimension ('to have'), a dimension referring to social relations ('to love'), and a dimension of human quality referring to the person's relationship to society, e.g. linked with the need for self-fulfilment ('to be'). To simplify somewhat, the way the church defines its mission in society, to preach and to help, is supposed to cover all three dimensions of welfare.[19]

This connection may be illustrated by the work of a diaconal organisation in the Church of Norway, The Norwegian Seamen's Church (NSC).[20] Though originally an organisation to serve the needs of Norwegian sailors, it seems to have succeeded in adapting to the changing patterns of travelling and migration of Norwegians, to cater for all sorts of temporary and more permanent migrants

---

[17] L. Qvortrup, 'Fra diakoni til velfærdsstat: diakoniens uddifferentiering [From diakonia to welfare state: the functional differentiation of diakonia]', in J.H. Schjørring and J.T. Bak (eds), *Velfærdsstat og kirke*, 79-102.

[18] E. Allardt, *Dimensions of Welfare in a Comparative Scandinavian Study* (Helsinki: Research Group for Comparative Sociology, 1975).

[19] Angell, 'Sacred Welfare Agents in Secular Welfare Space'.

[20] O.H. Angell, *Sjømannskyrkja som lågterskeltilbod: heim, organisasjon og institusjon med diakonal forankring [The Norwegian Seamen's Church as a low-threshold welfare service provider: a faith-based home, organisation and institution]* (Oslo: Diakonhjemmet Høgskole. Rapport 2011/6, 2011).

and travellers, such as lorry drivers, tourists, students, business people, and those who run away from a difficult situation at home as well as sailors.

The Norwegian Seamen's Church has as its main goal "to promote the kingdom of God by being a serving church in the everyday life of the world"; it "aims to create good encounters between people, be it inside or outside church premises".[21] A slogan for the organisation is that it wants to help people to manage their lives and to give them courage to put their faith in God.

The organisation has worked out a 'value document' specifying its goals further.[22] They may be summarised as follows (the four most relevant goals of the altogether five specified goals are presented here): The NSC aims at being:[23]

- A religious, social and cultural meeting place for Norwegians abroad (belonging).
- A resource in crisis situations, in the building of social networks and in 'relational counselling' (security).
- A church where people live their daily lives (outreach).
- An organisation characterised by 'generous guest friendship' ('guest friendship').

If we relate the goals or 'value expressions' cited from the value document to Allardt's concept of welfare, they seem to correspond primarily to the last two dimensions of welfare. We may link the spiritual or faith aspect of the value document with the 'to be' dimension of welfare. One of the things that are important to the NSC – and this may have something to do with Kalliala's statements – is that the social actions and interactions associated with all four goals take place in 'religious space', be it within or outside church premises. It gives social activity an imminent meaning as well as a meaning that transcends the imminent level, a symbolic or sign function. This is an aspect of 'church-based welfare work' that relates it to *diakonia*, by intention, specific meaning and through its sign function. A church-based welfare agency may be seen as a form of religious practice and in theological terms as closely linked with the concept of *diakonia*.[24]

---

21 Sjømannskirken, *Sjømannskirkens verdidokument [The Norwegian Seamen's Church: value document]* (Bergen: Sjømannskirken – Norsk kirke i utlandet, 2012), my translation.

22 Sjømannskirken, *Sjømannskirkens verdidokument*.

23 Angell, *Sjømannskyrkja som lågterskeltilbod*, 7.

24 Cf. Heitink, *Practical Theology*; A.V. Tønnessen, 'Velferdsstat og kirkelig diakoni i Norge etter 1945. Kritikk og fornyelse [Welfare state and church-based diaconia in Norway since 1945: Criticism and renewal]', in J.H. Schjørring and J.T. Bak (eds), *Velfærdsstat og kirke* (Copenhagen: Anis, 2005), 103-23.

The Concept of Hospitality

> Let brotherly love continue. Be not forgetful to entertain strangers: for thereby some have entertained angels unawares.[25]

NSC has as one of its goals to be an organisation characterised by 'guest friendship'. In Latin, guest friendship is *hospitalitas*, in English 'hospitality'. Thus, the concept of hospitality is closely linked with the concept of *diakonia*. In what follows I will draw on the British theologian Luke Bretherton's study of the understanding of the concept in the Christian religious tradition as he has worked it out in his doctoral dissertation on 'Christian witness amid moral diversity'.[26] The English word 'hospitality' derives from Latin *hospitium*, which originates from *hospes*, having a double meaning of both stranger, guest and guest friend (= host; innkeeper). The concept of hospitality in the Christian tradition is not explicitly defined in Bretherton's book. He starts his discussion introducing MacIntyre's conception of hospitality and takes it as his point of departure.[27] MacIntyre grounds his understanding in the virtue of *misericordia*, following Aquinas' definition of the concept, which denotes the virtue by which we relate ourselves to our neighbours, and by which "we supply what is needed by our neighbour".[28] In MacIntyre's view, hospitality is important for the functioning of society in general.

> It is important to the functioning of communities that, among the roles that play a part in their shared lives, there should be that of 'the stranger', someone from outside the community who has happened to arrive amongst us and to whom we owe hospitality, just because she or he is a stranger.[29]

To develop his understanding of the concept, Bretherton analyses its use in the Bible, in both the Old and the New Testament, and in the history of the church. The content of the concept in the Christian tradition may be summarised as follows: the Christian's neighbour to be welcomed is particularly "the vulnerable and friendless stranger".[30] To welcome this neighbour means, in practice, to accommodate or host, to make space and time for the stranger, to be ready to change one's life "in order that the vulnerable stranger may be accommodated".[31] Hospitality as actively welcoming the

---

[25] Hebrews 13:1-2.

[26] L. Bretherton, *Hospitality as Holiness: Christian Witness amid Moral Diversity* (Farnham, UK: Ashgate, 2006).

[27] A. MacIntyre, *Dependent Rational Animals: Why Human Beings Need the Virtues* (London: Duckworth, 1999).

[28] MacIntyre, *Dependent Rational Animals*, 125; Bretherton, *Hospitality as Holiness*, 127.

[29] MacIntyre, *Dependent Rational Animals*, 123.

[30] Bretherton, *Hospitality as Holiness,* 139.

[31] Bretherton, *Hospitality as Holiness*, 140.

stranger may be specified further to involve welcoming 'those with the least status':

> The imperative to welcome the weak and the vulnerable serves as a constant reminder to see and hear those members of society who are most easily marginalised, oppressed and rendered invisible.[32]

Though Bretherton's primary occupation is with how the church acts in a situation of moral plurality and discusses hospitality in the context of how 'Christians relate to their neighbours', who are not Christian or who do not share the moral values of the Church,[33] we may apply this principle for social practice more generally – and also to encompass neighbourly love, irrespective of whether the neighbour shares the person's or the collective's moral values or not, whether the neighbour is marginalised, oppressed or not. But the imperative to welcome the weak and the vulnerable serves as a constant reminder to see and hear those members of society who are most easily marginalised, oppressed and rendered invisible.[34]

We may distinguish *two forms of hospitality*, institutional – or institutionalised – and personal. This distinction had already been expressed in the preaching of the bishop of Milan, John Chrysostom, in the fourth century.[35] Though the two forms of hospitality may be analytically distinguished, institutionalised hospitality is always the practice of persons, though the persons, as part of a larger system, practise their hospitality within a more or less clearly predefined framework associated with their work role. The hospital represents an early form of institutional hospitality, and any charity organisation likewise exemplifies it, including the NSC, which we have introduced above to illustrate how *diakonia* may be related to welfare.

Diakonia, Hospitality and Welfare (Work)

How are these concepts related? In particular, how are *diakonia* and hospitality linked in the life and running of diaconal organisations? Let me first refer to a piece of our Nordic Christian heritage, i.e. the Christian church before the schism of 1054; *diakonia*, as it is presented by the Orthodox Church today: before the establishment of the Christian religion in the Roman Empire, hospitality was one of the core virtues of the Christian: "the giving of assistance and hospitality was part of the Christian's creed: every Christian was expected to provide lodging for three nights to any stranger who came to his

[32] Bretherton, *Hospitality as Holiness, 148.*
[33] Bretherton, *Hospitality as Holiness*, 138.
[34] Bretherton, *Hospitality as Holiness*, 148.
[35] Bretherton, *Hospitality as Holiness*, 140-41.

house."[36] After the establishment of the church, *diakonia* was institutionalised, e.g. as it was declared in the Council of Nicaea in 381: "Houses of hospitality must be built for the poor in every city of every diocese."[37] This explicit link between *diakonia* and hospitality is also preserved in the type of institution we still call 'hospital' and has been revived in the newer type of institution we call 'hospice', specialising in caring for terminally ill people. The hospital was first a church-based type of health institution (the institution is even older than its Latin name); while the founder of the modern hospice movement, Cicely Saunders, who established the discipline of palliative care, was rooted in the Anglican religious tradition – in their first phase, hospices were primarily established by religious orders.[38]

In a Lutheran context, the Lutheran World Federation explicitly includes hospitality as one dimension of *diakonia*, subsumed under the category '*Diakonia* of the table'.[39] Nordstokke relates the narratives in the New Testament about hospitality to the ethos of Antiquity, when 'communion at the table' not only meant eating together, but expresses 'friendship, mutual social acceptance and solidarity'.[40] The narratives about Jesus sharing a meal with outcasts therefore were provocative in the eyes of those who watched it.[41] Hospitality also includes advocacy. Hospitality in the form of sharing a meal or giving shelter to people on the margins of society (the homeless, persecuted people, asylum seekers and the like) may be perceived as provocative and possibly as a political protest, and might have serious repercussions for the church.[42]

We do not find the concept of hospitality in the English edition of the Church of Norway Plan for *diakonia*. But as the concept has been introduced, it may easily, in normative terms, be associated with the first two goals in the Plan's statement, in much the same way as the values specified in the NSC's value document.

Let me illustrate the relationship between welfare, hospitality and *diakonia* by way of two examples demonstrating, on the one hand, the moral 'power of hospitality', and on the other, the ambiguity of hospitality as *diakonia*. The first example concerns the Health Centre for Undocumented Immigrants (henceforth the Health Centre), a collaborative project between the Church City Mission (henceforth CCM) in Oslo, a faith-based welfare organisation in the Church of Norway, and the Norwegian Red Cross. The Health Centre was

---

36 WCC, IOCC and F. Ortaid, 'Introduction to Orthodox Diakonia': www.iocc.org/orthodoxdiakonia/index.php?id=p2

37 WCC, IOCC and F. Ortaid, 'Introduction to Orthodox Diakonia'.

38 C. Richmond, 'Dame Cicely Saunders: founder of the modern hospice movement', in *BMJ* 2005:331 (2005), 238.

39 LWF, *Diakonia in Context,* 32.

40 LWF, *Diakonia in Context*, 32.

41 See e.g. Matthew 9:9-13.

42 LWF, *Diakonia in Context*, 33.

established on the basis of a mapping out of the circumstances and social needs of undocumented immigrants in Norway. The mapping out concluded that the target group had comprehensive unmet needs, especially relating to health. The Health Centre is aimed at all people who do not have legal residence in Norway. It offers a range of health services that allow those who belong to the target group to consult a nurse, doctor, psychologist and physiotherapist, etc. All services are free. The Health Centre operates as a drop-in service, and is staffed by health professionals, mostly on a voluntary basis, who have taken a pledge of confidentiality. The clinic can therefore guarantee that under no circumstances will the patients' whereabouts or personal details be divulged to the police or immigration authorities. Literally, the Health Centre exemplifies hospitality in a 'church space'. But this form of social practice had a function in society beyond the meaning it had for those who were 'invited in' as 'guests'. The establishment of the Health Centre challenged the authority of the political system: when the Health Centre was opened, it created discussion in the media on the appropriateness of providing such care for people who had no legal right to be in the country. Members of the Norwegian parliament felt their political authority threatened enough to warn organisations that providing such help might have legal or financial repercussions. One could interpret the social practice of the CCM presented here as a way the organisation takes on its guardian role: it functions through its social practice as a 'critical voice' in society.[43] Such a statement in itself involves an attempt to project its practical activity on a more abstract level of understanding, giving it a symbolic meaning. This meaning may be constructed differently by different 'stakeholders', demonstrating that *diakonia* is not necessarily received with joy by all parties with a smaller or bigger stake in it. The agency of the CCM and the Red Cross together demonstrate the political aspect of *diakonia* as hospitality.

For the second example, I will again draw on empirical material from a study of The Norwegian Seamen's Church (NSC).[44] But first I will draw attention to the values specified in the NSC's value document). One of its organisational goals is to be 'an organisation characterised by "generous guest friendship"'. The Latin word for 'guest friendship' is *hospitium*, derived from the same word, *hospes*, as the English word 'hospitality'. By its very definition the ideological and value basis of the NSC links *diakonia*, welfare and hospitality. Thus, both the understanding expressed in the Church of Norway's Plan for *diakonia* and the goal formulations of the NSC may be related to the ethical concept of 'hospitality'.

My interest is next to demonstrate a potential ambiguity connected with institutionalised hospitality. First of all, there is a difference between a health

---

43 Cf. O.H. Angell, 'Church-Based Welfare and Public Religion', in *Nordic Journal of Religion and Society* 20:2 (2007), 179-93.

44 Angell, *Sjømannskyrkja som lågterskeltilbod.*

institution like the Health Centre and an organisation like the NSC in that the former will be much more structured in its operations than the latter, and what the staff do will be much more regulated and specialised. There will be more freedom for staff at a local Seamen's Church to form his or her role as a staff member than in a hospital – the freedom to shape the work role more, while the boundaries between work and leisure time will be much more blurred. To be a staff member in a NSC is more of a lifestyle than a job, as one of the interviewees expressed it. The practice of hospitality in the Health Centre will be a form of institutionalised hospitality carried out by the staff.

The following experience made me aware that institutionalised hospitality in this type of organisation, as experienced by those who encounter the organisation, is not totally determined by the character of the interactions with those who have a formal role in the system. A fairly young man entered the church one day. He was welcomed by a staff member. I sat him down at my table and talked with him. He was new in town, about to start a course at a school outside the city centre and was in the process of getting accommodation. He wanted to live near the school, but since he was new to the area, he was unable to correlate addresses given in property announcements with their location. One of the regular guests engaged himself seriously with the matter, found a city map, helped the young man find the addresses on the map, and gave him general information and advice. It struck me that the service this guest provided to the newcomer might well be seen as relevant to the organisation's practice of institutional hospitality. In this case the behaviour of the regular guest in an unplanned manner helped reinforce institutional hospitality. But just as the guest's behaviour contributed to reinforcing institutional hospitality, it could also, potentially, contribute to undermining institutional hospitality understood in quality terms, something that might be outside the control of the staff.[45] I did observe such happenings in the organisation. The incident I've described demonstrates that hospitality as *diakonia*, attending to the needs of the guests in an organisational setting and the creation of inclusive communities, is not always wholly in the hands of the organisation and its staff, but it can be a precarious thing.

To conclude this article, I want to raise the question whether the concept of hospitality may serve as a link between (church-based) *diakonia* and secular welfare work and welfare policy in our Nordic context. The double meaning of the word 'hospitality' in the sense I have used the word in this article in the context of *diakonia*, in practical social life implies that the 'guest', the person in need, may in other circumstances be the host, a provider of help, i.e. there is a shift of social roles. This shift may be based on principles of reciprocity and mutuality, but the guest-host shift may or may not apply to the same persons. For instance, at the organisational level, those who appear as 'hosts' in their role as representatives of a welfare organisation may in other circumstances

[45] Angell, *Sjømannskyrkja som lågterskeltilbod, 29.*

appear as 'guests' or help seekers in other welfare organisations. In a generalised way the principle of hospitality, involving the potential role shift among the members of society, may be institutionalised at the societal level in terms of general welfare arrangements. The potential shift of roles implied by the double meaning of hospitality shares common characteristics with the concept of 'solidarity' in the social democratic tradition.[46] With the structure of the Nordic model of public welfare system in mind, needs-based programmes, like social assistance, may be said to represent an institutionalisation of the principle of neighbourly love,[47] or hospitality based on an assumption that the host-guest role shift is not evenly distributed at this level, while the social security system is based on mutuality or solidarity in accordance with the social democratic tradition. However, such a link does not imply that there is any historical connection between *diakonia* and hospitality in the Christian tradition, and the structure of the Nordic welfare state. Be that as it may, in a research context the article indicates that an understanding and investigation of hospitality is most fruitfully based on an interdisciplinary approach, combining (at least) theological, cultural, sociological and social policy perspectives.

Bibliography

Allardt, E., *Dimensions of Welfare in a Comparative Scandinavian Study* (Helsinki: Research Group for Comparative Sociology, 1975).

Angell, O.H., 'Church-Based Welfare and Public Religion', in *Nordic Journal of Religion and Society* 20:2 (2007), 179-93.

Angell, O.H., 'Sacred Welfare Agents in Secular Welfare Space – the Case of the Church of Norway in Drammen', in Anders Bäckström and Grace Davie (eds), *Welfare and Religion in 21st Century Europe, Vol. 1: Configuring the Connections* (Farnham, UK: Ashgate, 2010), 89-115.

Angell, O.H., *Sjømannskyrkja som lågterskeltilbod: heim, organisasjon og institusjon med diakonal forankring [The Norwegian Seamen's Church as a low-threshold welfare service provider: a faith-based home, organisation and institution]* (Oslo: Diakonhjemmet Høgskole. Rapport 2011/6, 2011).

Blennberger, E., and M.J. Hansson, 'Vad menas med diakoni? [What do we mean by diakonia?]', in E. Blennberger and M.J. Hansson (eds), *Diakoni: tolkning, historik, praktik.* (Stockholm: Verbum, 2008), 13-27.

Bretherton, L., *Hospitality as Holiness: Christian Witness amid Moral Diversity* (Farnham, UK: Ashgate, 2006).

Church of Norway, *Comprehensive Diaconal Programme for the Church of Norway* (Oslo: National Council for the Church of Norway, 1988).

Heitink, G., *Practical Theology: History, Theory, Action Domains: Manual for Practical Theology* (Grand Rapids, MI: W.B. Eerdmans, 1999).

Johannessen, K.I., 'Diakontjenestens plassering i kirken [The placing of the diaconate in

[46] S. Stjernø, *Solidarity in Europe: The History of an Idea* (Cambridge: CUP, 2005).

[47] J.H. Petersen and L.H. Petersen, 'Nestekærlighed og velfærdsstat [Charity and the welfare state]', in J.H. Petersen, K. Petersen and L.H. Petersen (eds), *13 værdier bag den danske velfærdsstat* (Odense: Syddansk Universitetsforlag, 2007), 112-34.

the church]', in K.I. Johannessen, K. Jordheim and K.K. Korslien (eds), *Diakoni: en kritisk lesebok* (Trondheim: Tapir akademisk forlag, 2009), 29-43.

Kramer, R.M., *Voluntary Agencies in the Welfare State* (Berkeley, CA: University of California Press, 1981).

Kverndal, R., *The Way of the Sea: The Changing Shape of Mission in the Seafaring World* (Pasadena, CA: William Carey Library, 2008).

Lundström, T., and F. Wijkström, *Från röst till service? [From voice to service?]* (Sköndal: Sköndalsinstitutet, 1995).

MacIntyre, A., *Dependent Rational Animals: Why Human Beings Need the Virtues* (London: Duckworth, 1999).

Lutheran World Federation, *Diakonia in Context: Transformation, Reconciliation, Empowerment. An LWF Contribution to the Understanding and Practice of Diakonia* (Geneva: LWF, 2009).

Petersen, J.H., and L.H. Petersen, 'Nestekærlighed og velfærdsstat [Charity and the welfare state]', in J.H. Petersen, K. Petersen and L.H. Petersen (eds), *13 værdier bag den danske velfærdsstat* (Odense: Syddansk Universitetsforlag, 2007), 112-34.

Qvortrup, L., 'Fra diakoni til velfærdsstat: diakoniens uddifferentiering [From diakonia to welfare state: the functional differentiation of diakonia]', in J.H. Schjørring and J.T. Bak (eds), *Velfærdsstat og kirke* (Copenhagen: Anis, 2005, 79-102).

Richmond, C., 'Dame Cicely Saunders: founder of the modern hospice movement', in *BMJ* 2005:331 (2005), 238.

Sjømannskirken, *Sjømannskirkens verdidokument [The Norwegian Seamen's Church: value document]* (Bergen: Sjømannskirken – Norsk kirke i utlandet, 2012).

Stjernø, S., *Solidarity in Europe: The History of an Idea* (Cambridge: CUP, 2005).

Swatos, W.H. Jr., 'Differentiating Experiences: The Virtue of Substantive Definitions', in A.L. Greil and D.G. Bromley (eds), *Defining Religion: Investigating the Boundaries between the Sacred and Secular* (Amsterdam: JAI Press, 2003), 39-53.

Temple, William, *Christianity and Social Order* (Harmondsworth, UK: Penguin, 1942).

Tønnessen, A.V., 'Velferdsstat og kirkelig diakoni i Norge etter 1945. Kritikk og fornyelse [Welfare state and church-based diaconia in Norway since 1945: Criticism and renewal]', in J.H. Schjørring and J.T. Bak (eds), *Velfærdsstat og kirke* (Copenhagen: Anis, 2005), 103-23.

WCC, IOCC and F. Ortaid, *Introduction to Orthodox Diakonia* (Helsinki: International Orthodox Christian Charities (USA), Ortaid – Orthodox Church Aid from Finland (Finland), World Council of Churches – Diakonia and Solidarity Team (Geneva), 2005). www.iocc.org/orthodox*diakonia*/index.php?id=p2

Religion Between the Private and the Public: About Diaconal Studies as an Academic Field

Anders Bäckström

Introduction

In this article, I will discuss the place of religion between the private and the public sphere of society. I will argue that diaconal research that studies religion as a resource, both in relation to the individual and to the society at large, is capable of making a constructive contribution to a research area that is growing rapidly. The background to the presentation of this research area is the perspective that we have developed at Uppsala University over the years. This research has been linked with the analyses of religious, value-based and social change processes that are taking place in the European and especially in the western world. These changes have now had an effect on the Nordic countries through increased communication via media and through growing migration. Through these processes, the European north is moving closer to a global world.

This work has formed the basis for the idea of creating a researcher training programme we have called diaconal studies. A simple definition is that this research programme is concerned with the theological study of health and welfare or the interaction between theology/religion, health and welfare in a rapidly changing society. New disciplines, such as this researcher training programme is aiming for, arise either through offshoots from other disciplines or through mergers between two or more disciplines. Natural sciences are most often created through offshoots of new specialised disciplines – for example, in physics or chemistry – while social science disciplines are often created by linking subjects relating to a new focus area. The social/diaconal roles of churches or religious (diaconal) organisations in a changing society can be such a focus area if it includes the study of the values that lie behind (professional) practices in the area of social care. The study could indeed focus on civil society as such in which both religious and diaconal institutions are included.

The problem with previous diaconal research carried out in the Nordic countries has been its general focus on an institutional form of religiosity, such as the astate churches, that has been gradually marginalised through secularisation processes during the 20th century. This includes the specialisation of different knowledge areas in society, like medicine, education, law, the economy, etc. Religion has accordingly become such a specialised area. This also reflects the Nordic development towards a welfare state in which the Nordic national churches' social mission has been brought into the private sphere with spiritual guidance as the primary tool. During the process of secularisation, religion has become part of the private sector of society. Diaconal research focusing on this small field of diaconal practice is too limited to justify a separate government-funded university discipline.

Diaconal Studies as a broad concept

If, on the other hand, diaconal research is extended to include a broader area of social issues of society, it will become part of a general conversation of how to shape a future society in which religion takes a constructive part. Some examples include: a) the social and political consequences of religion as a social factor, b) the importance of modern pluralism for the development of democracy, and (as a consequence) religion as a voice in the public debate, c) the importance of legislation for a society's secular cohesion, especially through focusing on the place of religious minorities (and their human freedoms and rights) in this secular society, d) the importance of existential stress and the quest for health and well-being, e) the relativisation of religious convictions and scientific worldviews as part of the post-modern condition, and f) the growth of innovative social solutions in a society with minorities that find themselves to be non-citizens and therefore not eligible for social security. These examples could be multiplied.

The point I want to make is that it will most likely be difficult to argue that diaconal studies has a knowledge base of its own without broadening the research area to include significant social change processes of the society of today. At Uppsala University some of these research questions are dealt with within the interdisciplinary research programme called The Impact of Religion: Challenges for Society, Law and Democracy. This research programme is of course wider as it includes researchers not only from the Department of Theology but also from Law, Political Science, Medicine, the History of Ideas and Natural Sciences. It is, however, an example of how the study of *diaconia*, defined as the study of the relationship between theology/religion, health and welfare, can be developed and indeed include a theoretical reflection on practice. This design of the research area is close to the 'forefront of knowledge' and could attract extensive research resources from the Research Councils of the Nordic countries.

In sum: The starting-point for my argument is that the religious and social interaction has changed compared with the situation just a few decades ago. This has influenced society's development in a number of areas, some of which also concern the social and political role of religion. I will deal with these questions in the next section and point in particular to the new visibility of religion as both an asset and a problem. In the third section, I will give an account of the results of the projects on welfare and religion in a European perspective (WREP and WaVE), which highlight the question of whether the privatisation of religion is a necessary result of specialisation in modern society. On the basis of these accounts, I will then return to a discussion of the importance of the new social and religious conditions for the emergence of diaconal studies as an academic field.

Religion's New Visibility in the Private and the Public Sphere

Parallel development trends

There are several grounds for the increasing need for research on religion's place between the private and the public. The most important reason has to do with the tension between two diverging but parallel developments that are currently taking place in Europe. We have been used to the idea of development as a series of stages from the Age of Enlightenment towards higher levels of secular maturity. In simple terms, these stages can be called the pre-modern, modern and now the late modern or post-modern stage. In my previous work, I have shown that these stages cannot simply be seen as a sequence. Rather, they take place simultaneously, even into our present time. This means that the values and the social, economic and religious logic that is linked with the different stages are represented through different value cultures that coexist.[1]

However, the idea that culture develops towards a mature and rational stage has dominated social science research even into our time. The sociologist Bryan Wilson of Oxford is one example. In his influential book *Religion in a Sociological Perspective* from 1982,[2] he argues that modern society has led to the increased specialisation of knowledge and an increased pluralism of ideas with rational undertones, which in turn has led to religion mostly being assigned to the private sphere of the individual. This can be seen as an emancipation process whereby individuals and the state have broken free from religious authority. Religion has gone from belonging to the public sphere to becoming part of people's private lives. The Nordic countries are often cited as the best example of how this theoretical model works in practice.

In recent years, a number of books have been published that point to an ongoing opposite trend. One of the best-known of these is the report published in 2009 by The Economist journalists John Micklethwait and Adrian Wooldridge: *God is back. How the Global Rise of Faith is Changing the World.*[3] In the book, the writers argue that global communication is bringing

[1] Anders Bäckström, Ninna Edgardh Beckman and Per Pettersson, *Religious Change in Northern Europe. The Case of Sweden* (Stockholm: Verbum, 2004).

[2] Bryan Wilson, *Religion in a Sociological Perspective* (Oxford: OUP, 1982).

[3] John Micklethwait and Adrian Wooldridge, *God is back. How the Global Rise of Faith*

strong religious development in the world to Europe. On other continents, religion is to a greater extent considered an integral part of a technically and democratically advanced society. The world has come to the European countries, and the result is increased religious pluralism at the local level (what we call a multicultural condition). This has led to people saying that religion is on its way back as an authority in society. As I shall point out in the next section, it is important not to exaggerate the return of religion. On the other hand, the book's conclusion is probably true: if you want to understand the modern world, you cannot afford to ignore God – whether you believe in him or not. What is interesting about the book is that it illustrates an ongoing parallel development where religion is shifting from the private into the public sphere.

Has religion disappeared only to return?

It is important to recall that the idea of the return of religion (which is what the 'God is back' discussion is all about) is based on the idea that religion first disappeared from public life, only to later reappear. There is no evidence of a disappearance or reappearance. This is criticised by, among others, Hugh McLeod in his book *The Religious Crises of the 1960s.*[4] In his extensive survey, he refers to the fact that trends are always coming and going, and that the presence of religion in society is following different tracks depending on the different historical circumstances. It is also important to state that generalising theories, such as the secularisation theory, often have a normative aspect linked with them. For example, he doubts whether the idea of enlightenment can explain all the religious and social variation in the world. This is obviously not possible.

David Martin continues the same argument in his book *The Future of Christianity.*[5] In this book, he shows that there are different paths to modern society where religion plays very different roles. By distinguishing between the French, the American and the Russian revolutions, it is possible to see how three explicitly secular states deal with the presence of religion in very different ways. In the USA, religious freedom from the state has always been the most important issue, and religious groups have thus come to participate in the building of the nation, which results in a 'passive secularism'. In France, it is the state's freedom from religion that is the overriding goal. This leads to an active secularism, the political goal of which is the privatisation of religion. This is exactly what was incorporated into French law in 1905. In Russia, religion (Christianity) was first considered 'the opium of the masses', but is now, according to Vladimir Putin, Europe's rock. The absence of revolution in

is Changing the World (London: Penguin, 2009).

[4] Hugh McLeod, *The Religious Crises of the 1960s* (Oxford: OUP, 2007).

[5] David Martin, *The Future of Christianity. Reflections on Violence and Democracy, Religion and Secularization* (Farnham, UK: Ashgate, 2011).

the Nordic countries explains the co-operation between the church and the state during the 20th century. The Nordic interaction model can be considered a type of pragmatic secularism. It is obvious that the secular solutions that have arisen during the 20th century are not homogeneous.

This means that the discussion about the return of religion has more to do with the scientific community's surprise that religion has not disappeared in accordance with a modernisation thesis than with an actual return of religion. These discoveries have resulted in a newly awakened need in the social sciences for a theoretical analysis and integration of religion as a 'natural' or permanent phenomenon in western culture. This creates a need for in-depth studies in which diaconal research, which focuses on local conditions, can contribute substantially to the development of empirically based theory.

The cultural integration – about Nordic normality

The Nordic model, with a certain homogeneity and co-operation between the state and a number of different institutions, including national churches, has in practice facilitated the emergence of a welfare state emphasising individual freedom of choice and equal care for both women and men. The strong tension that prevailed in continental Europe between the Catholic church and the state, and which led to a weaker welfare state, is therefore absent in the Nordic countries. This means that the Nordic welfare model would hardly have come about without a Lutheran state church which, through its theology, gave the state a strong legitimacy.

However, the Nordic interaction model means that religion, in practice, has become invisible (latent) in everyday life. It manifests itself in times of national and individual crisis or transitions in life. Grace Davie calls this phenomenon 'vicarious religion', a type of vicarious religiosity practiced by a minority on behalf of a majority.[6] Vicarious religion can be seen as a welfare service provided by national churches as long as they define themselves as being open to all, democratically governed and geographically widespread.

At the same time, however, this practice of vicarious religiosity contributes to the majority of the Nordic population perceiving strong religiosity as something abnormal. Surveys have shown that many people in the Nordic countries, when asked about their religiosity, have a tendency to answer, 'I am not a religious person, but …' In his book *The Future of Christianity*, David Martin writes that the close relationship between the church and society in the Nordic countries has caused individuals to oscillate between the religious and the social sphere without being conscious of when they are in one or the other. He asks himself: why should a Danish (Nordic) citizen take part in the church service on Sundays when he or she can take part in society every day?[7] This still applies to large groups of citizens in the Nordic countries.

---

[6] Grace Davie, *The Sociology of Religion* (London: Sage, 2007).

[7] David Martin, *The Future of Christianity*, 2011.

The Nordic interaction model makes religion invisible in our day-to-day lives, but more visible in 'abnormal' situations. Interestingly, churches serve as public arenas for memorials relating to such events. This demonstrates that rituals, including rites of passage in the life of individuals, are given a public character. In practice, rituals and social activities link individuals with a collective memory, and religion thus serves as an arena for communication between individuals and the community. In practice, this is a welfare function that diaconal research must consider, since the process contributes to feelings of belonging and security.

Religious pluralism contributes to publicity

Increased religious pluralism makes it increasingly difficult for states and political parties to exclude religiously based views and demands from the public discourse arena. The Nordic countries have become part of the world both through the role of the media, where religion is often portrayed as dangerous or extreme, and through migrants coming from less wealthy parts of the world. This migration is reminiscent of migration to the cities in the early industrial society during the 19th century. Today, about 15-20% of the population of the Nordic countries is born in another country or have at least one parent born in another country (somewhat fewer in Finland). Migration has led to a new religious pluralism that challenges the secular thinking that peaked in the 1960s. That was when the welfare state was at its strongest and it seemed as though the economic development would go on for ever. This gave western countries a strong sense of optimism with regard to their own abilities. Cultures were radicalised, traditional values criticised, and 1968 became the year of the revolt against the 'establishment'. It was in the 1970s and later that the anti-institutional trend gained support and became clearer through a shift in values towards 'emancipative' freedom values at the private level, and consumer values and deregulation at the public level. This came to affect all tradition-bearing institutions, not least the national churches.[8]

Of the religions that are growing in Europe, Islam has been particularly difficult for secular states to handle, since it does not accept the division between the private and public spheres. Islam has diet, clothing and prayer rules that are of a public nature. Now that Muslims are making the transition from being immigrants to becoming citizens, the demand for Muslim values to be accepted is growing. The heated debate about freedom of religion shows that Europeans still consider freedom of religion to be freedom *from* all forms of religion, while religious pluralism and the multicultural community demand freedom to practise religion as shown in the example from the USA.

Statements by Angela Merkel, David Cameron and Nicolas Sarkozy, Europe's most powerful heads of state, demonstrate that these demands are

---

[8] Poppa Norris and Ronald Inglehart, *Sacred and Secular. Religion and Politics Worldwide* (Cambridge: CUP, 2004).

becoming increasingly problematic. They believe that the multicultural model has failed.[9] Despite the fact that their countries represent different secular models, which lead to different types of multicultural acceptance, they seem to claim that people of different ethnicities, languages and religions must adjust to the majority culture in order to become full citizens. We appear to have reached a point in the 21st century's development where the tendency for immigrant groups to retain their cultural and religious distinctiveness is perceived as an increasing social problem. Nationalist parties, not only in the Nordic countries, but across Europe, have taken a stand on this issue and gained political influence by combining popular religion and welfare traditions with a national 'us' feeling in a nationalistic dream of the future.

Increased religious pluralism, and the presence of Islam in particular, thus raise a number of questions about the visibility of religion that has consequences for the entire religious life. Criticism of religious symbols means that not only veils and minarets, but also crucifixes, are becoming political. Even celebrating the end of the school year in church buildings becomes a sensitive subject. The entire field of religion is suddenly becoming visible in the secular Nordic countries, and thereby the subject of a renewed debate about the place of religion in the public sphere. At the same time, it contributes to increasing churches' and religious organisations' sense of the political dimensions of religious life. This also concerns individuals who involve themselves in social issues. First and foremost, the new religious pluralism raises fundamental questions about what is public and what is private; in other words, questions that have been defined as private in the 20th century today require public political answers. This leads to unclear boundaries and generates a need for in-depth research on religion as a voice, identity marker, resource and agent. These are questions that can easily be integrated within an extended diaconal research framework.

Religion and Welfare in a European Perspective

Thirdly, I will discuss the results of the projects Welfare and Religion in a European Perspective (WREP) and Welfare and Values in Europe (WaVE). In order to understand the results, it is important to know that Europe is divided into three or four different welfare regimes, according to Esping-Andersen's (1990) terminology,[10] and that these welfare regimes have arisen in relation to different church traditions. The welfare regimes are: 1) the socio-democratic

---

9 James Kirkup, 'Muslims must embrace our British values, David Cameron says', in *The Telegraph*: www.telegraph.co.uk/news/politics/david-cameron/8305346/Muslims-must-embrace-our-British-values-David-Cameron-says.html 2011; 'Nicolas Sarkozy declares multiculturalism had failed', in *The Telegraph*: www.telegraph.co.uk/news/worldnews/europe/france/8317497/Nicolas-Sarkozydeclares-multiculturalism-had-failed.html 2011.

10 Gøsta Esping Andersen, *The Three Worlds of Welfare Capitalism*.

Nordic model of universal transfers, and with Lutheran state churches that have legitimised this social system (Sweden, Norway, and Finland); 2) the Anglo-Saxon liberal model of state control with a big voluntary component, plus an Anglican majority church with the same voluntary structure (England); 3) the constitutional Christian, democratic or conservative model based on subsidiarity (in practice, on the family), and on means-tested transfers and a strong Catholic church that has developed a social doctrine on subsidiarity (France, Italy and also Germany, which is actually bi-confessional); and, finally, 4) a rudimentary model that is found in the Mediterranean countries and in Eastern Europe, often with Orthodox majority churches (Greece, Romania). Croatia, Poland and Latvia have also been included in this group, with Catholic and Lutheran majority churches respectively. They actually belong to the group of post-communist states that have challenges of their own. The study entails a mapping out of the way in which welfare is organised, the prevalence of majority churches and their interaction with local authorities, and the social network of minority religions in a city in each country.

The basis for the welfare study

The basis for the studies is the conclusion that, from the 1990s onwards, states have started to seek alternative or less expensive welfare solutions because of the globalisation (and liberalisation) of the economy, and an ageing population that requires more expensive health and social welfare services. An important factor behind this is the increased tension between the state and the market, where deregulation of the state's authority had already begun in the 1970s with the oil crisis, an incipient global economy and unemployment.[11] Since the 1980s, the market has expanded, and in the 1990s it started to affect more and more areas. The market became almost like a separate being with its own 'clergy', and it has become identity-forming. The diminishing authority of the nation states has paved the way for market solutions, where care for the elderly in particular has become a sign of increased interest from (international) profit-seeking enterprises. The question of whether it should be allowed to make a profit on schools, health and social care services nonetheless remains controversial in the Nordic context.

The study was also based on the assumption that weaker relationships between the state and individuals, or between the state and the family, have increased the scope of what is called civil society or the third sector. This sector includes associations, co-operatives and not-for-profit organisations. These organisations have already gained a stronger position in society in all the European countries. The question, then, is what role civil society organisations should play. Is the primary function of these organisations 1) to be service

---

[11] Olofsson, Jonas, 'Välfärdspolitiska vägval', in: i Hans Swärd, Per Gunnar Edebalk and Eskil Wadensjö (eds), *Vägar till välfärd - idéer, inspiratörer, kontroverser, perspektiv* (Stockholm: Liber), 284-299

providers, 2) to create good citizens, 3) to serve as a critical voice in the social debate, or 4) to create innovation? Normally, organisations must be able to correspond to all aspects of civil society functions, but in practice the emphasis has often come to be placed on one or two aspects.[12] The question is: what is the primary task of churches and religious organisations? Is it, for example, possible to combine the roles of service provider and critical voice without them coming into conflict with each other?

Finally, the study was based on the theoretical discussion about modern society's necessary differentiation, and the importance of this development to the privatisation of religion.[13] What bearing does increased social commitment have on the discussion of religion's place between the private and the public spheres? Is there a de-differentiation process going on as a consequence of current social changes?

General observations

Churches and religious organisations have always been concerned with caring for people in need. As exclusion and a new type of poverty are becoming apparent in society, churches and religious organisations are therefore drawn into the discussion about the grounds for solidarity and care. Increased costs in all European countries contribute to a similar set of problems, even though welfare systems differ between Northern and Southern Europe. This has led to the establishment of what is called the two-thirds society, with a group that is lacking a social network, but also in the form of a new hierarchy between the rich and the poor. Class society is returning. Poverty and exclusion are obviously defined as relative to the European context. It is not the type of poverty you find in so-called Third World countries, but the kind of exclusion experienced by people who live in the midst of a consumer society without being able to gain any benefit from this society's goods and services.[14]

To a certain extent, the new exclusion has ethnic and religious undertones, and it is probably here to stay. In a comparative study, Friedrichs showed that exclusion and poverty have generally been located in certain districts of European cities.[15] All signs indicate increased diversification in the European countries, partly between different religious/ethnic groups, partly between different social classes, and partly between women and men. The problem escalates when religious/ethnic and social factors work together. This can lead to unrest among the citizens of the respective countries and form the basis for

---

[12] Angell, Olav Helge, 'Diakonia and Hospitality', this volume, 155-167.

[13] José Casanova, *Public Religion in the Modern World* (Chicago, IL: University of Chicago Press, 1994).

[14] Zygmunt Bauman, *Work, Consumerism and the New Poor* (Buckingham, UK: Open University Press, 1998).

[15] Jürgen Friedrichs, 'Social Exclusion and Segregation in urban areas'. Paper presented at the final conference of the European Commission Project, *Faith-Based Organisations and Social Exclusion in European Cities*, 25-26 November 2010.

reduced tolerance of religious and ethnic minorities. In the European Union, the big question is how social cohesion can be preserved and strengthened amid this social and religious diversification.[16]

It is in this context that we must see the increased involvement of churches and religious or diaconal organisations in social issues. This not only applies to the rest of the European continent, but also very much to the Nordic countries. The Easter Appeals in 2005 and 2010 in Sweden, where the government was approached by the Ecumenical Council complaining about the treatment of immigrants and of people on sick leave, are part of this trend. The question is also whether the deregulation of the welfare state means that the Nordic countries are approaching a continental family-based welfare society where care becomes more individualised and means-tested. Are we moving from a welfare state to a welfare society that all political parties can agree on? Does this mean that the organisations of civil society are filling a void created by the slow withdrawal of the welfare state? These are complicated questions to which there are no obvious answers, especially in the Nordic countries which have a well-developed transfer system. In the Nordic countries, the organisations of civil society largely complement the state welfare organisation.[17]

The main results of the European studies

The most important results of the European welfare studies (WREP and WaVE) can be summarised as follows:

- Churches and religious organisations see themselves primarily as complementing state welfare organisations (contributing quality values);
- The deregulation of the nation state has given both for-profit and not-for-profit organisations greater leeway within the framework of civil society (with more religious schools and retirement homes);
- Churches and religious organisations are perceived as religiously inclusive (no faith requirement applies to receive support), and are also more open than local social authorities, as they do not register the help-seeker;[18]
- Majority churches serve as arenas for interaction between majority cultures and minority religions, and thereby fulfil an important function in relation to integration;

---

[16] *World and European Sustainable Cities. Insights from EU research 2010*. Brussels: European Commission. Directorate-General for Research, 2010.

[17] FACIT-Project, *Faith-Based Organisations and Social Exclusion in European Cities.* Research Project funded by the European Commission Seventh Framework Programme 2008-2010, 2010: www.ua.ac.be/oases

[18] Olofsson, Jonas, 'Välfärdspolitiska vägval', in: i Hans Swärd, Per Gunnar Edebalk and Eskil Wadensjö (eds), Vägar till välfärd - idéer, inspiratörer, kontroverser, perspektiv (Stockholm: Liber) 284-299.

- Ethnically or religiously diverse minority groups (often Muslim, but also Protestant) help to develop social networks that strengthen the group internally (bonding), but also externally (bridging), through contact with other religious groups and local authorities;[19]
- The role of religious organisations is often of an innovative nature in that they quickly identify new groups in need of social security;
- There is a great difference between evangelically/charismatically oriented religious groups, which develop their own 'social industry', and liberal religious groups, which prefer to co-operate with governments and social authorities;
- Women predominate in all countries, either as employees in social services in Northern Europe or as 'volunteers' in family care in Southern Europe;
- Churches and religious organisations tend to adapt to government regulations – which means that the deregulation of the nation state also leads to new regulation of religion through different types of signed agreements through the new tendency of contracting into society;
- The role of churches and religious organisations as moral or ethical voices promoting solidarity has increased in a world characterised by a new type of exclusion and poverty. It is this function that contributes to increasing the presence of religion in the public sphere, and which means that religious leaders (e.g. bishops) are expected to participate in the political debate about these questions.[20]

The studies show that, despite all the deregulation of states and churches, the Nordic and the continental welfare models remain surprisingly stable. They are enduring structures that are not easily changed. It is also obvious that in both models, men predominate as decision-makers and women as providers, but in different ways. In Northern Europe, women are employees in social services or nursing, and in Southern Europe, they are providers of family care.

We can also see that the similarities between the cities surveyed are greater than the differences between the countries and the different welfare regimes. This shows that there are social problems that are common to all cities, although at different levels. It is also the same groups of persons that are in need of care in the cities surveyed, i.e. homeless people with drug addiction or mental problems, single (older) women with dependent children, and persons belonging to migrating groups (such as illegal immigrants) that gather in suburban areas. These studies show that it can be difficult to unite contract-based care with criticism of such care, especially in Southern Europe, where a representative of the independent organisation and a representative of the local

---

[19] Klas Borell and Arne Gerdner, 'Frivilligt socialt arbete i svenska muslimska forsamlingar [Tradition, organisation, integration]', in *Socionomens forskningssupplement* 29, 2011, 34-43.

[20] Pål Kjetil Botvar and Ulla Schmidt, *Religion i dagens Norge. Mellom sekularisering og sakralisering* (Oslo: Universitetsforlaget, 2010).

authorities can be one and the same person (or belong to the same local organisation, e.g. Caritas). On the whole, contract-based care gives states the possibility of retaining control, including over society's religious life.[21]

Conclusion

In this article, I have tried to show that there are ongoing research programmes that focus on the new visibility of religion and on the challenges this represents to society and its democratic and legal structure. The starting-point for projects is often increased religious and social diversification seen as a problem. This applies in particular to the presence of Islam and the 'risks' associated with the introduction of Sharia law, because such a practical application would jeopardise the idea of secular legislation as a guarantor of cohesion. Together this means that the Nordic discussion of cultural normality no longer functions in the way that most Nordic citizens have been used to. The majority of the Nordic population still oscillates between the church and society without having a clear awareness of when they are in one or the other sphere. However, increased religious pluralism has made this oscillation more visible in a way that Nordic citizens have not been prepared for, and highlights the need to hear religious voices in the democratic discourse. This has also resulted in a lack of clarity as to what place these religious voices should be allowed to have. According to the modernisation thesis, public discourse should be free from religious input. The lack of clarity can explain why the representatives of secular society have become more active in the religious debate.

On the whole, the rapid changes in society with increased global communication contribute to uncertainty about our cultural identity. Am I the same person I was when I was born in the 1940s? Are my children the same, not to mention my grandchildren, who were born in the 2000s? Is there a greater sense of fellowship across national boundaries (ethnic/religious) than among members of the same housing association? Nationalist parties have taken a stand in this national identity discussion and won political power in Europe. The question is how we can develop a national identity for the present without using religious minorities as a threat.

The results of the welfare studies raise interesting theoretical questions that concern the secular state's fundamental idea of a clear division between the religious and secular spheres. Throughout the 20th century, secularisation theory has been based on such a gradual separation. From the 1960s onwards, a parallel development has pointed in the opposite direction, even though alliances between different players can be of a more temporary nature. Behind these trends, we find a social and religious diversification issue that has yet to be resolved, but also an increased need for complementing welfare services.

---

[21] James A. Beckford, 'The Return of Public Religion? A Critical Assessment of a Popular Claim', in *Nordic Journal of Religion and Society* 23, Vol. 2, 2010, 121-36.

Recent developments now contribute to making churches and religious organisations more socially active and politically involved in questions concerning the fight against poverty at the national as well as the international level.[22] The point is that society's specialised institutions certainly endure, but that religion is permeating various social institutions in new and unexpected ways. Research into the relationships between welfare and religion in a European perspective is just one example of how these social changes are affecting the Nordic countries.

New preconditions for diaconal research

Today, religion is found not only in the private social sphere. Instead, religious organisations and phenomena are found in both the private and the public spheres at the same time, and studies of diaconal welfare that churches and religious organisations contribute, are evidence of this. I began by saying that diaconal research has been strongly connected with the conditions that prevailed during the 20th century, when the welfare state grew strong, and economic and social conditions laid the foundations for a shift in values towards emancipative values of freedom. The research followed the development and became focused on individual care and spiritual guidance.

We are currently seeing a broadening of diaconal research towards the interaction between theology/religion, health and welfare in a global and multicultural context. It is this broadening that corresponds with the processes of the 21st century that I have described in this article. This broadening of research is not only noticeable in Uppsala-based research, but is also found in Nordic and German universities and university colleges. On the whole, practice-related and locally based diaconal research corresponds with what Danièle Hervieu-Léger (2000), among others, has called the development from (religious) convictions to (religious) activities, a development that corresponds with the relativisation of convictions and the increased importance of actions for both private and collective identities.[23] She therefore calls for more action-based research because, in practice, values can become manifest in different forms. Against this backdrop, diaconal research as an academic field with its own researcher training programme has the prerequisites for focusing on an area of research which is certainly broad but which meets a fundamental empirical need to study values and religious dimensions over and above traditional definitions.

---

[22] Anders Bäckström and Grace Davie, 'Welfare and Religion in Europe: Themes, Theories and Tensions', in Anders Bäckström, Grace Davie, Ninna Edgardh and Per Pettersson (eds), *Welfare and Religion in 21st Century Europe, Vol. 2: Gendered, Religious and Social Change* (Farnham, UK: Ashgate, 2011), 151-71.

[23] Daniele Hervieu-Leger, *Religion as a Chain of Memory* (Cambridge: Polity Press, 2000).

Together, this shows that religion, in practice, appears in different ways in different sectors of society, and is assigned different roles that transcend the distinction between the private and the public. New interaction models are developing in society, which leads to the paradoxical situation that religion is gaining more influence in other institutions in society, while it is decreasing in scope within its own institution. We can now see that the space created by the slow weakening of the welfare state is being filled by both ideal and commercial organisations and (international) companies.[24] This 'marketisation' of welfare is also spilling over into religion, which takes on forms that are similar to the market. All this needs to be studied in more detail. On the whole, there is a growing need for research into the tension between the quality-based private sphere, where the health and welfare of individuals are central, and society's need for public welfare solutions. These solutions take different forms in the European context, but very much meet similar social challenges. Comparative studies should be able to provide a basis for theoretical analyses of religion's place in a late modern society where the interaction between specialised spheres is increasing. With such an orientation, diaconal studies should have the characteristics to enable it to develop into a separate academic field with strong support from the scientific community.

Bibliography

Bäckström, Anders, Ninna Edgardh Beckman and Per Pettersson, *Religious Change in Northern Europe. The Case of Sweden* (Stockholm: Verbum, 2004).

Bäckström, Anders, Grace Davie, Ninna Edgardh and Per Pettersson (eds), *Welfare and Religion in 21st Century Europe, Vol. 1: Configuring the Connections* (Farnham, UK: Ashgate, 2010).

Bäckström, Anders, and Grace Davie, 'Welfare and Religion in Europe: Themes, Theories and Tensions', in Anders Bäckström, Grace Davie, Ninna Edgardh and Per Pettersson (eds), *Welfare and Religion in 21st Century Europe, Vol. 2: Gendered, Religious and Social Change* (Farnham, UK: Ashgate, 2011), 151-71.

Bauman, Zygmunt, *Work, Consumerism and the New Poor* (Buckingham, UK: Open University Press, 1998).

Beckford, James A., 'The Return of Public Religion? A Critical Assessment of a Popular Claim', in *Nordic Journal of Religion and Society* 23, Vol. 2, 2010, 121-36.

Borell, Klas, and Arne Gerdner, 'Frivilligt socialt arbete i svenska muslimska forsamlingar [Tradition, organisation, integration]', in *Socionomens forskningssupplement* 29, 2011, 34–43.

Botvar, Pål Ketil, and Ulla Schmidt, Religion i dagens Norge. Mellom sekularisering og sakralisering (Oslo: Universitetsforlaget, 2010).

Casanova, Jose, *Public Religion in the Modern World* (Chicago: University of Chicago Press, 1994).

Davie, Grace, *The Sociology of Religion* (London: Sage, 2007).

Esping-Andersen, Gøsta, *The Three Worlds of Welfare Capitalism* (Cambridge: Polity

[24] Leis-Peters, Annette, 'Diaconal Work and Research about Diakonia in the Face of Welfare Mix and Religious Pluralism in Sweden and Germany', above, 139-154

Press, 1990).

FACIT-Project, *Faith-Based Organisations and Social Exclusion in European Cities.* Research Project funded by the European Commission Seventh Framework Programme 2008-2010, 2010 (www.ua.ac.be/oases)

Friedrichs, Jürgen, 'Social Exclusion and Segregation in urban areas'. Paper presented at the final conference of the European Commission Project, *Faith-Based Organisations and Social Exclusion in European Cities*, 25-26 November 2010.

Hervieu-Leger, Daniele, *Religion as a Chain of Memory* (Cambridge: Polity Press, 2000).

Impact of Religion. Challenges for Society, Law and Democracy, 2008: www.impactofreligion.uu.se

Kirkup, James, 'Muslims must embrace our British values, David Cameron says', in *The Telegraph*: www.telegraph.co.uk/news/politics/david-cameron/8305346/Muslims-must-embrace-our-British-values-David-Cameron-says.html 2011.

Martin, David, *The Future of Christianity. Reflections on Violence and Democracy, Religion and Secularization* (Farnham, UK: Ashgate, 2011).

McLeod, Hugh, *The Religious Crises of the 1960s* (Oxford: OUP, 2007).

Micklethwait, John, and Adrian Wooldridge, *God is back. How the Global Rise of Faith is Changing the World* (London: Penguin, 2009).

'Nicolas Sarkozy declares multiculturalism had failed', in *The Telegraph*: www.telegraph.co.uk/news/worldnews/europe/france/8317497/Nicolas-Sarkozydeclares-multiculturalism-had-failed.html, 2011.

Norris, Poppa, and Ronald Inglehart, *Sacred and Secular. Religion and Politics Worldwide* (Cambridge: CUP, 2004).

WREP – Welfare and Religion in a European Perspective. A comparative study of the role of the churches as agents of welfare within the social economy. Project description (Uppsala Institute for Diaconal and Social Studies, No. 4/2003, 2003).

Wilson, Bryan, *Religion in a Sociological Perspective* (Oxford: OUP, 1982).

World and European Sustainable Cities. Insights from EU research 2010 (Brussels: European Commission – Directorate-General for Research, 2010).

Reports from the WREP-Study

1) Bäckström, Anders, Grace Davie, Ninna Edgardh and Per Pettersson (eds), *Welfare and Religion in 21st Century Europe, Vol. 1, Configuring the Connections* (Farnham, UK: Ashgate, 2010).
2) Bäckström, Anders, Grace Davie, Ninna Edgardh and Per Pettersson (eds), *Welfare and Religion in 21st Century Europe,. Vol. 2: Gendered, Religious and Social Change* (Farnham, UK: Ashgate, 2011).
3) *WaVE – Welfare and Values in Europe. Transitions related to Religion, Minorities and Gender.* Research project funded by the European Sixth Framework Programme (FP6), conducted in twelve countries and covering February 2006 to February 2009. Presentation of the Research Project (Uppsala: Uppsala University, 2006).

Reports from the WaVE-study

1) Bäckström, Anders (co-ordinator), *Welfare and Values in Europe. Transitions related to Religion, Minorities and Gender. National Overviews and Case Study Reports, Volume 1. Northern Europe: Sweden, Norway, Finland, England.* Acta Universitatis Upsaliensis. Studies in Religion & Society No 4, Uppsala: Uppsala University, 2011.
2) Bäckström, Anders (co-ordinator), *Welfare and Values in Europe. Transitions*

related to Religion, Minorities and Gender. National Overviews and Case Study Reports, Volume 2. Continental Europe: Germany, France, Italy, Greece. Acta Universitatis Upsaliensis. Studies in Religion & Society No 5, Uppsala: Uppsala University, 2012.

3) Bäckström, Anders (co-ordinator), *Welfare and Values in Europe. Transitions related to Religion, Minorities and Gender. National Overviews and Case Study Reports, Volume 3. Eastern Europe: Latvia, Poland, Croatia, Roumania.* Acta Universitatis Upsaliensis. Studies in Religion & Society No 6, Uppsala: Uppsala University, 2013.

Part 3

Practical Perspectives

Bridge-Building and Go-Between: The Role of the Deacon in Church and Society

Kari Jordheim

This chapter is based on material collected during the World Assembly arranged by the Diakonia World Federation in the summer of 2013 in Berlin. The Diakonia World Federation's members are associations, organisations and communities of deaconesses, deacons, diaconal brothers and sisters, diaconal ministers and other church workers.[1] On one of the first days I handed out a questionnaire, and 48 people volunteered to answer my questions. In addition to these I also received several brochures and documents about the role of deacon and the diaconate in different churches. My informants represent twenty countries from all continents and 22 church denominations. They represent Lutheran churches from Europe, America and Africa, different types of Methodist churches, as well as representatives from the Anglican Church, the Episcopalian Church, the Batak Christian Protestant Church in Indonesia, the Reformed Church in Switzerland, the United Church of Canada, etc.

The two main questions that I will focus on and discuss in this chapter are the questions: 'What are the most important tasks in your job?', and 'How would you describe your role as a deacon/deaconess/diaconal worker in the church and in society?'

Many of the responses talk about being a servant, but also being a bridge-builder – building bridges between the church and local society, between the daily life of the people in the community and the liturgy in the church, and between individuals in the community. Based on these practical experiences, I discuss the role of the deacon as one who 'goes between', using the theory of the Australian theologian John Collins to shed light on this perspective. But I also use documents from organisations like Eurodiaconia, LWF (Lutheran World Federation) and WCC (World Council of Churches) to discuss the role of the deacon in different contexts today.

[1] Diakonia's tasks: reflects on the nature and task of *diakonia* in the biblical context, links and gathers those who are engaged in diaconal work worldwide, encourages, supports and empowers the development of groups doing diaconal work, and is a living experience of ecumenical relationships:
www.diakonia-world.org/en/main/whoweare.shtml

Method

The questionnaire I used had seven questions. The first four relate to information about nationality, church denomination, place of work and title. Among the titles, the alternatives were: deacon, deaconess, diaconal worker, others. The three main questions were:

> How does your church describe *diakonia*?
> What are the most important tasks in your job?
> How would you describe your role as a deacon/deaconess/diaconal worker in the church and in society?

In this chapter I will not compare the different denominations, but when I quote my informants, I will give their denomination and country in brackets to show the variety. Among the responses I find that most of the informants are deacons (total 19) or deaconesses (total 23). Diaconal worker, diaconal minister, reverend, priest and volunteer are also categories mentioned, but they are mentioned only 1-3 times each.

I made a matrix of all the answers and numbered them consecutively, and show these numbers after the quotations in the text.

What is a Deacon?

Diakonia is an integral part of 'being church', and in principle *diakonia* is the responsibility and task of the whole church and not only of specialists. In this way *diakonia* has many practitioners, both volunteers and employed, varying with different confessional traditions and specific circumstances. The group of volunteers is the biggest, and the fact is that most diaconal work is done by lay people. All baptised are challenged to live in a diaconal way "as an expression of a new lifestyle empowered by God's Holy Spirit."[2]

Some people have professional training and competence to do diaconal work, in congregations, organisations or institutions. Among these groups we find deacons, deaconesses and diaconal pastors. Other professions may be nurses and other health workers, social workers, teachers, but also people with administrative or economic competence who are all working to secure the professionalism and quality of diaconal work.

Deacons and deaconesses have been trained and employed for diaconal work in an explicit way. From the very beginning, such education was interdisciplinary.

Deaconesses were trained as nurses, but they also received solid theological training. In Germany, this is often referred to as a 'double qualification', bearing in mind the two distinct spaces, clinic and church, in which the student

---

[2] LWF, 2009:69.

is qualified to act.[3] Deacons and deaconesses today also have this double qualification that enables them to work both in the church and in society, and they can have their training from different health professions, social work, education, etc.

In many churches there has been established a diaconate as a part of the church's ministry. In the Lutheran church in Sweden and in Brazil, deacons are recognised as an integral part of the ordained ministry, while other churches reserve the term 'ordination' for pastors, and use the term 'commissioning' or 'consecration' for deacons when they start their official ministry.[4] In other churches, like the Catholic and Anglican churches, we can find the so-called 'transitory diaconate', which means that before a person can be ordained a priest, she or he should be part of the order of deacons for a time.

The situation for deacons varies in different church traditions but can be summarised as follows:

- Some deacons have mainly liturgical functions and are regarded as in transit to other church positions.
- Some deacons work in the social field within the church, involved in educational ministries, community-building, pastoral care and so on.
- Some deacons are commissioned by the church to serve in institutions for care-giving and/or social welfare outside the church.
- Some deacons are volunteers and have their own diaconal institution within the church and are represented on church governing bodies.[5]

Diakonia belongs to the essence of the church as part of the 'serving church.' This author holds to the view that the ministry of deacons ought to be fully recognised within the church. It should be more than a stopgap for those in transit to other church positions. The vision that *diakonia* is at the heart of the church should also become visible in church structures and church policy-making. To find answers about this it is necessary to do further research into the position of the deacons and also into questions about ordination.

In my meeting with deacons and deaconesses in the Diakonia World Federation, I received several presentations of the role of the deacon in different churches, and in the following I will present some of them.

The Church of Scotland said the following about the role of the deacon:

> A Deacon is a man or woman who, under a call from God, has pledged himself or herself to the service for Jesus Christ and His Church, and has been selected, trained and ordained according to the doctrine and discipline of the Church of Scotland. The office of deacon is recognised by the Church to be a distinctive, life-long Office within the ministry of the Church, and to be agreeable to the Word of God … We (the deacons) tend to serve in areas of great need and scarce resources. We 'grow where we're planted', discerning the gifts and the needs of

[3] LWF, 2009:75.
[4] LWF, 2008:71.
[5] Eurodiaconia, 2004:28.

> the community; working with individuals and groups at grassroots level, nurturing relationships, offering pastoral support, training and education; aiming at all times to equip people with skills that gifts may be shared to the benefit of each, to build bridges between church and world, to minister to one another; contextualising the gospel in our day to day living.[6]

The Uniting Church in Australia recognises two expressions of ordained ministry: the Ministry of the Word and the Ministry of Deacon. Together with the whole people of God, they share in the mission of God in the world. They say:

> Deacons in the Uniting Church are called to be, along with the scattered members of the congregations, a sign of the presence of God in the everyday world; to be especially aware of the places in the community where people are hurt, disadvantaged, oppressed, or marginalised and to be in ministry with them in ways which reflect the special concern of Jesus for them; to recognise, encourage, develop and release those gifts in God's people which will enable them to share in the ministry of caring, serving, healing, restoring, making peace and advocating justice as they go about their daily lives ... Deacons work in community programmes including counselling and health care; new housing projects; advocacy in social welfare; rural resource ministry; justice and education ministries; children's and family ministries, and with youth and young adults. Some deacons work in congregations with a focus on diaconal ministry and fostering the diaconal ministry of the whole people of God.[7]

From *South Africa the deacon from the Anglican Church* gave me the Charge to the Deacons, and here I want to refer some of the main points that express the position of the deacon:

> God calls you (the deacon) to a special ministry of humble service. In the name of Jesus Christ, you are to serve all people, and to seek out particularly the poor, the weak, the sick and the lonely. As a deacon in the Church you are to study the Holy Scriptures, to seek nourishment from them, and to model your life upon them. By your word and example, you are to make Christ and his redemptive love known to those among whom you live and work and worship. You are to interpret to the church the needs, the concerns and hopes of the world.[8]

From *the Methodist Church in Britain* I received a brochure telling about how deacons work in a wide range of settings, with different people, in ways that appear to encompass many different objectives.

> Much of this diversity has arisen as a result of deacons seeking to respond flexibly to the changing needs of the Church in different times and places.

---

[6] The Church of Scotland, Act of General Assembly, 1998.
[7] Report on Ministry in the Uniting Church, 1991 Assembly.
[8] Charge to the deacons in the Anglican Church in South Africa.

> Deacons also bring diverse gifts to their ministries and place these at the disposal of the Church. The Methodist Church in Britain seeks to match these gifts to the needs of particular places by moving and placing deacons through its 'stationing' process. Deacons emphasise how they see their ministry as inherently creative. They see their ministry as contributing towards the wider mission and ministry of the whole Church. They do this by linking together aspects of presence, service, discernment, witness and enabling others.[9]

A deacon from the *Anglican Church of Australia* expresses it this way:

> The deacon is ordained to a ministry reaching out from the church to the world, serving those in need. Some deacons remain as permanent deacons while others remain deacons for a period of time (usual a year) and are then ordained as priests.

In the *Church of Norway* there are written qualifications requirements and service arrangements for deacons stating that the deacon is the leader of the caring ministry in the congregation, and that this is expressed through "loving your neighbour, creating inclusive communities, caring for creation and struggling for justice".[10]

According to the Norwegian Association of Deacons, the deacons may have different tasks and profiles based on local needs and variations in expertise, but all deacons should have a special focus on those at the margins and try to build inclusive communities. Among the deacon's tasks it is especially mentioned that the deacon has good opportunities to co-operate with different groups in local society because of his/her broad competence. In this way the deacon is often a bridge-builder between church and society.[11]

The quotations above show how different churches express the role of the deacon in their written documents. In the following I will refer to the answers from the deacons themselves.

What are the Most Important Tasks for a Deacon?

In my survey I asked the question: what are the most important tasks in your job? The answers in my questionnaires cover many different activities. To make it easier to give an overview I have grouped the tasks under different headings. It is possible to recognise tasks of a caritative character, educational tasks, pastoral and liturgical tasks, administrative tasks and advocacy work.

Among the *caritative tasks* there are many different activities:

Several visiting programmes; visiting the elderly, nursing homes, hospitals, disabled people, etc. Different counselling tasks include social, spiritual and

[9] The Methodist Church in Britain, *Making Connections*.

[10] Definition in Plan of *diakonia*, The Church of Norway, 2008.

[11] Det norske Diakonforbund [The Norwegian Association of Deacons].

medical counselling. A statement says, "the provision of medical advice to Aids/HIV patients". Some have mentioned soup lunches or other food programmes, and social work with those in need of economic support. Also work for victims of domestic violence is mentioned, looking after teenagers in custody, helping immigrants with food, cleaning, taking care of orphans, etc; crisis counselling, talking to people in difficulty and also those needing more acute help. Several types of fellowship group are mentioned – for people in grief, for people with cancer, for people in difficult family situations.

From India, a deaconess describes her ministry among children, taking care of orphan boys and meeting the educational, medical and spiritual needs of women and poor children in rural villages. "The children I minister to are Hindu, and by showing God's love and care we spread the gospel."

Several of the deacons/deaconesses in my survey tell about *tasks of a more educational character.* Some mention that they support programmes for training deacons. Others are teaching nurses. A deacon from the United Methodist Church in the USA says, "I am educating youth and adults about the meaning of the Gospel, and our moral imperative to love the neighbour." A deaconess from Indonesia says, "The most important task in my job is to train the young people to be able to do *diakonia* ministry; for children, old people, church ministry, and to guide the poor, street people." From Tanzania a deaconess says, "The most important task is to teach others how to serve poor people." From Scotland a deacon talks about Christian education in local primary schools through regular school assemblies. This deacon has also produced a 'Bible alive' programme for primary children (9-10 years of age). A deacon from the Church of England tells about the training of lay members for outreach ministries, and empowering others to *diakonia* through service and example. A brochure about deacons in Australia says; "Deacons have a special task to educate the church on justice issues and community needs."[12]

Many of the answers tell about *pastoral and liturgical work of different types*, and a deacon from the Church of England express a totality of the work in this way:

> Being available in prayers, on the margins to serve where needed; parish work, hospital chaplaincy, preaching and teaching, pastoral care, spiritual direction, inter-faith work, social justice and wherever I am needed/asked to go. Taking all this back into the liturgy to enable and encourage others to serve.

From South Africa, a deacon in the Methodist Church tells about "preaching at worship services of the congregation, preaching at geriatric centres, conducting Bible studies, conducting funeral services mainly to non-church members of the community". Others explain that they are preaching the word of God, offering prayers with and for the community, the church and the world,

---

[12] Deacons in the Uniting Church of Australia.

and sharing in a ministry of hospitality at the Eucharist. "The main task of my preaching is to relate the world to God to its practical application in everyday life." One answer is short but clear on this, just saying – "My task is to be a deacon in the liturgy."

The *administrative tasks* are expressed very explicitly in the material by some leaders. A German priest is leading a diaconal company running hospitals, nursing homes, facilities for the disabled, and educational institutions with about 3,000 persons working there. Another answer from Switzerland expresses the work of a leader in a diaconal foundation. A third answer comes from a deacon in England who is doing leadership in a church high school (11-16 years). He expresses that he is "empowering young people to take leadership, facilitating strategic development". There is also an answer from a Mother Superior telling how she administers the Motherhouse and supervises the sisters. These answers all come from leaders in defined leadership positions, but it is easy to find administrative tasks also 'between the lines' in answers from deacons in congregations. An Episcopalian deacon from the USA tells about work to establish links between the parish and the community.

Much organisation and administration is needed to arrange all the activities the deacons and deaconesses talk about, and several mention the necessity of teamwork among the parish staff, and teamwork with members of the congregations and other groups in local society.

Advocacy work is also part of what deacons do. this is mentioned several times in different ways in my material, both under this question and the next. The actual word is used several times, like the voice from Canada saying, "I am doing advocacy for the marginalised." And from Switzerland – about the role of the deacon: "Advocacy for diaconal challenges in church and society."

To be advocate for people in need, and to act boldly as transformative signs of hope, is a challenge for *diakonia*, and several of the deacons tell how they advocate for peace and justice.

> In society my role is to discover injustice and needs, and bring these to the attention of the Christian community and others, and help to bring resources to bear in helping find creative solutions (United Methodist Church, USA).
>
> Working with community groups as advocate for the homeless and addicted.
>
> Advocate for justice, sharing in the church's justice ministries, standing beside people who are disadvantaged or oppressed, encouraging others to work for justice and calling the church to costly actions (Uniting Church in Australia).[13]

A deacon from the Anglican Church in Canada also expresses the need for advocacy for deacons in the Anglican tradition. Others express advocacy work

---

[13] Deacons in the Uniting Church of Australia.

by referring to access to healthcare for all, working with social justice, bringing the church to attentiveness about prejudice.

Diaconal activities are always conditioned and challenged by concrete contexts, and all contexts are multifaceted and require an interdisciplinary approach. My way of grouping the tasks could have been different, but in my material I found these categories useful.

The Role of the Deacon – in the Church and in Society?

The main question in my survey was the last one: how would you describe your role as a deacon – in the church and in society? Here I find a lot of different answers, and to indicate the variety I will give some examples. Many informants express the main task to be the love of Christ in action, 'the gospel in action',[14] both in the church and in society. 'Serving people' is mentioned in several answers, and service is expressed both as service in the congregation and in society, and also as service for Christ.

It is of course not surprising that the word 'service' is frequently used since that is the translation of the Greek work *diakonia*. 'My role is to serve people in need' is the short answer from a deaconess in Tanzania, or 'to be among people as one who serves', as a deaconess from Guyana says. But longer answers also express service as a main focus.

> To participate in God's love for the whole creation and further God's reign by: helping to equip and encourage all the baptised to serve as Christ served, companioning and serving the suffering and the needy in such a way that they may know Christ's love, and that Christ is served and comforted, helping the church to see the needs present in God's world and to respond out of Christ's love in word and action, to proclaim the Word of God (Evangelical Lutheran Church in America).

It seems as if most of the informants experience their role in the church and in society as being very much linked together, and that the main purpose is always to meet people where they are and to engage in practical ministries of care; to be present and listen on the margins. Responses don't reflect on whether the 'person in need' is inside the church or not. Some express more explicitly how their role in the church and in society gives rise to different challenges, and how they feel the need of trying to link these contexts together. Several use the expression of being a 'bridge-builder'.

> Being a bridge-builder. Being the gospel message alive in a language that children/young people/adults can relate to (Church of Scotland).

[14] Church of Norway National Council 2008.

> Bridge-builder between daily life and the liturgy of the church (Church of England).

> Fostering partnerships and creating bridges between churches and social service agencies, to be better informed of need, and being better prepared to be equipped for meaningful service (Lutheran, USA).

> In my local community we have spent a lot of time creating trust and good relationships with the authorities. I work a great deal with the health system where I am a resource person. I try to be in different places in society to show that I want to co-operate, and after 21 years people know me. I also write in the local newspaper. I hope to be a bridge-builder from the church to local society (Church of Norway).

Quite a few use the concept of being a bridge-builder, but we also find that the expression 'go-between' is used to explain how the deacons view their role. It may seem as if the two expressions are used in a similar way, especially in a statement like this:

> As a deacon I am a representative of God making the servant ministry of Christ present for God's people. I am the 'go-between' taking the church into the community and bringing the concerns and needs of the people to God. I build bridges and facilitate linkage between church and culture. It is primary my role to help the congregation make the fundamental connection between worship and service (Methodist Church, South Africa).

In one of the answers the informant expresses the deacon as being between the church and the secular society:

> Living in a luminal place between church and secular society, called the 'gospel zone'. Bringing an accessible version of church to government, social agencies and the secular university. Breaking down the focus on buildings as the only way of being church (Anglican Church, Canada).

From the Evangelical Lutheran Church of America, a deaconess sums up her role in church and society in this way:

> Care-giver, chaplain, spiritual director, teacher, preacher, leader, facilitator, planner, listener, encourager, event planner, curriculum designer, writer, prayer, follower of Christ, singer, fundraiser, publicity person, companion, equipper, trainer, ponderer, lover. I sing for the dying. Equip and challenge the healthy and gifted, and gather together people from every faith and 'no faith' to discuss what matters, and serve together for a better world.

Perhaps it is time to ask – what does the deacon *not* do?

From Humble Servant to Advocate

It is striking to see how many of the deacons and deaconesses use the words 'bridge-builder' and 'go-between' to explain their role in church and society. This relates to an interesting development in the identity of deacons from *humble servants* to *advocates.*

The Protestant renewal of *diakonia* in the 19th century is looked upon as the starting-point of diaconal ministry as we know it today. The diaconal revival in Germany inspired church leaders in many European countries to establish diaconal institutions focusing on caritative work and education, especially within social work and nursing. Over the years this led to a stronger rise of congregational *diakonia* as well. The focus of the deacons' and deaconesses' role at this time was on servanthood – to serve the neighbour in need, to meet practical needs in church and society. As mentioned earlier. the word 'deacon' comes from the Greek word *diakonos* which means 'service', and the service is a response to the need of people. The main understanding seems to be that the *diakonos* was a servant who served at the table, and that humble service was the main focus.[15]

In my material we can see that many of the informants focus on service, like the following statements connected with the question in my research about what deacons do: 'the special ministry of humble service', 'serving those in need', 'to serve as Christ served'.

John Collins' Reinterpretation of the Deacon's Role

As already mentioned in the introduction chapter of this book, the Australian theologian John Collins questioned the interpretation of the deacon's role as serving at the table and as 'humble service for the poor'. According to Collins, the Greeks were familiar with the word 'deacon' as a title for someone who was involved in the accomplishment of a task or in the delivery of a gift, but also as waiters at religious festivals that included meals.[16] In Collins' presentation it seems as if the *diakonos* was never standing alone and independent in his tasks. Behind the *diakonos* there was always a person or a group of people to whom the *diakonos* was responsible in carrying out a task. The *diakonos* stands in relation to someone else who has mandated a task to him or her.[17] Rather than being a humble servant, Collins says that the deacon is a 'go-between' entrusted with an important message. The deacon is doing something in the name of another. As an agent, the deacon has a mandate as well as a personal obligation.[18]

---

[15] Oftestad, 2001:237.
[16] Collins, 2002:90-91.
[17] Collins, 2002:89.
[18] Collins, 1990:194.

Critical voices have been raised against Collins' interpretation, but it seems as if Collins' study of *diakonia* is important for a broader understanding of the role of the deacon. The British writer and lecturer in Biblical studies, Paula Gooder, in an article named 'Diakonia in the New Testament: A Dialogue with John N. Collins' offers some interesting reflections on this. She writes:

> It (Collins' theory) represents a shift of perspective on the understanding of *diakonia* in New Testament and other early texts that cannot be ignored. Whether one agrees with Collins or not, his case is so persuasively put that it must be explored and debated. In my view the most significant and persuasive outcome of Collins' interpretation is that ministry is not primarily about caring for one's neighbours but about fulfilling a task commissioned by a master (whether this be in the case of a 'normal' servant or in the case of a servant of God or of the church). This change of focus is immensely helpful as it centres the attention on the primary motivation of ministry which is the fulfilling of God's calling, not just the care of one's neighbour.[19]

The Deacon's Role of Go-Between

When my informants have used the concept 'go-between', they are talking about how they bring the church in and out of the community by offering help and support to those who suffer, and encouraging others to use their gifts, and then bringing the concerns and needs of the people back to the church and to God. They express an understanding of a 'two-way' sense of direction.

According to John Collins' theory, the deacon's role is to be a messenger from the master (God) to his people. The deacon is given an important task by an important authority. The role of the deacon is not to humble oneself, but an awareness that God loves and sends. Service is to be seen as a service of God: *why* the deacon does this service, more than on an awareness of love (God's love) for one's neighbour, and *how* this love is expressed. Paula Gooder writes:

> We must be very clear that adopting this view does not mean that we abandon humble care for our neighbour; rather that we focus more on why we do it. The primary reason for caring for our neighbour is doing what God requires. This has roots far back in the Judæo-Christian tradition and passages such as the famous Micah 6.8: 'what does the Lord require of you but to do justice, and to love kindness, and to walk humbly with your God?' It is also supported by the often cited 'Servant of the Lord' in Isaiah. The Isaianic servant songs are regularly used by people to illustrate the biblical background to a doctrine of service. It is important to recognise, however, that the role of the servant is not menial waiting at table but the fulfilment of God's vision for those in Exile.[20]

---

[19] Gooder, 2008.
[20] Gooder, 2008.

Reading Collins this way will not undermine the importance of humble care for one's neighbour within the Christian tradition. As followers of Christ, all Christians are called to follow Christ's example and wash each other's feet, to seek not to be first but to be last, to subvert hierarchies and the love of power which characterises all societies, whether ancient or modern. But as Gooder says:

> What this redefinition does, however, is to question whether this understanding is the basic understanding of *diakonia* in the New Testament. It is possible that one's commissioned task would be humble care for others. What Collins' theory denies is that this is always the case in all instances of *diakonia*. What Collins tries to do is to disentangle the notions of humble service and *diakonia*. He does not deny that the two do have connections; he just argues that they are not synonymous. In this I find his theories entirely convincing.[21]

The consequence of Collins' theory is perhaps to widen the role of the deacon from the situation where the deacon's role has been characterised primarily in terms of humble service for people in need. The role of the deacon is instead associated with the carrying out of a commissioned task, a task commissioned by the church, the bishop, or God himself. This opens up a greater reflection on the specific role of the deacon. At the same time, it is important to say that when we open this broader reflection, the purpose is not to remove it from the requirement all Christians have, not only the deacons: to love and take care of one's neighbour.

Go-Between = Bridge-Builder

According to Collins' theory, the classical Greek use of the word *diakonia* points to the mission of a go-between role, being a messenger or even an ambassador. The concept had a principal focus on the direction from the authority to the people. Collins as a theologian focused on the word *diakonos* from a theological and ecclesiological perspective. The messenger received his significance from God who sent him.

The concept of the go-between role has been explored further in the diaconal field – both in theory and in practical diaconal work. The Norwegian Professor of *Diakonia*, Kjell Nordstokke, has processed Collins' thoughts in several of his books, and we also recognise the concept of go-between and bridge-building in several other documents, as in *Diakonia in Context*[22] from the Lutheran World Federation, in the report from Eurodiaconia *Diaconal*

[21] Gooder, 2008.
[22] LWF, 2009.

Identity: Faith in Social Care,[23] and in the document *Theological Perspectives in Diakonia in 21st Century*[24] from the World Council of Churches.

The concept of go-between also focuses the tasks, as expressed in John 20:21b: "As the Father has sent me, I also send you."[25] Today the concept is used quite often about one who has been mandated to restore relationships, to heal and to reconcile – as we can read in the LWF study document *Diakonia in Context.*[26] The concept seems to be used in a very similar way to the concept of being a bridge-builder, and in fact, deacons were already in ancient times crossing bridges between the people and the church. In *Diakonia in Context* we can read:

> The task of being a bridge-builder is integral to the very nature of *diakonia*. In the Ancient Church, the deacon was called 'the ear and the mouth of the bishop'. It was the deacon who had the responsibility to bring the stories from the margins, from the lives of the poor and the sick into the church. The mission of go-between is successful if distances can be bridged. When this happens, diaconal involvement can contribute to transformation of the church – both in its centre and periphery.[27]

I see that many of the deacons in my research are using the word 'bridge-builder' to describe their role, and they are building different bridges between the church and the society. For deacons doing practical work, it is natural to look at the task also from the perspective of social studies. From this perspective relationships are central. Diaconal activities are relational, in the sense that all diaconal activity, including those addressing immediate needs, are embedded in a comprehensive mandate of building relationships. Many of my informants are talking about being a bridge-builder – between the church and local society, between daily life and the liturgy of the church.

> I am the 'go-between' to take the church into the community and bringing the concerns and needs of the people to God. I build bridges and facilitate passage between church and culture.

Another informant expresses her role this way:

> My role is accompanying people in grief, loneliness, and joy and celebration – a ministry of presence.

As a diaconal method, accompaniment seeks to overcome isolation and exclusion, and to identify pathways that may offer opportunities for a broader

[23] Eurodiaconia, 2010.
[24] World Council of Churches, 2012.
[25] The New Testament, New King James Version.
[26] LWF, 2009:46-47.
[27] LWF, 2009:46.

sharing in mutual solidarity. A go-between needs the capacity to listen to different versions of a story, and to see why such differences emerge. Then there is the necessity of really going between, of building bridges of understanding and acceptance. Again, this is related to communion-building, of identifying processes of reconciliation and of inclusion. There are endless situations which call for the diaconal involvement of bridge-building, both inside and outside the church. The picture of the deacon as a bridge-builder is recognising this perspective. A bridge is a construction made to carry people both ways.

It is possible to say that the two concepts are expressing the same thing, but there are also some differences. I think that my informants use the concepts in parallel, but I would like to focus on another small difference. The picture of a bridge is something built to give access from one place to another. The concept of go-between is more open. It can be more like a movement between people at different places and in different situations. For a deacon both aspects are important, both to be able to build more permanent bridges and to be able to move between people in changing situations and in varying contexts.

Neither a go-between nor a bridge-builder can be silent. Communication is a basic component. This communication often needs to be patient and diplomatic, but there are also situations when communication has to be prophetic, lifting up the voice of the silent and the suffering.[28] Deacons and deaconesses must also act as advocates for people in need and as signs of hope. The mission of go-between is successful if distances can be bridged. The task of being a bridge-builder is integral to the very nature of *diakonia*. When this happens, diaconal involvement can contribute to transformation within the church – both in its centre and on its periphery.

Conclusion

In this chapter I have presented some results from a qualitative study among deacons and deaconesses. The study was done during a World Assembly arranged by the Diakonia World Federation in the summer of 2013. These deacons and deaconesses have been trained and employed for diaconal work, and I have asked them what they actually do in their job in congregations and institutions. The answers show that they are working with a wide range of tasks, and I have categorised these into caritative tasks, education, pastoral and liturgical tasks, administration and advocacy tasks. Each category shows that *diakonia* looks different in different contexts, but that there are a lot of similar experiences and reflections connected with the role of the deacon in the church and in society.

It would seem that the answers from the deacons and the deaconesses of today correspond with the understanding of the deacon as a servant of people in

---

[28] LWF, 2009:47.

need, but not only that. The answers very much underline that deacons also see themselves as bridge-builders and advocates. Deacons and deaconesses describe in many ways their identity in the answers they have given, and this identity is not limited to just *one* understanding of the word *diakonos*. The practical work of deacons widens the traditional concept to include that of servant, go-between, bridge-builder and advocate. I want to close with a statement from an informant about her understanding of her role as a deacon:

> Imaging what the best experiences of care is.
> Sometimes waiting alongside people in need.
> Drawing others into caring ministry.
> Speaking out on behalf of others about what is unjust in the community.
> Listening on the margins and engaging in conversations, transformations.
> Bridge-builder between daily life and the liturgy of the church.
> Enabling a ministry of hospitality of table and by being open church.
> Reflect on grassroots theology and practice (Church of England).

Bibliography

Church of Norway National Council, *Plan for diakonia in the Church of Norway* (Church of Norway National Council: 2008).

Collins, John N., *Diakonia. Re-interpreting the Ancient Sources* (New York: Oxford University Press, 1990).

Collins, John N., *Deacons and the Church. Making connections between old and new* (Leominster, UK: Gracewing, 2002).

Det norske Diakonforbund: www.diakonforbundet.no/index.php/diakon (accessed 6 March 2014).

Diakonia World Organisation. www.diakonia-world.org/en/main/whoweare.shtml (accessed 5 February, 2014).

Dietrich, Stephanie, Kari Karsrud Korslien and Kjell Nordstokke (eds), *Diakonen – kall og profesjon* (Trondheim: Tapir Akademisk forlag, 2011).

Eurodiaconia, *Diaconal Identity: Faith in Social Care. A Reflection from Eurodiaconia* (Brussels: Eurodiaconia, 2010).

Eurodiaconia, *To be and to do – Diaconia and the Churches* (Brussels: Eurodiaconia, 2004).

Gooder, Paula, *Diakonia in the New Testament: A Dialogue with John N. Collins,* in Ecclesiology 8/2006; 3, No. 1:33-56.

Lutheran World Federation, *Diakonia in Context: Transformation, Reconciliation, Empowerment. An LWF Contribution to the Understanding and Practice of Diakonia* (Geneva: LWF, 2009).

Oftestad, Alf B. (ed), *En bok om kirkens diakoni* (Oslo: Luther Forlag 1980).

The New Testament – New King James Version 1982.

World Council of Churches, *Theological Perspectives on Diakonia in 21st Century* (Colombo, Sri Lanka 2012).

Reports/brochures

The Church of Scotland, *Diaconal Ministry. Variety of Gifts, variety of service* (Act of General Assembly 1998).

The Uniting Church in Australia, *Deacons in the UCA. Celebrating 20 years in 2012.*

Charge to the deacons in the Anglican Church in South Africa (received 2013).

The Methodist Church in Britain, *Making connections* (University of Durham, 2012).

Diakonia as Action: Some Perspectives on Diaconial Professional Practice

Kari Karsrud Korslien

Private faces in public places
Are wiser and nicer
Than public faces in private places

W.H. Auden[1]

This article focuses on the relationship between knowledge about *diakonia* and *diakonia* as action. The author assumes there is a paradigm shift in reflections about *diakonia*, and this shift indicates renewed understanding of deed and action. 'Diaconal action' is used in this article to describe Christians' deeds and acts for responsible service. In recent literature on *diakonia* the method 'see – reflect – act' is recommended in practical *diakonia*. Several values are held to be of core importance in diaconal praxis, and the author reflects on how they are articulated in professional diaconal work and what kind of professionalism diaconal workers need. The author is herself trained as a deacon, a social worker and a teacher in *diakonia*. This article gives some perspectives on diaconal professional practice based on interdisciplinary knowledge and experiences from diaconal and social work.

Paradigm Shift

The paradigm of *diakonia* as humble service has changed into an understanding of *diakonia* as solidarity work and advocacy among and with the marginalised and poor. Our challenge as Christians is to develop *diakonia* that boldly acts in favour of suffering and marginalised people, committed to the cause of lifting up justice, peace and the integrity of creation.[2] The Church of Norway explains *diakonia* as the gospel in action expressed through loving your neighbour, creating inclusive communities, caring for creation, and struggling for justice.[3] The change indicates care for both people and creation. Both professionals and

[1] From W.H. Auden, 'Shorts'.
[2] LWF, *Diakonia in context,* 16.
[3] Church of Norway, *Plan for diakonia* (Oslo: Church of Norway, 2008). Plan of diakonia was adopted in 2007 and translated into English in 2009.

volunteers are invited to participate in the field of *diakonia*. Nordstokke uses the term *diakonia* to indicate a certain praxis, a social framework that gives a specific identity as church in its widest understanding, and a disciplined reflection (theory) in order to systematise what is being done in a professional way.[4] Nordstokke focuses on a specific praxis conceived of as diaconal, expressing a distinct identity as a church, and at the same time, a disciplined and critical reflection on what is being done. 'Professional praxis' as a term refers mainly to professional diaconal work. What is meant is activity performed by deacons or other professional workers engaged in the field of *diakonia*. The paradigm shift mentioned above is an expression of what deacons and other professionals, together with others in the field of *diakonia*, are able to create. When 'praxis' is used as a term in this article, it is reflecting the whole field of professional diaconal work in co-operation with vulnerable people, but also with volunteers from church congregations. Praxis is therefore done by a set of participants who may or may not have specific professional qualifications.

In the following I will use some characteristics given by Kjell Nordstokke and John Collins to discuss renewed *diakonia* as action.[5] Like Nordstokke and Collins, I ask what kind of diaconal praxis is to be seen as a result of the new understanding of *diakonia*. Nordstokke and Collins list some items that may belong to the new paradigm of *diakonia* in our time. These characteristics are: 1) A new role as agent, 2) A new authority, 3) A new language, 4) A new logic and 5) New methods. This list indicates clear shifts in diaconal work, and the introduction of new values. The question however is how they can lead to a renewed *diakonia* in action. In the following I will focus on some ways to take this further, affirming the assumption that the discussion of how *diakonia* could be done will continue, since *diakonia* is both a dynamic and contextual phenomenon.

Expand Key Methods

Nordstokke and Collins claim that the role of professionals in the field of *diakonia* has changed

> … from a role of professional employee, where others are often reduced to being clients, to a role of facilitator, animator and enabler. The intention here is to give others, especially those on the periphery, a status as subjects and agents who also operate within God's project with humankind.[6]

---

[4] Kjell Nordstokke, *Liberating diakonia*, 103.

[5] Kjell Nordstokke and John Collins, 'Diakonia – theory and praxis', in *Liberating diakonia* (Trondheim: Tapir, 2011), 41-53

[6] Nordstokke and Collins, 'Diakonia – theory and praxis', 46.

This role is intimately linked with the claim of a new authority, outlined as a change from servility and silent service into prophetic *diakonia.* When referring to this new language, they present it as an inclusive way of speaking where the perspective of the voiceless and disempowered is defended. The new logic implies praxis as a starting-point for critical reflection and for developing knowledge based on experience. In their discussion of new methods they state:

> In this time when new mechanisms of exclusion are at work in both church and society, *diakonia* has a special mandate to identify mechanisms of inclusion, to point at possible opportunities of diaconal praxis, and to develop methods that express its new role, new authority, new language and new logic.[7]

The call for new methods in a new paradigm of *diakonia* is clearly value-based as it builds on arguments from both theology and ethics. As a diaconal church, we may however ask how people engaged in *diakonia* will be able to realise this vision in action.

One important method that has been developed has given a deeper insight when searching for a renewed *diakonia* as action – and one which is presented in the LWF study document *Diakonia in Context* – is the method of 'see – reflect – act'.[8] For professional diaconal workers this method offers useful tools for linking theory with praxis. The first step in the method, to see, refers to a thorough analysis of what is being done as a response to diaconal challenges, by using the insight of social sciences and other relevant disciplines, in order to get an authentic picture of the context in which the diaconal action takes place.[9] The second step, to reflect, is more hermeneutical and seeks to interpret what is seen and analysed. The dialectic interaction between what we see and how we reflect is of great importance and helps to develop interdisciplinary knowledge. The third step, to act, will bring insights from the first two steps into the arena of diaconal action. It is however interesting that the description of this method differs a bit from what Leonard Boff has described in his book *Salvation and Liberation* where he labelled the method as 'see, judge and act'. He emphasises the importance of the perception of misery and underlines ethical religious indignation and protest against injustice.[10] In his view, the emotional reaction may be the first impulse that sparks action. It seems as though seeing and sensing are interconnected. In this article, sensing is interesting when seen in connection with the inspiration of action, the quality of action and professional practise.

---

[7] Nordstokke and Collins, 'Diakonia – theory and praxis', 47.

[8] LWF, *Diakonia in context.*

[9] LWF, *Diakonia in context*, 59.

[10] Leonard Boff, 'Salvation in liberation: The theological meaning of Socio-historical Liberation', in Leonard and Clodovis Boff, *Salvation and Liberation in Search of a Balance between Faith and Politics* (Maryknoll, NY: Orbis, 1984), 1-13.

Bearing in mind the five above-mentioned characteristics for new *diakonia*, and as a further reflection on relevant methods in *diakonia*, it may be interesting to ask: who are the professionals in the field of *diakonia*? What kind of knowledge is already familiar and activated in the process of developing specific diaconal work organised by the churches, diaconal institutions or organisations? Are, for instance, the values of empowerment and participation applied in the everyday life of *diakonia*? Does the logic start with experience and praxis, or is the logic based on other traditions? For example, when working with vulnerable children, most of us would most likely conclude with the importance of action and empowerment as critical issues. The children's descriptions of both their situations and their ideas of what kind of help is needed are part of the solution. Moreover, we must recognise the significance of relational competence among professionals. From a theological perspective, *diakonia* is a collaborative project where God, professional diaconal workers and fellow human beings are imagined to share. In such a case, the professional herself and her understanding of involvement and relationship will be of great importance. Personal development is often seen therefore as a necessary part of the professional training and equipping of diaconal workers. *Diakonia* in action is in many ways dependent on professional practitioners and their willingness to explore how to build competence, including competence as a possible facilitator, animator and enabler, in co-operation with others.

Some Challenges

Financial crises, social chaos and political paralysis challenge the church to assume new roles in arenas of needs. It seems however that the church quite often struggles to reach out to the most vulnerable. *Diakonia* has been criticised for not being bold enough in its action, and for not addressing the most important diaconal challenges.[11] I see the validity of this critical point of view, and also recognise the relevance of what has been described as 'heterotopic *diakonia*'.[12] Such *diakonia* aims at working together with and among marginalised groups on their own conditions both inside and outside the church. It remains an important challenge to open up typical church-based arenas for others than those who apparently belong to traditional church activities in the first place. On the other hand, I like to ask what kind of consequence an outsourcing of challenging *diakonia* causes to the inclusive

---

[11] Charlotte Engel, 'Social Work in the Church of Sweden – For whom and why? A religious-sociological study of a deaconry dilemma', in Charlotte Engel, *Svenska kyrkans sosiale arbete – för vem och varför? En religionssosiologisk studie av ett diakonalt dilemma* (Uppsala: Ersta Söndal Högskola, 2006), 255-64.

[12] Trygve Wyller, 'Heterotopisk diakoni', in Roger Jensen, Dag Torkildsen and Aud V. Tønnesen (eds), *Kirke, protestantisme og samfunn* (Trondheim: Tapir akademisk forlag, 2006), 309-23. See also Wyller (ed.), *Heterotopic Citizen New Research on Religious Work for the Disadvantaged* (Göttingen: Vandenhoeck & Ruprecht, 2009)

fellowship in ordinary congregations. Both traditional and heterotopic praxis are interesting to analyse according to renewed *diakonia*. According to the rapport *Seeking Conviviality: Re-forming Community Diakonia in Europe*, it seems *diakonia* has two possibilities: one is to create a stronger diaconal identity in ordinary congregations while the other is to organise diaconal work outside the institutional church with bigger or smaller groups of marginalised people.[13] The question is whether the first one becomes too traditional, and also in which way the other is different from the first one. It might be too difficult to organise both within the same geographic space. However, I find it interesting to develop *diakonia* in a way that gives opportunity to all involved, both traditional and non-traditional participants, to be engaged in diaconal activities with the possibility of making choices when developing *diakonia* locally without any separation between the two forms.

In my opinion, separation is not only about the work itself, but about attitudes towards participants. When they are categorised as people with specific challenges or as a target group, they are often treated differently from the core groups of the congregation. An example could be addicts and members of Bible study groups who are invited to church during the week. The Bible study group members are often looked upon as a part of the church and defined as insiders, while the others are often associated with target groups and in a way defined as outsiders. Critically, I like to ask if the congregation operates a two-tier system of membership. On the other hand, there may be participants who like to be a part of the fellowship, but don't recognise themselves as a part of the congregation. On the other, some people appreciate being included in activities, but not on the same ideological grounds and conditions as the core group. In developing diaconal competence, diaconal workers need tools to renew ways of practising fellowship and being engaged with people of different mindsets and opinions. Diakonia is created in a field where the community consists of people with different opinions and varying degrees of association with the ideological foundation. In a way, *diakonia* as action challenges our compassion and willingness to open up for diversity. It is a question of what we see as a diaconal church, how we reflect on, and how we choose to take action in, renewed *diakonia*.

The Process of Learning

To make a fully authentic picture of the situation in diaconal work is perhaps unrealistic, but professional diaconal workers have some new and interesting tools in order to obtain a more trustworthy picture of the situation, relationships and challenges in the field of praxis. To get a fuller picture, we may learn with

[13] LWF, *Seeking Conviviality: Re-forming Community Diakonia in Europe* (Geneva: Lutheran World Federation, 2013).

others in a systematic way, by the method called 'Exposure'.[14] In brief, Exposure is a process of learning. Exposure is only possible in groups; people from the field of *diakonia* can practise Exposure together to improve their local diaconal work, and it may be an interesting way of developing diaconal competence. The method indicates systematic reflection on what you are seeing, what you feel about what you are see, and lastly what you think about what you are seeing and feeling.[15]

According to the method used, this will expand one's horizon of understanding. The group spends time in one place, which may or may not be familiar to participants, and a key factor is that they have no specific task or role to perform. This may be unusual for many people in the field of *diakonia* who are often occupied with relationships, responsibility and tasks. "Everyone in the group should use their senses, all of them, to deeply observe the place to which they are sent."[16] Often they pass through the same area several times in silence. Later on, they should write down what they have seen.

Other exercises are given in a process with the purpose of creating room for reflection, but first of all the participants enter an imagined room of emptiness. This room, called 'empty space', gives the opportunity to be aware of ready-made concepts and interpretations. As an exercise, they should try to reduce the impressions to one symbol which they then draw on a piece of paper and later share with the group. Afterwards the group takes part in more explicit exchange about what was seen and experienced linked with their own lives. They enter a place in silence and reflect upon their life story. All of them make a rope with knots that they tie for special events in their life. They don't share the events, but share what it's like to reflect upon these events in the context where they have been sitting or walking around while seeing and reflecting. This is not a strictly therapeutic move, but a way of opening up for reflections and insight. This experience will often be of value in relation to others later on, and a way of learning to open up and grasp challenges one is not familiar with. Sharing with others, hearing each other's stories based on experiences from one and the same place, lead to richer and more varied stories than we are able to figure out as individuals, and in this way Exposure is a process of learning by diversity. My experiences with Exposure, together with master students in *diakonia,* convince me that it has great relevance for professional work in a diversified context.[17]

---

[14] Tony Addy, 'New approaches to community-based work, social service, and Diakonia. Challenges from the CABLE Approach', in *Diaconia. Journal for the Study of Christian Social Practice.* 4:2 (Göttingen: Vandenhoeck & Ruprecht, 2013), 194-215.

[15] Per Starke, *Exposure – som synsätt, forhöllningssätt och arbetssätt* (Lund: Arcus, 2010).

[437] Addy, 'New approaches to community-based work', 201.

[17] In Stephanie Dietrich, Kari Karsrud Korslien and Kjell Nordstokke, *Diakonen – kall og profesjon* (Trondheim: Tapir, 2011). Arild Notland and Kari Karsrud Korslien have written about the method and about their experiences in a Norwegian context.

Prejudices are often the reason for not developing diaconal work. It may therefore be interesting to reinforce the perspective of marginalised and vulnerable people with whom *diakonia* should be developed. In order to ensure such development, *diakonia* should be established in areas that are outside the comfort zone of deacons, pastors and other professionals. Instead of taking over responsibility from the various marginalised groups they would like to create *diakonia* together with, they should create opportunities to act and to be participants in developing a relevant *diakonia*. The roles of facilitator, animator and enabler are important in creating a new *diakonia*, and even more so the role of listener. A professional who is able to motivate others based on such roles is performing what we could call diaconal competence, creating space for action where deacons and other professionals, together with other participants, promote a renewed praxis. We define it as a public space for action where people are equal, and everyone is invited to participate under the same conditions and are equally free to talk and act. Working in programmes of Exposure may offer a fresh start and would fully enable professional work on empathy, trust and the interpersonal relationships based on personal subjects.[18] Such work develops participants in the diaconal field. When experience of Exposure confronts us with this 'empty space', hopefully it may afterwards more easily open up opportunities for action, diversity and co-operation.

Working Together in the Field of Diakonia

Within the field of *diakonia,* professionals, vulnerable people and volunteers are involved. In most congregational activities people participate because they are members. This is not necessarily the case when it comes to diaconal work. People are free to attend and have no status as client or patient. In spite of life's differences, people are defined as one common fellowship in the spirit of Christ. The Norwegian Plan for Diakonia states: "There are periods in life when we have the ability and possibility of giving, while at others times we need to receive. Reciprocity is a key word."[19] Every Christian is called to participate in God's project with humankind, but as deacons or other professionals we are given a specific responsibility to create open space for action among people. However, as Jesus has shown, we should do it by taking a step back, allowing others to initiate diaconal effort. Such co-operation among all involved is one way of exploring renewed *diakonia*, but it may be asked whether taking a backwards step is enough. If the involvement and engagement come from others, hopefully they will be able to create new and open spaces for *diakonia* themselves without the assistance of professional leaders. The role of professional diaconal workers may therefore be flexible and contextually oriented.

---

[18] Addy, 'New approaches to community-based work', 203.
[19] Church of Norway, *Plan for Diakonia*, 9.

We are aware of the fact that fresh initiatives often empower others to take new initiatives themselves. I do not think deacons or other leaders will have any problems in taking a backwards step, but as leaders of diaconal work in the congregations there may be a lot to learn from what is called 'boundary leadership'. The practice of boundary leadership may be of interest as a specific method in diaconal work.[20] Boundary leadership is defined as the practice of leadership in the 'boundary zone', the space between settled zones of authority where relationships are more fluid, dynamic and itinerant. When professionals and others in the field of *diakonia* co-operate with marginalised people or others in need, this can be an example of being in the boundary zone. Professionals have to build trust and companionship where people often conclude that there are no possibilities. For instance, the boundaries arise from social, economic and cultural differences. But at the heart of the idea of boundary leadership lies a way of seeing such boundaries that appear disconnected but in reality are not. Leaders are working together across the boundaries of public, private and community-based agencies. Professionals may therefore practise a kind of flexible leadership where possibilities are seen and confirmed. In company with others, deacons or other professionals may have a team that animates others to be in charge as creative leaders and interpreters. The role as listener, coach and supervisor may be more important in those cases than the role as a facilitator, but it depends on the congregation and the context.

The Principle of Intersubjectivity

In my opinion, professionals must be familiar with opportunities in the boundary zone and develop their personal skills with particular emphasis on relation-based skills. A Norwegian philosopher, Hans Skjervheim, explains the importance of intersubjectivity in his essay *Participants and Spectator*.[21] In a conversation with someone, the author says: "The cost of living is bound to increase even more." Skjervheim explains there are two fundamentally different attitudes: I can participate and let myself get engaged in his problem and make a judgement in return. The relationship is triangular – between the other, me and the subject matter – in such a way that the latter is shared between us.[22] But I may also take a different attitude by not letting myself get involved with his problem or caring about the subject he refers to, but simply registering the fact that he refers to it. I register the fact that he says the cost of

[20] Gary R. Gunderson and James R. Cochrane, *Religion and the Health of the Public: Shifting the Paradigm* (New York: Palgrave Macmillan, 2012), 120.

[21] Skjervheim, *Mennesket* (Oslo: Universitetsforlaget, 2002), 20-35, is written in Norwegian, but there is an English version of his most important works published on the occasion of his 70th birthday: Hans Skjervheim, *Selected Essays, In Honour of Hans Skjervheim's 70th Birthday* (Bergen: Department of Philosophy, 1996), 127-41.

[22] Skjervheim, *Mennesket*, 2002: 21.

living will increase. We then have a dual relationship where we do not share the subject matter. As Skjervheim explains, it is like a Chinese box: myself in relation to my subject matter, or fact, and my subject matter, which is in relation to his subject matter. "Each lives in his own world, where the other is a fact for the ego in the ego's world."[23] In other words, the possibility of being involved with each other through something we share have been spoilt.

When the other is seen just as a patient or a client, she or he will often be treated as an object. But it may be the same if the other is seen as a person in need, and the concern for his or her situation is restricted without taking an interest in or care for the whole person. *Diakonia* is oriented by the teaching of Jesus – that everyone is equal before God and belong to the same fellowship even if our opportunities in life differ. This is part of our belief and also our vocation: to take each other seriously, create more inclusive fellowship, empowering each other when it is necessary and taking seriously the challenges that really matter in life. If *diakonia* is to count, it must have an impact on issues that actually matter to people. The ethical position indicated by Skjervheim underpins the importance of serious engagement. That position influences both logic and language. The logic in *diakonia* starts out with believing in people's possibilities and their right to be active citizens and to build society together. This is not a 'new' logic, but it is basic when it comes to believing in an inclusive fellowship where we are all vulnerable and dependent on each other. In my opinion, hospitality is a concrete way of living together with people of different mindsets. It has been said that Skjervheim was a 'friend of the thought of others', and in my opinion that seems to be a kind of inspiring hospitality. The diversity between people allows us to see a richer picture. When giving space for this diversity, the churches become even more attractive as people's real life is reflected in a more authentic way. People involved in *diakonia* are able to see, reflect and act, but *diakonia* as praxis, its identity and our reflections about methods, will always present new challenges because the inter-human condition, according to Skjervheim, in principal is equivocal, not unequivocal.[24] As I see it, his thoughts are a warning against reducing both people to objects, and *diakonia* to behaviour and actions performed by rote.

The Change of Language

The paradigm shift also has an influence on language. The change can be described as a transition from the dichotomy 'them and us' to 'we', because we all belong to the same fellowship where all have status as subjects and agents who together operate within God's project with humankind. This requires us to

---

[23] Hans Skjervheim, *Selected Essays*, 128.

[445] 'The Forgotten Theme: Intersubjectivity' is described further in *Objectivism and the Study of Man,* in Skjervheim, *Selected Essays*, 34-42.

mutually respect each other and people of other faiths, bearing in mind that inclusiveness can never be forced. As stated in *Diakonia in Context*, the human imperative comes first.[25] It seeks to uphold human dignity, to restore broken relationships, and to promote healing and reconciliation to communities. *Diakonia* in action incorporates compassion, inclusiveness, mutuality, respect and accountability as basic values. It seeks ecumenical alliances and has participation, accompaniment and empowerment as its primary methods. Those methods should be essential in diaconal praxis. It is not just in the process of seeing that we should learn from each other, as the method of Exposure teaches us. This attitude is also necessary in reflection and action. In my opinion, performing diakonia is neither a result of a linear nor a chronological process. All involved are dependent on each other and will be influenced by each other. This kind of open-minded attitude is therefore both a way of being and acting. What we see, sense and reflect may change our way of both seeing and acting together. This dynamic process may renew diakonia. We encourage each other, invite and open up, but at the same time we may risk making mistakes and failing. Doing *diakonia* is, in my opinion, a project of hope and we need imagination in order to create new opportunities for even more people to be included in the life and work of the common fellowship. The language we use in *diakonia* must be developed in a way that gives voice to many, and provides trust and faith to a polyphonic expression of *diakonia*.

Conclusion

As Christians, we can be sure that *diakonia* has a future if we risk embarking on new forms of engagement and action, and showing our presence outside our comfort zone. Our response to injustice may help us to get inspired to build better societies together with people who are most affected by injustice. However, we have to work at different levels to succeed. Injustice and the abuse of power can also take place in church congregations. People in the field of *diakonia* have a call to be prophetic about injustice, but *diakonia* must also speak out when indifference prevents development.

People who are involved should assess diaconal work together. We should always seek to develop our competence and praxis, evaluate whether this really is a renewed *diakonia* where people are taking part and are able to share each other's worlds. Sometimes we may recognise what is happening when *diakonia* based on right values is being renewed, but at other times we may not be so sure. As a foundation, we should remember that mercy and justice are twins and we need both of them. The only way we can see if renewed *diakonia* works is in people's ability to feel empathy and compassion with each other in fellowships where people are free to talk and act. In my opinion, all of us should go on trying to develop *diakonia* together. There is no recipe for every

[25] LWF, *Diakonia in context*, 90.

single situation. But we may believe that relations, personal skills, education, and God's good cause, will encourage us all to serve each other as people who also have the opportunity and potential to make a difference. We have to be pathfinders when we follow the greatest commandment: "You shall love the Lord your God with all your heart and with all your soul and with all your strength and with all your mind, and your neighbour as yourself" (Luke 10:27).

We have to deal with the challenge of methods. Contexts will differ, but all contexts have something in common; people should always have the right to talk and act in public, and to participate, and should never be treated like facts or objects. In this way, *diakonia* belongs to mankind.

Bibliography

Addy, Tony, 'New approaches to community-based work, social service, and Diakonia. Challenges from the CABLE approach', in *Diaconia. Journal for the Study of Christian Social Practice,* 4:2 (Göttingen: Vandenhoeck & Ruprecht, 2013).

Auden, W. H., *Collected Shorter Poems 1927-1957* (London: Faber & Faber, 1966).

Boff, Leonard, 'Salvation in liberation: The theological meaning of Socio-historical Liberation', in Leonard and Clodovis Boff, *Salvation and Liberation In Search of a Balance between Faith and Politics* (Maryknoll, NY: Orbis, 1984).

Church of Norway, *Plan for Diakonia* (Oslo: Church of Norway, 2008).

Engel, Charlotte, 'Social Work in the Church of Sweden – For whom and why? A religious-sociological study of a deaconry dilemma', in Charlotte Engel, *Svenska kyrkans sosiale arbete – för vem och varför? En religionssosiologisk studie av ett diakonalt dilemma* (Uppsala: Ersta Söndal Högskola, 2006).

Gunderson, Gary R., and James R. Cochrane, *Religion and the Health of the Public Shifting the Paradigm* (New York: Palgrave Macmillan, 2012).

Korslien, Kari Karsrud, and Notland Arild, 'Metodiske overveielser I diakonalt arbeid', in Stephanie Dietrich, Kari Karsrud Korslien and Kjell Nordstokke, *Diakonen – kall og profesjon* (Trondheim: Tapir, 2011).

Lutheran World Federation, *Diakonia in Context, Transformation, reconciliation, empowerment. An LWF contribution in the understanding and practice of Diakonia* (Geneva: LWF, 2009).

Lutheran World Federation, *Seeking Conviviality: Re-forming Community Diakonia in Europe* (Geneva: Lutheran World Federation, 2013).

Nordstokke, Kjell, *Liberating diakonia* (Trondheim: Tapir, 2011).

Nordstokke, Kjell, and John Collins, 'Diakonia – theory and praxis', in *Liberating diakonia* (Trondheim: Tapir, 2011).

Skjervheim, Hans, *Mennesket* (Oslo: Universitetsforlaget, 2002).

Skjervheim, Hans, *Selected Essays. In Honour of Hans Skjervheim's 70th Birthday* (Bergen: Department of Philosophy, 1996).

Starke, Per, *Exposure – som synsätt, förhöllningssätt och arbetssätt* (Lund: Arcus, 2010).

Wyller, Trygve, 'Heterotopisk diakoni', in Roger Jensen, Dag Torkildsen and Aud V. Tønnesen (eds), *Kirke, protestantisme og samfunn* (Trondheim: Tapir akademisk forlag, 2006).

Wyller, Trygve, *Heterotopic Citizen New Research on Religious Work for the Disadvantaged* (Göttingen: Vandenhoeck & Ruprecht, 2009)

Mapping Out and Mobilising Diaconal Assets

Kjell Nordstokke

We must be the change we want to see in the world

Gandhi

In international co-operation for development,[1] the term 'asset' has been given more attention over the last few years.[2] It is now customary to talk about an asset-based approach as an alternative to the needs-based approach that for a long time has been dominating.[3] This change can also be linked with the stronger emphasis on rights-based development work, which presents targeted people as 'rights-holders', based on the assumption that every person is given basic rights, and that she or he possesses knowledge and skills that should be affirmed and promoted.

This article aims at bringing about a better understanding of 'assets' in relation to so-called faith-based organisations (FBOs) and their role as agencies in development work. It is my assumption that the term 'asset' is a useful concept in presenting their distinct identity and added value. Special attention will be given to FBOs which present themselves as church-based specialised ministries and whose work may be described as diaconal.[4] It has been asked

---

[1] I am applying the term 'development' in a merely descriptive sense, referring to initiatives undertaken by public or voluntary actors in order to promote social welfare in poor countries, mainly in the global South. Using this term, I am fully aware of its questionable ideological connotations and the criticism held, for instance, by theologians in Latin America.

[2] For a presentation of this development, see Kjell Nordstokke, 'Faith-Based Organizations (FBOs) and their Distinct Assets', in Kenneth Mtata (ed), *Religion: Help or Hindrance to Development?* (Leipzig: Evangelische Verlagsanstalt, 2013), 225-42.

[3] Gunderson and Cochrane, *Religion and the Health of the Public*. See especially the section 'Changing the Language: From Deficits to Assets', 44-46.

[4] Since the mid-1850s a rich variety of diaconal institutions have been established in northern Europe and in other parts of the world, belonging to what has been called the modern diaconal movement which intends to renew what was understood as the diaconal ministry in the Early Church. Diaconal institutions are by nature faith-based, but represent a distinct type of FBO as they, in a Christian perspective, will understand their mandate to perform services targeting people who suffer or are victims of injustice and need. *Christian Aid* in the UK, *Bread for the World* in Germany, and *Norwegian Church Aid* are examples of this kind of organisation.

whether FBOs represent added values that can be documented in the performance of their work.[5] Does this give them comparative advantages when it comes to the effectiveness or the sustainability of what is being done?

My interest in this article goes beyond the question of values. I want to focus on assets and how they contribute to the achievement of goals in the work performed by diaconal organisations. Another assumption here is that such assets are often under-communicated in professional work, and that there is a need that they be mapped and described. That will be the main task of this article.

Understanding Assets

The fact that the term 'asset' is assumed by many to belong to the realm of economics, may make some suspicious of using it in development work. We observe, however, that the term 'asset' is frequently used also in other contexts, for example, within sociology, and then as a sort of parallel to the expression 'social capital' that has been shaped by leading sociologists like Pierre Bourdieu and Robert Putnam. Bourdieu distinguishes between three forms of capital: economic, cultural and social. He defines social capital as "the aggregate of the actual or potential resources which are linked to possession of a durable network of more or less institutionalised relationships of mutual acquaintance and recognition".[6] Putnam, on the other hand, points at two basic factors when describing social capital, civil participation and social trust, both fundamental for the development of democracy and social cohesion according to his understanding.[7]

It is quite obvious that social assets are intimately connected with people's worldview, value systems, and also their spirituality. Does this make it sensible also to talk about 'religious assets' which would mean elements rooted in peoples' faith that can be activated so that people are empowered to assume a role in society, to care for others and to promote justice and human dignity?

Social, cultural and also religious assets are then understood to belong to the kind of resources that form social capital. While sociologists might recognise their value in the formation of society, it requires interdisciplinary research to study their nature and potential.

One significant example of such interdisciplinary research is the African Religious Health Assets Programme (ARHAP – now IRHAP, as African has been replaced by International) that has brought together social scientists,

[5] Carole Rakodi, *Are religious organizations different*? (ontrac: Newsletter of INTRAC, No. 46, September 2010); Rick James, *What is Distinctive About FBOs? How European FBOs define and operationalize their faith* (INTRAC: Praxis Paper 22, 2009).

[6] Pierre Bourdieu, 'The forms of capital', in J. Richardson (ed), *Handbook of Theory and Research for the Sociology of Education* (New York: Greenwood, 1986), 241-58.

[7] Robert D. Putnam, *Bowling Alone: The Collapse and Revival of American Community* (New York: Simon & Schuster, 2000).

health experts, theologians and others with the purpose of gaining a better understanding of the interface of religion and public health, mainly in southern Africa.[8] They clearly verified the strong position of FBOs in delivering health services in that region. It has been estimated that half of such service is delivered by Christian churches and organisations in many countries in sub-Saharan Africa, a number that recent research claims to be an exaggeration.[9] This reality indicates the close link between religion and health in people's life. The study, however, brought the researchers beyond these empirical facts, or 'tangible religious health assets' as they were called. They also identified what were referred to as 'intangible religious health assets', elements that relate to people's spirituality and faith practices. In matters of health, illness and healing they were found to play a pivotal role.

With these findings in mind, the research team started a process of mapping out the different kinds of religious health assets (RHAs) that were activated in the process of healing and recovery. The term 'healthworld' was invented, inspired by African linguistic expressions (like *bophelo* in Sesotho) that refer to people's holistic conception of health, as framed by the background store of inherited or socialised knowledge that defines their being in the world.

> The idea of a healthworld ... designates the complex web of elements that shape how health and well-being is understood, relationally rather than atomistically, ecologically rather than reductionistically.[10]

Healthworld is the space where religion and health align and where different assets are mobilised, empowering people to be active subjects in the struggle for health and well-being.

From this understanding it is clear that the quest for health is about much more than health institutions and health workers. It links with a much wider web of relationships and practices, and the assets represented by them. Some of these RHAs are tangible, such as hospitals, clinics and dispensaries. Others are intangible: practices such as, for instance, intercession, visitation and blessing – assets that are rooted in faith and which foster hope, care and resilience. Those who fall ill will interpret sickness as something that affects not only their body and mind, but also their social and spiritual life, but in such a way that all dimensions may contribute to the process of healing and of coping with one's health situation. As a woman said after being visited by her friends that were singing and praying for her, "I am healed, even if I am not yet cured."

My question relates to development work where FBOs are involved and deliver services. Is this a space where religious assets, both tangible and

---

[8] James R. Cochrane, Barbara Schmid and Teresa Cutts (eds), *When Religion and Health Align. Mobilizing Religious Health Assets for Transformation* (Dorpspruit, RSA: Cluster Publications, 2011).

[9] http://www.plosone.org/article/info%3Adoi%2F10.1371%2Fjournal.pone.0048457

[10] Cochrane, Schmid and Cutts, *When Religion and Health Align*, xx.

intangible, can be mapped and their role studied? As I am focusing on diaconal practitioners, my interest is the 'diaconal space' where people are motivated and mobilised by their Christian faith to engage in processes of promoting human dignity and of constructing a just and participatory society. Is it possible within this space to identify diaconal assets, tangible and intangible resources that may make a difference in the struggle for a better world?

Mapping Out Diaconal Assets

Diaconal assets are then basically perceived as elements that bring diaconal practice into being and doing, assets that motivate, mobilise, transform and empower people, congregations and organisations for diaconal involvement. This view recognises that such involvement may take different forms, as already stated above. At the same time it emphasises that the connectivity between the different expressions is an asset it itself. The fact that individuals, congregations and specialised organisations relate to and support each other mutually, as for instance when engaged in the HIV and AIDS work, add value and quality to what is done.

Diaconal assets are thus elements that form and sustain diaconal practice, in that they orient, guide and correct diaconal agents when performing their work. This makes it clear that we are dealing with both tangible and intangible assets. The distinction between them should, however, not be regarded as too strict; in fact, they are interwoven and mutually foster each other.

In the following, a number of tangible diaconal assets will be listed, followed by a list of intangible assets. For the sake of clarity, I shall group them under some main headings:

Tangible assets

d) *Practice*. We are here referring to the impressive record of longstanding diaconal involvement, some would say since the time when the church was founded. Care for the sick, the elderly and the poor has always been considered a ministry of the church and has within some church traditions been named 'diaconal service'. In recent times such service has taken the form of programmes and projects, of service delivery, of educational programmes, of advocacy and the promotion of human rights.[11] Together they represent a vast tradition, and we also see that these assets have often found new expressions in order to respond to new challenges.

---

[11] Because of limited space, it is not possible to illustrate what is here stated, by empirical facts. Instead I refer to ACT Alliance whose members altogether employ 25,000 staff and mobilise about $1.5 billion annually for its work in humanitarian aid, development and advocacy: www.actalliance.org/what-we-do (accessed 8 January 2014).

e) *Institutions and structures*. Included here is the wide variety of diaconal establishments such as hospitals, training centres, offices, etc. that have been set up to deliver services: diaconal organisations – local, national and international – represent such assets, but also local congregations, national churches and ecumenical bodies.

f) *Human resources*. Diaconal involvement depends on skilled personnel with a strong commitment to what they are doing. Many of them combine professional competence with a strong personal motivation founded on their faith. In many diaconal activities the role of women is also being promoted, both as professional workers and as leaders in decision-making processes.

g) *Economic resources*. Diaconal involvement is made possible thanks to funds and foundations, properties, but also to donors and financial supporters, private and public.

h) *Communication resources*. Publications, educational material and forms of communication are assets that are used to promote attitudes, responsibilities, opportunities and the relevant competence in order to work for change.

When looking at these tangible assets, they may give the impression that they very much depend on western patterns of organising development work, with its dependency on financial resources and professional performance. In this perspective, diaconal involvement may appear as being implemented 'from above'.

A focus on intangible assets presents a different angle and opens up a window for seeing *diakonia* 'from below' with prime attention given to the role and resources of ordinary people.

Intangible assets

a) *The collective memory of the past*. This includes a variety of narratives, from the biblical stories about Jesus who set an example when caring for the sick, the hungry and the poor, to 'diaconal heroes' throughout the history of the church – personalities such as Francis of Assisi, Mother Teresa, Bartholomé de las Casas, and Dom Hêlder Cámara. In addition to such outstanding people, this also includes ordinary women and men that are known from people's own history and community. They may be founding mothers and fathers, people who have pioneered diaconal involvement. This 'cloud of witnesses' encourages and inspires one to follow their example, and nurture the faith that it is possible to make a difference. Stories of healing, of transformation, reconciliation and empowerment in the past will make people confident that something similar is possible today.

b) *Rites and rituals*. Within faith communities people share moments that foster and strengthen their faith, hope and love. This is experienced in church services, when singing and dancing together, even in funerals. Sacraments and rites of intercession, blessing and consecration will often strengthen peoples' understanding of being called by God and their vocation to serve one's neighbour. They will serve as concrete signs of God's caring love, even in times of suffering and struggle.

c) *Ethos*. Communities of faith will propagate value systems and attitudes that promote the practice of justice, fairness, inclusiveness, mercy and care. Such an ethos is related to the concept of human dignity, of life being sacred and the vocation to protect and defend human life.

d) *Relationships*. The sense of belonging together, of being part of an extended family, will contribute to the notion of being a subject with tasks to fulfil. It will motivate the practice of hospitality and visitation as expressions of mutual care, and also empower people for active citizenship.

All these elements form people's worldview, and their basic understanding of what is real, what makes sense, and what gives meaning. They are diaconal assets because they will mobilise ordinary people to do something for the common good and empower them to engage in processes that promise a better future for themselves and the community they belong to.

All these assets, both the tangible and the intangible, underpin the role that diaconal organisations have gained as actors within civil society engaged in development work. It makes is understandable why they are often preferred partners of popular movements, local authorities and international agencies, including government agencies that manage official development money. Again, we can list a number of broadly recognised assets that are often associated with FBOs, and with them also diaconal organisations:

a) *Trust*. FBOs have a longstanding commitment to people's well-being, often, for instance, thanks to health and social services that have been delivered for decades and that have built confidence far beyond the community of active Christians. This can also be noted in Muslim countries where in some cases such services have prevented a hostile climate developing towards Christians.

b) *Moral authority*. When dealing with sensitive issues, as for instance Female Genital Mutilation (FGM), the support of local religious leaders will make a tremendous difference in addressing the topic as well as in efforts of changing attitudes and practices. The same is seen in HIV and AIDS campaigns. FBOs are able to link with local congregations and religious leaders, motivating them to take a leading role in initiatives of changing sensitive cultural practices and promoting ethical behaviour, care and health services.

c) *Pioneering practice*. Diaconal agencies have often had the role of introducing new health and social practices. In the 19th century they were among the first to establish services for physically and mentally disabled persons, which meant a significant change in the life situation of those involved, but also for their recognition as members of society. Diaconal work has also promoted the role of women and thereby given a witness to gender equity. In many contexts diaconal initiatives are responding to situations of discrimination, of neglect of human rights, and of social marginalisation due to irresponsible political leadership.

These assets allow us to see why diaconal agencies, even in challenging political contexts, may play a distinct role as social agents, especially when dealing with sensitive issues. This also reveals why advocacy can be an integral part of diaconal work. Public witness gains more weight when rooted in committed service that is recognised and trusted. This is important to bear in mind when diaconal involvement in some cases takes upon itself what may be designated a prophetic role, which means raising its voice in situations where people, especially the poorest and most vulnerable, are victims of the abuse of power and the lack of justice and equal rights.

In my opinion, it is of paramount importance that professional diaconal agencies understand the potential of diaconal assets and know to relate to them when performing their work. This has, however, not always been the case. Instead, diaconal assets are often under-communicated or even neglected, and especially the intangible ones. The consequence is not only missed opportunities of articulating the distinctiveness of professional diaconal involvement and its added value, but even more so the inability to activate such assets as basic resources in securing a higher level of local participation and a sense of ownership when projects and programs are implemented, as sustainability and lasting effect to a large degree depend on how these activities are embedded in the worldview and value systems of those involved.[12]

Nomenclature, or: Language Matters

Does it make any difference for FBOs, and especially for diaconal agents, what terminology is used when describing their work, its goals and methodology? When projects are presented to public donors applying for funding, it is not common to make reference to matters of faith and religion. Secular professional language is normally used. Does this express a shyness regarding own identity and the added value of a faith-based organisation? Or does it indicate a lack of professional understanding of the potential of the social capital of religious practitioners, and in particular of diaconal assets?

Language does matter, also in professional performance. Names express identity and frame the space of interpretation. The term 'development' is embedded in a secular worldview and aims at processes of economic growth and modernisation according to western models. Can this concept fully convey

[12] Knud Jørgensen, 'Sustainability of Churches: Assumptions and Realities in Partnerships', in Hanns Hoerschelmann (ed), *Mission and Development. In Search for a Mission Strategy for the Mekong Region* (Hong Kong: Mekong Mission Forum Publication, 2011), 59-66.

the vision and the values of diaconal work? Does it recognise the role of spirituality and the importance of human dignity?[13]

It has therefore been discussed whether diaconal practitioners should develop concepts and expressions accordingly. This was on the agenda of the Ecumenical Conversation on Diakonia at the World Council of Churches assembly in Busan, South Korea, in November 2013, with the following recommendation being made:

> Churches, ecumenical partners and the WCC must respond to the signs of the time by developing a common diaconal language. We are faith-based and rights-based and we need to identify what this means in practice including defining both our mandate, our core values and mapping our diaconal assets.[14]

This statement gives voice to several concerns. First, it points to the intimate link between identity and performance, between what diaconal agencies *are* and what they *do*. Diaconal organisations are faith-based *and* rights-based, and it is the connection between these two expressions that shapes not only the identity, but also the manner, in which diaconal activity takes. Both faith and rights mark the area of action and the diversity of assets that may be mobilised as belonging to this space. Here is found the distinctiveness of diaconal being and activity. It gives diaconal organisations a unique opportunity for presenting their comparative advantages as agents in civil society and as partner organisations.

Secondly, the above statement responds to what is called 'the signs of the time'. One of them is that religion is back in the public arena. Since the turn of the millennium, matters of faith are no longer considered irrelevant in the development debate, nor is religious neutrality maintained as a basic requirement by governmental bodies when they support non-governmental organisations, including FBOs, financially. It is now acknowledged that development work is a complex matter; it requires more than technical expertise and the transfer of financial and other resources. Spirituality and values are recognised to be of fundamental importance in the processes of promoting social change and empowering people to struggle for their rights.[15]

How can diaconal agents contribute to a sober reflection on the relationship between development and religion? On the one hand, they will reject the practice of using religion and religious leaders for promoting development goals, without acknowledging their distinct nature and objectives. Such a practice would mean reducing them to mere instruments in the development

---

[13] For a broader reflection on the relation between *diakonia* and development work, see: LWF, *Diakonia in Context*, 76-81.

[14] Report from the WCC 10th Assembly in Busan, South Korea.

[15] Gerard Clarke, 'Faith matters: Faith-based organisations, civil society and international development', in *Journal of International Development*, 18 (2006), 835-48; Kenneth Mtata (ed), *Religion: Help or Hindrance to Development?*

business. Diaconal organisations may be tempted to use a similar approach: their identity would however require a different methodology. The fact that they themselves are faith-based gives them an inside perspective and a profound awareness of shared identity, values and assets. Their shared diaconal space implies not only belonging together, but also the opportunity of acting together.

This does not mean uncritical acceptance of whatever is claimed and practised in the name of religion or *diakonia*. It is important to bear in mind that diaconal agents often operate within asymmetric power structures, and constantly need to ask themselves whether they exercise power in a responsible manner. Assets, both tangible and intangible, may be abused as tools of silencing people or undermining their dignity. Anne-Marie Holenstein is right in observing that "religions and faith communities can be effective as 'angels of peace' and as 'warmongers'".[16] The ambiguous role of religion and religious leaders should however not lead to hasty conclusions. First of all, the picture is more faceted. We have many examples of religious leaders who have taken a significant leading role in promoting responsible action and change. It is also a reality that Christian congregations in many places are the only existing social structures that are functioning, and thus able to support community-based development work. Competence is therefore needed in order to analyse how faith and religious practice impact the environment of development work. In the past it has often been the case that development workers, among them also employees of diaconal organisations, have been marked to a large degree by 'religious illiteracy'. Diaconal agents should have a leading role in developing professional competence in this regard, and be able to use 'a religious lens' when engaged in development work.[17]

Already Socrates is quoted for having spoken about 'a battle of names'.[18] As Jill Olivier has documented, there is power in naming, and within development theory secular and instrumental thinking has dominated the tradition of defining social practices.[19] There is a need to break this religious-secular construction, and critically apply an interdisciplinary, and thereby more holistic, approach when defining reality and analysing social practice.

In a theological perspective, this is linked with a holistic understanding of being human, and one in which the spiritual dimension is an integral part. It

---

16 Anne-Marie Holenstein, 'Governmental donor agencies and faith-based organizations', in *International Review of the Red Cross,* 87:858 (June 2005), 367-73.

17 Annette Dietschy, 'On the Role of Religion in Development Co-operation. A First-hand Report from the Discussion among Governmental and Non-Governmental Development Agencies in Switzerland', in Nordstokke (ed), *Serving the Whole Person,* 223-35.

18 Plato, The Dialogues of Plato, Vol. 1 (New York: Random House, 1937), 678.

19 Jill Olivier, '"An FB-oh?": Mapping the Etymology of the Religious Entity Engaged in Health', in Cochrane, Schmid and Cutts (eds), *When Religion and Health Align*, 24-42.

also implies that intervention in relation to one dimension, be it the physical, the mental, the social or the spiritual, may have consequences for the three others. Spiritual care may energise a person to recover physically, mentally and socially. Similarly, spiritual empowerment may foster social and political engagement.

As we have seen, religious assets bridge the different dimensions of being human. They open up a view of reality that corresponds with the biblical vision of the world as God's household (Greek: *oikonomia*), the whole inhabited world, as a space where all inhabitants are gifted and called to be householders (*oikonomoi*), co-responsible for the well-being of all that belong to the 'house'. This holistic perspective resists the opinion that development in the first place is a matter of economy in its modern (or post-modern) sense, aimed at markets and profit, and a matter reserved for economists and their expertise. The biblical view of women and men being created in the image of God proclaims that human dignity implies possessing ability and competence – in other words, of contributing to assets, and independent of their social status. Indeed, language matters!

Concluding Observations

As stated at the WCC Busan assembly, it is important to initiate a process of mapping out diaconal assets and describing their potential in development work. Due to the fact that diaconal work is interdisciplinary, this research must itself be interdisciplinary, bringing together insights from both the social and human sciences, including theology and religious studies.

One of the aims of this exercise should be to develop professional competence that acknowledges diaconal assets and ability to act on and relate to them. Hopefully that would contribute to a professional practice that will avoid people interpreting change as disability or the breaking up of the social and cultural order. They will instead see themselves as promoters and agents of new times to come. This could also contribute to overcoming the gap between helpers and beneficiaries, and of the paternalistic separation between those who know and those who are considered ignorant, between the powerful and the powerless.

For diaconal organisations it should be of pivotal importance to promote such an asset-based approach in development work, and to use methods that seek to uncover and use the strengths within communities, instead of focusing on needs. People get motivated and empowered when focus is given to their abilities and skills rather than pointing to what is lacking. It is assumed that this approach will reduce dependency on external practitioners; instead it will create active citizenship and mobilise the community's own ability of finding sustainable solutions.

The idea of promoting active citizenship has become fundamental to international *diakonia*. It recognises the importance of civil society in development work as an arena where faith-based agents also have a significant role in influencing public life and of promoting democratic practices in decision-making processes. In addition, it takes into consideration what has been named 'the new geography of global poverty', a shift in the sense that there are fewer poor countries in the world today as compared with earlier decades, while larger groups of poor people live in many middle income countries.[20] This requires new strategies and working methods by development agents. Traditional projects will have to be replaced by more comprehensive involvement with the aim of establishing social and political mechanisms that will allow a fairer distribution of welfare goods. Here diaconal organisations have the advantage of partnering with local religious communities, and of linking with the richness of assets they represent, and with people of faith that may be empowered to act as responsible citizens, committed to promoting a better life for all.

Bibliography

Bourdieu, Pierre, 'The forms of capital', in J. Richardson (ed), *Handbook of Theory and Research for the Sociology of Education* (New York: Greenwood, 1986), 241-58.

Clarke, Gerard, 'Faith matters: Faith-based organisations, civil society and international development', in *Journal of International Development,* 18 (2006), 835-48.

Cochrane, James R., Barbara Schmid and Teresa Cutts (eds), *When Religion and Health Align. Mobilizing Religious Health Assets for Transformation* (Dorpspruit, RSA: Cluster Publications, 2011).

Dietschy, Annette, 'On the Role of Religion in Development Co-operation. A First-hand Report from the Discussion among Governmental and Non-Governmental Development Agencies in Switzerland', in Kjell Nordstokke (ed), *Serving the Whole Person. The Practice and Understanding of Diakonia within the Lutheran Communion* (Minneapolis, MN: Lutheran University Press, 2009), 223-35.

Holenstein, Anne-Marie, 'Governmental donor agencies and faith-based organisations', in *International Review of the Red Cross,* 87:858 (June 2005), 367-73.

Gunderson, Gary R., and James R. Cochrane, *Religion and the Health of the Public. Shifting the Paradigm* (New York: Palgrave Macmillan, 2012).

James, Rick, *What is Distinctive About FBOs? How European FBOs define and operationalize their faith* (INTRAC: Praxis Paper 22, 2009).

Jørgensen, Knud, 'Sustainability of Churches: Assumptions and Realities in Partnerships', in Hanns Hoerschelmann (ed), *Mission and Development. In Search for a Mission Strategy for the Mekong Region* (Hong Kong: Mekong Mission Forum Publication, 2011), 59-66.

Lutheran World Federation. *Diakonia in Context: Transformation, Reconciliation, Empowerment. An LWF Contribution to the Understanding and Practice of Diakonia* (Geneva: LWF, 2009).

Mtata, Kenneth (ed), *Religion: Help or Hindrance to Development?* (Leipzig: Evangelische Verlagsanstalt, 2013).

[20] Andy Sumner and Richard Mallett, *The Future of Foreign Aid: Development Cooperation and the New Geography of Global Poverty* (Basingstoke, UK: Palgrave Macmillan, 2013).

Nordstokke, Kjell, 'Faith-Based Organisations (FBOs) and their Distinct Assets', in Kenneth Mtata (ed), *Religion: Help or Hindrance to Development?* (Leipzig: Evangelische Verlagsanstalt, 2013), 225-42.

Olivier, Jill, '"An FB-oh?": Mapping the Etymology of the Religious Entity Engaged in Health', in James R Cochrane, Barbara Schmid and Teresa Cutts (eds), *When Religion and Health Align. Mobilizing Religious Health Assets for Transformation* (Dorpspruit, RSA: Cluster Publications, 2011), 24-42.

Plato, *The Dialogues of Plato, Vol. 1* (New York: Random House, 1937).

Putnam, Robert D., *Bowling Alone: The Collapse and Revival of American Community* (New York: Simon & Schuster, 2000).

Rakodi, Carole, 'Are religious organisations different?' (ontrac: Newsletter of INTRAC, No. 46, September 2010).

Sumner, Andy, and Richard Mallett, *The Future of Foreign Aid: Development Co-operation and the New Geography of Global Poverty* (Basingstoke, UK: Palgrave Macmillan, 2013).

Preparation for Ministry in a Cross-Cultural Society: Christian Care and Counselling in a Multicultural Context

Edwina Ward and Anneliese Schäpers

Introduction

So that pastoral care-givers may gain a fuller understanding of human persons within global society, it is necessary to explore the ways in which culture, humanity and individual uniqueness all work together. Many pastoral care-givers feel that the phrase often quoted by Kluckholn and Murray (1948) – "we are like all others, we are like some others, we are like no other"[1] – still holds true for the present day in coming to an understanding of the Christian care-giver and the pastoral counsellor's role in serving the people of God in ministry.

Christian care-givers accept that human beings, despite wide cultural differences, hold basic characteristics and traits in common. We all experience a common humanity, while at the same time we are diverse in our cultural expressions and experiences. The existence of dominant cultures cannot mean that one culture is inherently superior to another at this stage in our global world. The intercultural and multicultural counsellor must move from her or his culture into another and then back again, providing help at the 'cutting edge' of cultural insights ('interpathy'). This would mean that we resist making others like ourselves in the stereotypes of our culture. Rather, the Christian pastoral care-giver is required to help those in need within the context of the other person's culture, values, assumptions and beliefs. This challenges the person being helped to find their way to wholeness as defined by the society in which they live. This would also imply knowledge of the God of all creation and cultures.

Our task will be to look at major issues in multicultural counselling and Christian care. The interface of pastoral care and counselling and trans-cultural theological reflection will be explored. Areas of missiology, theology, anthropology and psychology will be integrated in the discourse. As pastoral

---

[1] C. Kluckholn and H. Murray, *Personality in Nature: Society and Culture* (New York: Alfred Knopf, 1948) – in the Introduction.

care-givers we will further explore the process of human change and growth in counselling and recognise different approaches to persons in another culture.

As such, it is true that all forms of counselling are inseparable from the cultural assumptions and the personal bias of the counsellor. Different cultural systems will find expression in different styles of therapy and different approaches. These approaches will demonstrate the eclectic styles of counsellors who themselves are from many cultures. Because of this, it is necessary to argue that effective pastoral counselling should involve reflection on the significance of both the counsellor and the 'client' as each lives in a different world in order for the therapeutic process to take place.

Dealing with a focus on pastoral care and service in multicultural societies, it would be deemed necessary to include spiritual and cultural resources as central to the work and role of the pastoral care-giver. As a pastoral care-giver it is necessary to recognise that in different geographical areas and contexts what is needed is the freedom to recognise what is of value in their historic traditions. Similarly, we need to reject what blocks the opening of the way for effective counselling, using the skills to initiate a model which in turn will liberate and empower the relationship between the pastoral care-giver and the client.

On the African continent it may be necessary to look at the mystical and supernatural world found in the African context. As we explore interculturality and multiculturality in Africa, we need a constant awareness of the reality of racism and oppression.[2]

In short, this chapter confronts the Christian care-giver and counsellor with the tasks of moving from cultural isolation (encapsulation)[3] to living, working and caring across cultural boundaries.

Training of Pastoral Care-givers for Pastoral Counselling and Care-Giving

Over the past 70 years the training of pastoral care-givers has changed radically. For a process like Clinical Pastoral Education (CPE)[4] to be incorporated into South Africa and indeed into the whole of Africa, even more

[2] A study of racism can be found in articles by Atkinson, Morten and Sue, 1989, and Ponterotto and Borodovsky, 1991.

[3] D.W. Sue and D. Sue 1990 and Pedersen 1990 – all these theorists discuss the need for a multicultural perspective in counselling, with the counsellor acquiring a personal knowledge of their own racial and cultural heritage.

[4] Clinical Pastoral Education (CPE) is a programme where participants are trained in clinical environments to accompany persons suffering and in need of pastoral care and counselling. In effect, this is training and education necessary for *diakonia* – the social ministry of the church, in solidarity with marginalised and suffering people. The ministry of the church is expressed in caring for one's neighbour, and the struggle for justice and peace.

radical changes had to be made to include the cultural heritage of the African peoples. Africans live in a multicultural society held together by common humanity, yet traditions, values, customs and languages distinguish them. When introducing CPE in South Africa, the many elements of the African culture had to be learned and understood. To take into account the attitudes, gender roles, identity, traditions, ethnicity and customs of multicultural society required a study of communication styles and religions, and a grasp of the supernatural nature of African belief systems.

My own doctorate, written in 2001, was entitled, The Contribution of Clinical Pastoral Education to Pastoral Ministry in South Africa: Overview and Critique of its Method and Dynamic, in View of Adaptation and Implementation in a Cross-Cultural Context. I was particularly concerned with the process of cross-cultural dynamics in the multicultural society of Africa. I explored the complexity of transferring a tried and tested process from one culture to another. This thesis explicitly acknowledged the important contribution of Africa to theology. One prevalent element is 'narrative theology' where people write or tell stories through their own life experience. As Pobee states, "God is present, active and alive in the midst of human beings." This is living praxis (which is itself another living element). An African narrative theology of inculturation is not just a theoretical or intellectual exercise; it is praxis. It is practical theology and pastoral theology, often being 'written' by people and communities in and through their everyday experience. This practical inculturation forms an important part of both pastoral and missionary ministry. This praxis is a significant dimension of applied inculturation and functional African Christianity.[5]

Before we continue, it is necessary to clarify some terms and issues likely to be raised.

Monoculturalism implies that we human beings are all the same: we judge one another by saying that our core values and cultural norms are all the same, along with our class and our social group. This means that monoculturalism is not neutral. White western cultures are expressed as the norm to which we all conform. Other cultural beliefs are thus suppressed in their expressions, beliefs, practices and values. Pastoral counselling takes place privately, in one-to-one sessions and confidentiality.

Cross-cultural implies that they are totally different from us: cultural differences are recognised. This term is used to attempt to capture the complex nature of the interaction between people who are influenced by different social contexts and origins, and by different cultures. These differences around the individual can provide an identity for the whole group, the whole tribe, the

[5] J.S. Pobee, *Kenosis: Christian faith in an African context* (Mambo occasional papers, 1992), 52.

whole clan. In this respect we refer to David Augsburger (1986).[6] His main argument is that counsellors should be culturally capable (with) the ability to join with another in their culture whilst retaining one's own. So counsellors have an interpathic understanding of the other. The problem in this approach is that there remains an 'us and them' mentality. We learn about them. White counsellors are seen to be superior to a black client, so that if the client is white and the counsellor is black there may be unconscious stereotypes. A further definition of cross-cultural counselling by Sue would include an understanding of counselling as a relationship in which "two or more of the participants differ in cultural background, values and lifestyle".[7] Cross-culturalism over-emphasises difference, and educational multiculturalism over-emphasises cultural difference.

Multicultural implies that we should learn as much as we can about them: We are looking for healthy race relations so that we can properly understand our differences. We study religious rites, play activities, family patterns, gender roles, education and even eating habits within each group. Of course, this leads to stereotyping and creates expectations of 'sameness' among all who are in that same group.

Interculturality implies that every human is like all others, like some others and like no other.[8] All humans are humans physiologically, psychologically and cognitively. We are like some others because of the socialisation process, worldviews, customs and forms of social relationships. We are like no other as we have personal characteristics, like fingerprints, and dental shaping.

Culture is broadly defined by some to include race, ethnicity, class, religion, sex, age and so on. As such, when we talk about multicultural counselling, we would include not only ethnic and racial minorities but also women, gays and lesbians, and those who are different from us, like those who are HIV-positive. The 'us and them' syndrome. Yet Whites in South Africa would call to name the other cultures as Blacks, Coloured and Indian people, as being of a different culture.

Pastoral is not taken to simply mean a reference to the ordained Christian, but to what it might mean in a post-modern context. The image of pastor as 'shepherd' is valid, but with the new associations of leading, healing, nurturing, empowering and liberating. The concept of Jesus as the Good Shepherd offers

---

6 David W. Augsburger, *Pastoral Counseling Across Cultures* (Philadelphia, PA: Westminster, 1986).

7 D.W. Sue and D. Sue, *Counseling the Culturally Different: Theory and Practice* (New York: Wiley, 1981), 8-16.

8 E.Y. Lartey, *In Living Color: an Intercultural Approach to Pastoral Care and Counseling* (London: Cassell, 1998).

a unifying theme, but the image of the shepherd is accepted as Jesus the servant, brother and companion in the present context.[9]

Ubuntu[10] as a root metaphor is an intercultural approach to praxis-thinking. The notion of *ubuntu* is linked to hospitality and the generosity of giving freely to another without any thought of repayment. It is a philosophy and a way of life. *Ubuntu* is both a religious and a philosophical concept that defines an individual in relationship with others. The African asserts "I am because we are" – and since we are, therefore I am.[11]

Umuntu ngumuntu ngabantu. A person is a person through others. It is argued that for Africans, humanity is first and foremost found in the community. Individuals acquire their basic identity through their relationships with others, and they enjoy a feeling of security as long as their relationships are in harmony. The values of interdependence in and through relationships rates higher than individualism and personal independence.[12]

In order to deal with an intercultural approach within the southern African context, we should deal with the construct which dominates the mindset of Africans.[13] Within the spirituality of the African, a socio-cultural analysis should take into consideration the importance of the concept of *ubuntu.*[14]

Training as a Pastoral Care-Giver

Today it is noted that most pastoral counselling and Christian care programmes tend to offer a multicultural focus in the training module. Students who are called to *diakonia*, to be pastoral care-givers in mission locations away from their country of origin will attend training programmes which address the need to develop multicultural awareness, knowledge and skills. At present these

---

[9] R. Hunter, *Dictionary of Pastoral Care and Counseling* (Nashville, TN: Abingdon Press, 1990).

[10] Julius Gathogo (2008:42-43). The concept of *Ubuntu* is explored in African philosophy in the *Journal of Theology for Southern Africa*, 130, March 2008, 42-43.

[11] J.S. Mbiti, *Introduction to African Religion* (Nairobi: East African Ed. Publishers, 1994).

[12] M.P. Moila, 'The Role and Function of the Pastoral Counsellor in the Present Crisis in South Africa', in *Africa Theological Journal*, 18:3 (1989).

[13] A. Berinyuu, *Pastoral Care to the Sick in Africa. An Approach to Transcultural Pastoral Theology* (Frankfurt: Peter Lang, 1988:5). In this book Berinyuu states that most Africans believe that everything, including humans, is in a constant state of relationship with one another and with the invisible world, and that people are in a state of complete dependence upon those invisible powers and beings. Life is a liturgy of celebration for the victories and /or sacrifices of others.

[14] *In the Words of Nelson Mandela*, London (Penguin). The spirit of *Ubuntu* – that profound African sense that we are human only through the humanity of other human beings – is not a parochial phenomenon, but has added globally to our common search for a better world (2005:82). Quotation taken from an unpublished article by Prof Daniel J. Louw, 'Hermeneutics of Intercultural Pastoral Care' (2013).

modules tend to deal with cultural differences from a purely intellectual perspective without reference to the socio-political complexities of counselling, such as discrimination, oppression and racism. Thus most students in cross-cultural counselling training do not have enough practical experience in their training, or in their personal daily lives, with ethnic or racial minorities. We believe that all forms of counselling are cross-cultural, and that cross-cultural issues need to be seen as central to pastoral counselling situations. Because someone may belong to a particular group does not make that person competent in the knowledge or skills needed to be a competent pastoral counsellor.

As stated by Sue, we are becoming a global society that is multiracial, multicultural and multilingual.[15] In the past, society operated within a monocultural and monolingual perspective, referred to as the 'encapsulated counsellor'. This monocultural approach is documented as demonstrating the ineffectiveness of traditional counselling approaches and techniques when applied to racial and ethnic minority populations, mainly due to ineffective training.[16]

Clinical Pastoral Education as a Skills Training Foundation

During the Clinical Pastoral Education programme which lasts either one month or three months and takes place in a clinical hospital setting, the participants come from cultures all across Africa and may speak as many as 22 different languages. The common language for communication is English which may in itself be cause for many misunderstandings. We try to emphasise that the worldview of the pastoral care-giver and client may well be vastly different, each bringing their own experiences of oppression and personal biases. The minority client is likely to approach Christian care and counselling with a great deal of suspicion concerning the pastoral care-giver's motives in a cross-cultural context. Most of the clients or patients in the hospitals of KwaZulu-Natal, are isizulu- or Xhosa-speaking and cannot comprehend that a black counsellor cannot speak their language! Those participants in the CPE programme who have been living in South Africa and studying at seminary or university have usually picked up enough Zulu to make simple conversation with the clients/patients. This bilingualism should be a major goal for the counsellor as it encourages good listening, trust and confidentiality.

A further acknowledgement for the Christian counsellor is that racial and ethnic minorities are bi-cultural and function in at least two different cultural

---

[15] D.W. Sue, 'A conceptual model for cultural diversity training', in *Journal of Counseling and Development*, Vol. 70 (1991), 99-105.

[16] F.A. Ibrahim and P.M. Arrendondo, 'Ethical standards for cross-cultural counseling: Counselor preparation, practice, assessment and research', in *Journal of Counseling and Development* 64 (1986), 349-52.

contexts. We are often heard to say that the African person is 'Christian by day and traditional by night', meaning that part of their culture is to consult traditional healers when seeking healing for illnesses such as HIV and AIDS.

A further potentially harmful practice is that pastoral care-givers who are not trained in cross-cultural knowledge and skills are unethical and can be harmful. Pedersen and Marsella note:

> A serious moral vacuum exists in the delivery of cross-cultural counselling and therapy services because the values of a dominant culture have been imposed on the culturally different consumer. Cultural differences complicate the definition of guidelines even for the conscientious and well-intentioned counsellor and therapist.[17]

It seems that an obstacle in getting the white Christian counsellor to understand the implications of monoculturalism is that the white culture is such the dominant norm that it acts as a screen which prevents the client from opening the lines of communication and trust to even the most well-intentioned counsellor.

Cross-cultural Competencies of the Pastoral Care-Giver[18]

The culturally skilled pastoral care-giver is one who is actively in the process of becoming aware of his or her own assumptions about human behaviour, values, biases, preconceived notions, personal limitations, and so forth. They accept how they are a product of their cultural conditioning, and how that is reflected in their counselling and the work they do with other cultures. They respect the adage 'counsellor, know thyself' which disallows biases, values, or 'hang ups' to interfere with the counsellor's skill in working with the clients.

A culturally skilled pastoral care-giver/counsellor, is one who actively attempts to understand the worldview of his or her culturally different client without negative judgements. It is vitally necessary that the pastoral care-giver understands and shares the worldviews of clients, and shows respect and appreciation for their differences and beliefs. The pastoral care-giver should accept the client unreservedly.

A culturally skilled pastoral care-giver is one who is in the process of actively developing and practising appropriate, relevant and sensitive intervention strategies and skills in working with culturally different clients. The pastoral care-giver should effectively use methods and define goals

---

[17] P.B. Pedersen and A.J. Marsella, 'The ethical crisis for cross-cultural counseling and therapy', in *Professional Psychology*, 13 (1982), 492.

[18] In their article 'Multicultural Counseling Competencies and Standards: A Call to the Profession', D.W. Sue, P.M. Arredondo and R. McDavis have written extensively on the competencies required of the counsellor working in a cross-cultural society in *Journal of Counseling and Development*, Vol. 70 (March/April 1992), 477-86.

consistent with the life experiences and cultural values of clients. Sue and Sue state:

> These three goals stress the fact that becoming culturally skilled is an active process, that it is ongoing, and that it is a process that never reaches an end point. Implicit is recognition of the complexity and diversity of the client and client populations, and acknowledgement of our own personal limitations and the need to always improve.[19]

We look at cultural competency in three dimensions: (a) beliefs and attitudes, (b) knowledge, and (c) skills.[20] The first section deals with the pastoral care-givers' attitudes and beliefs about the client. There is a need to check the biases, and stereotypes. The second section accepts the good knowledge and understanding of the pastoral care-giver's own worldview and the specific knowledge around the cultural groups he or she works with, understanding the socio-political influences in the community. The last section deals with the specific skills and intervention techniques needed in working with clients from different cultures. Here we emphasise the specific skill of *listening* to the verbal and non-verbal messages given during the counselling interview, and the ability of the pastoral care-giver to acquire the skill of meta-listening.

What follows is an outline of the three dimensions mentioned above under the requirements of a culturally skilled pastoral care-giver who is working in a multicultural environment.

Pastoral care-giver/counsellor awareness of own values and biases

- To be sensitive to one's own cultural heritage, and to value and respect the differences of others.
- To be aware of how their own cultural background and experiences influence psychological processes.
- To recognise the limits of their competences and expertise.
- To have specific knowledge about their own racial and cultural heritage, and to possess knowledge about how oppression, discrimination, racism and stereotyping affect them personally.
- To be aware of communication styles and how language may affect genuine listening to the client.

---

19 D.W. Sue and D. Sue, *Counseling the Culturally Different*, 146.

20 S. Sue, 'Training issues in conducting therapy with ethnic-minority clients', in P.B. Pedersen (ed), *Handbook in cross-counseling therapy* (Westport, CT: Greenwood Press. 1990).

Pastoral care-giver/counsellor understanding of the worldview of the culturally different client

- Willingness to contrast their own beliefs and attitudes in a non-judgemental fashion.
- Awareness of any preconceived notions of the other person.
- Knowledge of the life experiences, cultural heritage and historic background of the clients. Understanding of the socio-political influences upon the life of the client, such as poverty, powerlessness and stereotyping, all of which leave major scars.
- Counsellors may become actively involved with the community outside the counselling setting. Attend social and political events, celebrations, meetings and tribal functions.

Pastoral care-givers'/counsellors' developing intervention techniques and strategies.

- Respect the clients' religious and spiritual beliefs and the indigenous helping and healing practices.
- Value bilingualism and understanding of unspoken beliefs and taboos.
- Knowledge of the family structures, hierarchies, values and beliefs of the client and his or her community.
- Engage in a variety of verbal and non-verbal helping responses.
- Counsellors are not averse to seeking consultation with traditional healers, or religious and spiritual leaders and practitioners, when counselling culturally different clients.[21]

The Need to Understand Interculturality

Working in a cross-cultural and multicultural society for the 'outsider' is a challenge and a rewarding ministry. Living at the end of the twentieth century, the concept of interculturality emerged to demonstrate that an intercultural paradigm could be more appropriate than the existing concepts on inculturality.[22]

---

[21] S. Sue, 'Training issues in conducting therapy with ethnic-minority clients' (1982).

[22] The differences between inculturality and interculturality are not great. The first emphasises interpenetration while the second emphasises exchange. Bellagamba (1987:99) refers to inculturation as the attempt to create a spirituality which is rooted in the basic experience of life. The theological justification for inculturation is sought in incarnational theology: "An incarnated spirituality would be a great gift to Africans" (Bellagamba 1987:104). This footnote is taken from the research of Prof Daniel J. Louw of Stellenbosch University, South Africa, in his unpublished article mentioned above, 'Hermeneutics of Intercultural Pastoral Care' (2013).

In the book written by Bate,[23] we read of the connection between inculturation and healing. Bate feels that an understanding of the sickness-healing process is required to analyse culture. This 'theological key' is of importance for the interpretation of sickness and healing within African contexts.

Bate argues that inculturation implies a re-appropriation of contextual culture. As such, it addresses the issue of unity and plurality within the church, and also places the contextual manifestations within an historical framework.

The notion of inculturation is accepted when we believe that culture is a way of life in a given time and place, complete with values, symbols and meaning. Bate also suggests that culture represents the human locus of people's context. In Africa the human being cannot be understood as being separate from cultural values and issues. The human person is embedded in his or her culture. Culture is seen as a sacred mystery and encompasses the entire life of a people, their morals, religious beliefs, social structures, economic and political systems, plus their forms of music and dance, rituals and the total creative spirit.

A Christian counsellor from another culture outside Africa should ask the question, "How should I encounter people coming from a different background without being caught in the web of prejudice and stigmatisation, along with the threat of discrimination?" How do we deal with diversity, difference and stereotyping with strangeness in a multicultural context?[24] The aim is to create a shared space, a friendly empty space, as Henri Nouwen once put it, for co-existence and co-understanding (National Catholic Reporter, 1979). This creation of a friendly empty space and 'being present' is described as 'hospitality'. In his small but meaningful book *Reaching Out*, Nouwen states:

> Hospitality, therefore, means primarily the creation of a free space where the stranger can enter and become a friend instead of an enemy. Hospitality is not to change people, but to offer them space where change can take place … is not a method of making our God and our way into a criteria of happiness, but the opening of an opportunity to others to find their God and in their way.[25]

Interculturality in pastoral care is less about technique in counselling and more about the quality of the interaction and the encounter. The 'outsider' pastoral care-giver is challenged to face the concern of encountering people coming from a different background, with different values, customs and beliefs. According to Lartey,[26] three basic principles are called for: contextuality (the framework of beliefs and worldviews), multiple perspectives (the listening to and the dialogue within that different perspective), and

---

[23] S.C. Bate, *Inculturation and Healing. Coping-healing in South African Christianity* (Pietermaritzburg, RSA: Cluster, 1995), 19.
[24] Augsburger, *Pastoral Counseling Across Cultures*, 101.
[25] Henri Nouwen, *Reaching Out* (Glasgow: Collins, 1975), 51.
[26] E.Y. Lartey, *In Living Color*, 11.

authentic participation (mutual concern for the integrity and dignity of the other). Interculturality is more than the traditional process for empathy in counselling. This cultural empathy (interpathy),[27] is based on uniqueness and differences. Empathy is the skill used by a counsellor to spend a little time 'in the shoes', as it were, of the other, but without becoming just like the other; whereas interpathy also recognises the unique differences of the other and allows them to stay separately within their own culture.

Thus we can say that intercultural care is about the following:

a) Intercultural sensitivity.
b) Understanding language, metaphors and symbols describing meaning in life.
c) The challenge for a Christian counsellor is whether his or her approach can move into a trans-cultural identity regarding anthropology. Human identity is determined by grace and not by culture.
d) Healing is about change in perspectives and a different position in life, and implies a multi-eco-systemic intervention,[28] with a repositioning and reframing in terms of the spiritual network which includes ancestors and the spirit world.
e) Intercultural care should be understood in terms of ubuntu, the reaching out to the whole community, tribe and clan, to healing relationships before the individual person can be healed.
f) Finally, intercultural care deals with tribalism, ethnicity, power issues, gender inequality and religious diversity. It is sensitive to the social environment such as marriage, family and clan relationships and affiliations. It deals with stigma and discrimination, and is involved with marginalised groups in society. Poverty as a socio-cultural and economic problem is part of intercultural care.[29]

Understanding Mission and Culture

The *missionary model* was the focus on cultural assimilation.[30] For many years in the missionary history of Africa, African culture was viewed from a colonial Christian perspective as intrinsically wrong.[31] Non-Christian religion was influenced by sin and imperfection. Thus total transformation was required for the indigenous culture, with no form of accommodation by incorporation. This approach cannot be maintained within practical theology. Human beings cannot

---

[27] Augsburger, *Pastoral Counseling Across Cultures*, 29.

[28] Schneider-Harpprecht, 'Was ist interkulturelle Seelsorge?', in Daniel J. Louw, 'Hermeneutics of Intercultural Pastoral Care', 61.

[29] This is a summary of findings written by Daniel J. Louw in his unpublished article, 'Hermeneutics of Intercultural Pastoral Care'.

[30] Villa-Vicencio, *Theology and Culture in South Africa* (1994), 116.

[31] Benezet Bujo explains the impact of foreign missionaries in *African Theology in its Colonial Context* (Faith and Cultural Series – New York: Maryknoll, 1992), 37-49.

be separated from cultural issues and values in the African perspective. Culture in itself is an expression of the creative and imaginative human spirit.

According to Dwight N. Hopkins, "Culture is where the sacred reveals itself. As a result, one only knows what she or he is created to be and called to do through the human created realm of culture."[32] We find meaning and purpose in life through our culture and we express this in symbolic forms. Culture can therefore be called a structured strategy for survival: it gives a sense of belonging to a social group; a system of expressed ideas or concepts; an indication of general behaviour and patterns for daily living.

Practical Pastoral Counselling

Putting into practice academic theology and practical theology is a key component in a training programme such as Clinical Pastoral Education. There must be links between the study of scripture and pastoral counselling, between ethics and cross-cultural caring, between what we say and what we believe, and through our actions which demonstrate our beliefs. These connections begin to show themselves while working with 'living human documents', people who challenge our very beliefs, our theology, our moral values and our self-identity when we are in a cross-cultural counselling situation. The seven functions of pastoral counselling (guiding, healing, sustaining, reconciling, nurturing, liberating and empowering) surface as some of the most important skills the counsellor draws on.

A complete outline of these functions may be found in the book by Lartey,[33] and in the original work by Clinebell.[34]

Cultural Information in the Counselling Process

Cultural information refers to all the data in one's culture that gives insight into the pastoral concern or conflict presented. Society today has learned to appreciate a culture that does not identify all good with the church and all evil with the world. The church and the world mutually affect each other. Like tradition and experience, culture can be both positive and negative, and at times also ambiguous. Don Browning describes culture as a "set of symbols, stories (myths), and norms for conduct that orient a society or group cognitively, effectively, and behaviourally to the world in which it lives".[35] It is critical for ministers and counsellors to reach an informed understanding of those to whom

[32] D.N. Hopkins, 'Black Theology: The Notion of Culture Revisited', in *Journal of Theology for Southern Africa,* 124 (2005), 83.

[33] E.Y. Lartey, *In Living Color*, chapter 3.

[34] H.J. Clinebell, *Basic Types of Pastoral Counseling* (Nashville, TN: Abingdon Press, 1966), 38-40.

[35] Don S. Browning, *The Moral Context of Pastoral Care* (Philadelphia, PA: Westminster, 1976), 73.

they minister. The minister needs to know what data is needed and available to inform a pastoral counselling decision.

The following could be some of the questions to pose as they relate cultural information to the counselling session: *Does culture play an important role in this event? What are the key cultural values that are present? Does ubuntu have any significance in this event?* This model focuses on identifying sources of information to use in theological reflection within the counselling process.

Four Approaches to Understanding South African Culture

How can cultural categories be best comprehended within a multicultural society such as South Africa? Xolile Keteyi,[36] a South African author, wrote a short but important book which was published posthumously. He suggests four approaches to understanding culture in the African consciousness.

The first is the 'ethnic group', in which the symbol and skills of each cultural group provides a valued worldview for the people. This provides them with their identity. The second is the 'dominant heritage', which delineates people according to their European, Asian or African heritages. The third approach is the 'Black urban culture with is linked together with the Anglo-Boer culture'. This approach is identified around the pivot of oppression. The Anglo-Boer culture which was the culture of white domination is totally rejected as a model for black people. In this culture black people are seen as workers and labourers with very few rights. Finally, Keteyi concludes with this hopeful observation: "Thus even though the cultures are in tension and criticise one another, in their capacity to assimilate, they represent different manifestations of one human culture".[37]

It is Theresa Okure, a Nigerian scripture scholar, who suggests that we look at the model offered in scripture (Philippians 2:6-8). Okure explains that the image is that of dying to oneself to welcome new learning, and new experiences and new understandings of what it means to be part of the whole of humanity.[38] This emptying of self involves becoming aware of the cultures around us and learning to accept that being different and being diverse is how God created the human family.

Listening Skills in Cross-Cultural Counselling

For those who have studied the basic skills of counselling and pastoral care, the importance of *listening and attending* would appear to be obvious. In order for

---

[36] X. Keteyi, *Inculturation as a Strategy for Liberation* (Pietermaritzburg, RSA: Cluster, 1998).

[37] Keteyi, *Inculturation as a Strategy for Liberation*, 27.

[38] T. Okure, *Inculturation of Christianity in Africa* (Eldoret, Kenya: AMECA Publications, 1990), 65-66.

the counsellor to hear God's revelation or truth, the counsellor must be a good listener. Listening focuses on "… the words and the silences, the emotions and ideas, the situation in which the conversation takes place".[39]

In multicultural and intercultural counselling, a most important quality of the counsellor is the capacity to listen. In the book by Virginia Satir,[40] in which she writes predominantly on family counselling, she stresses the art of communication within the family (community) and the importance of listening. She writes: "Listening and looking require one's full attention. We pay a heavy price for not seeing and not hearing accurately: we end up by making assumptions and treating them as facts."[41]

The art of listening is not just hearing the words spoken but, of equal importance, observing non-verbal expressions, facial expressions and body behaviour. From attending to the speaker to the interpreting of what has been spoken we find many steps. According to Fr Michael Jamail, OMI, the basic decision in listening is to decide whether we are the speaker or the listener in the counselling situation.[42] To counsel needs a firm intention and internal preparation to be present to the other. Creative listening demands energy, time, honesty and trust. Fr Jamail discusses two kinds of listening: passive and active listening:

a) *Passive Listening*. This is non-interference with words, questions or any other action on the part of the counsellor. This type of listening offers comfortable silence without judgement. During this time an inner world can open up and the listener gains an insight into the client's feelings and an in-depth understanding of their worldview. At this moment empathic listening takes place. This kind of listening from a counsellor is inclined to be more acceptable to a western client since African clients prefer a counsellor to be concrete and verbal in the counselling situation.
b) Active Listening. This demands participation in what has been verbalised by the counsellor. The listener interprets what is being said and checks that the message heard was comprehended correctly. "What I have understood you to be saying …" "You are feeling … because … and that makes you …" This response from the counsellor lets the client know that his or her feelings are understood, the context of the conversation is credible, and the client's behaviour is congruent with their feelings and emotions. The counsellor is also attentive to the tone of voice, the choice of words and to body language. In active listening, the listener needs to decode the words by clarifying the correctness of

[39] J. Whitehead, *Christian Life Patterns* (New York: Doubleday, 1982), 96.
[40] Virginia Satir, *The New Peoplemaking* (Mountain View, CA: Science & Behavior Books, 1988).
[41] Satir, *The New Peoplemaking*, 70.
[42] Fr Michael Jamail offers a workshop on Listening. This DVD is available from the CPE library.

the interpretation of the meaning of the words. This is the skill most needed in cross-cultural counselling. Understanding the meaning of words, myths, stories and cultural nuances implied in the conversation. This method of listening is called 'meta-communication', which is taken from the Greek, meaning 'beyond' To listen beyond the words that are spoken …listening between the lines, being present to interpret a quiver in the voice, see a tear, to interpret what is not being verbalised.

In offering a *ministry of presence* in the form of care and counselling, and those skills used for pastoral intervention such as empathy and listening, we believe that 'presence' to another is important, as Moila explains:

> In South Africa, a physical Christian presence is of vital importance because crisis situations are the order of the day, especially among young African people. People in these situations feel much better when they see they are suffering in solidarity with others. Thus physical Christian presence opens a window of liberation through granite walls of suffering. In moments of crisis in the lives of most black South Africans, it can say more than the words of a thousand sermons. By this I mean to say that it is possible at times to counsel people in crisis, through one's own silent body.[43]

Being present is often all that is necessary when a client is in distress. As human persons, we need to know that we are like all others, like no other, and yet we belong to the whole of humanity as people who need one another.

Outcomes of the Pastoral Encounter in a Multicultural Relationship

As pointed out by Arredondo,[44] the pastoral encounter is by no means a one-way experience. Both the pastoral care-giver and the client begin to realise that each is a recipient of the counselling process. Each party learns from the other what it means to accept another culture and to acknowledge that we are all unique, we are different and we are learners in the cross-cultural communication process. This means that pastoral counselling becomes a give-and-take experience, with neither the counsellor nor the client holding the dominant culture. Therefore a new understanding emerges between two persons who were from different cultures, and now a new culture of understanding and communication emerges. Service is given by the pastoral care-giver and received by the client, and in turn the pastoral care-giver is the recipient of a new ethos in care-giving.

---

43 M.P. Moila, 'The Role and Function of the Pastoral Counsellor', 206.

44 F.A. Ibrahim and P.M. Arredondo, 'Ethical Standards for cross-cultural counselling, 351-52.

Conclusion

After 19 years and some 26 CPE programmes, we can evaluate the process with some objectivity as we look at the results of the transitions from an American model into the African model.

We realise that the three-week module is sufficient because rarely can a participant take more leave from their place of employment or study. This module of 120 hours of supervised training is adequate for those learning the skills of pastoral care-giving. This timeframe is also required by the university and the seminary for credit in the Master's programmes.

We have decided to cut down on the number of written assignments and to require only three verbatim reports per student. This means that in a small group of six, who are under one supervisor, the participants evaluate 18 verbatim reports, sometimes using them for practical role play, sometimes putting themselves in the shoes of the patient, and sometimes 'living the verbatim' in the first person as the pastoral care-giver.

- The greatest difficulty in the present CPE programme is the question of communication. Language in a cross-cultural environment is the largest barrier. Patients do not comprehend how a fellow black person cannot speak their language of isizulu.
- Knowledge of the customs and traditions is not fully respected. The care-giver may be inclined to have prejudices against other tribal groups or even belittle their belief system.
- The meaning of the present moment and of true listening and keeping respectful silence is only learned in the third week. There is now a new emphasis in the first week. Learn to LISTEN and keep silent when offering dignity and respect for the stories of the patients.

The care-giver in his or her enthusiasm is inclined to feel the need to offer advice, or to interfere with the beliefs, traditions and customs of the patient.

These points above go to show that pastoral care-givers feel the need to reach out, to care for and to love their neighbour, yet sometimes to the detriment of the inner person they seek to serve.

The role of the cross-cultural pastoral care-giver is a difficult task, requiring patience, the willingness to learn another person's culture, and an openness to accept the other as unique in the sight of God.

Bibliography

Atkinson, D., G. Morten and D.W. Sue, *Counseling American Minorities: A Cross-cultural perspective* (Dubuque, IA: Brown, 1989).

Augsburger, D.W., *Pastoral Counseling Across Cultures* (Philadelphia, PA: Westminster, 1986).

Bate, S.C., *Inculturation and Healing. Coping-healing in South African Christianity* (Pietermaritzburg, RSA: Cluster Publications, 1995).

Berinyuu, A.A., *Towards Theory and Practice of Pastoral Counselling in Africa* (Frankfurt: Peter Lang, 1988).

Berinyuu, A.A., *Pastoral Care to the Sick in Africa* (Frankfurt: Peter Lang, 1988).

Bellagamba, A., 'New Attitudes Towards Spirituality', in Aylward Shorter (ed), *Towards African Christian Maturity* (Kampala, Uganda: St Paul, 1987).

Browning, Don, *The Moral Context of Pastoral Care* (Philadelphia, PA: Westminster, 1976).

Browning, Don, 'The Introduction to Pastoral Counseling', in Wicks et al (eds), *Clinical Handbook of Pastoral Counseling* (New York: Paulist, 1985).

Bujo, B., *African Theology in its Social Context* (New York: Maryknoll, 1992).

Clebsch, William, and Charles R. Jaekle, *Pastoral Care in Historical Perspective* (New York: Jason Aronson, 1967, reprint 1975).

Clinebell, H.J., *Basic Types of Pastoral Counseling* (Nashville, TN: Abingdon, 1966).

Gathogo, Julius, 'African Philosophy as expressed in the Concepts of Hospitality and Ubuntu', in *Journal of Theology for Southern Africa,* 130 (2008), 42-43.

Hopkins, Dwight, N., 'Black Theology: The Notion of Culture Revisited', in *Journal of Theology for Southern Africa*, 124 (2005), 83.

Hunter, Rodney, *Dictionary of Pastoral Care and Counselling* (Nashville, TN: Abingdon, 1990).

Ibrahim, F.A., and P.M. Arredondo, 'Ethical standards for cross-cultural counselling: Counselor preparation, practice, assessment, and research', in *Journal of Counseling and Development* 64 (1986), 349-52.

Keteyi, X., *Inculturation as a Strategy for Liberation* (Pietermaritzburg, RSA: Cluster, 1998).

Kluckohn, C., and H. Murray, *Personality in Nature: Society and Culture* (New York: Alfred Knopf, 1948).

Lartey, E.Y., *In Living Color: an Intercultural Approach to Pastoral Care and Counseling* (London: Cassell, 1997, reprint 1998).

Louw, D. J., 'A Mature Faith. Spiritual Direction and Anthropology', in *Theology of Pastoral Care and Counselling* (Louvain, Belgium: Peters Press, 1999).

Louw, D.J., *Cura Vitae. Illness and the Healing of Life* (Wellington: Lux Verbi, 2008).

Louw, D.J., 'Hermeneutic of Intercultural Pastoral Care. From "psyche" to "position" within the Healing Dynamics of Life' (*Cura Vitae*). Unpublished paper (2012).

Mandela, Nelson, *In the Words of Nelson Mandela* (London: Penguin, 2005).

Mbiti, J.S., *Introduction to African Religion* (Nairobi: East African Ed. Publishers, 1994).

Moila, M.P., 'The Role and Function of the Pastoral Counsellor in the present crisis in South Africa', in *Africa Theological Journal*, 18:3 (1989).

Nouwen, Henri, *Reaching Out* (Glasgow: Collins, 1975, reprint 1979).

Nouwen, Henri, article published in the *National Catholic Reporter* (USA: June 1979). Title unknown.

Okure, T., P. van Theil, et al, *Inculturation of Christianity in Africa* (Eldoret, Kenya: AMECA Gaba Publications, 1990).

Pedersen, P.B., and Marsella, A.J., 'The ethical crisis for cross-cultural counselling and therapy', in *Professional Psychology,* 13 (1982), 492.

Pedersen, P.B., 'The constructs of complexity and balance in multicultural counselling, theory and practice', in *Journal of Counseling and Development,* 68 (1990), 550-54.

Ponterotto, J., and M. Borodovsky, *Handbook of racial/ethical minority counselling research* (Springfield, IL: Charles Thomas, 1991).

Satir, Virginia, *The New Peoplemaking* (Mountain View, CA: Science & Behavior Books, 1988).

Schneider-Harpprecht, 'Was ist interkulturelle Seelsorge?' in Daniel Louw, *Hermeneutics of Intercultural Pastoral Care* (2013). Unpublished paper.

Sue, S., 'Training issues in conducting therapy with ethnic minority clients', in P.B. Pedersen (ed), *Handbook in cross-cultural counselling therapy* (Westport, CT: Greenwood Press, 1990), 275-80.

Sue, D.W., and D. Sue, *Counselling the Culturally Different: Theory and Practice* (New York: Wiley, 1981, reprint 1990).

Sue, D.W., 'A conceptual model for cultural diversity training', in *Journal of Counseling and Development,* 70 (1991), 99-105.

Villa-Vicencio, C., 'Theology and Culture in South Africa: Beyond Multi-culturalism', in *Theology Today* 51/2 (1994), 115-26.

Ward, E.D., *The Contribution of Clinical Pastoral Education to Pastoral Ministry in South Africa: Overview and Critique of its Method and Dynamic, in View of Adaptation and Implementation in a Cross Cultural Context.* PhD thesis (UKZN: 2001). Unpublished in complete book form.

Ward, E., 'Authority and Empathy in Pastoral Care', in *Bulletin for Contextual Theology in Africa*, 7:2 (June. 2001).

Whitehead, James, and Evelyn, *Christian Life Patterns* (San Francisco, CA: Harper Collins and New York: Doubleday, 1982).

Index

Editors and Contributors

Editors

Stephanie Dietrich, b. 1966. Associate professor at Diakonhjemmet University College, Norway. Studied theology in Neuendettelsau, Erlangen and Oslo. DrTheol from MF Norwegian School of Theology in 1998 with thesis 'Das schweigende Gebet. Zur fundamentaltheologischen Grundlage des Gebets in ökumenischem Blickwinckel' ['Silent prayer. On the theological basis for understanding prayer in an ecumenical context']. 1991-98, teacher and PhD scholar at MF. 1998-2007, senior advisor on ecumenical theology/Church of Norway Council on Ecumenical and International Relations. Since 1997, associate professor at Diakonhjemmet University College. For many years involved in a number of national and international bi- and multilateral ecumenical dialogues, and especially work on the understanding and practice of *diakonia* in an ecumenical context and the deacon's ministry. 2006-12, member of presidency of CPCE (Community of Protestant Churches in Europe), and since 20012 convenor of Church of Norway Theological Committee. Has edited several books (in Norwegian) and published numerous articles on *diakonia* and ecumenical theology.

Knud Jørgensen, b. 1942. MTh from University of Copenhagen, PhD in Missiology, Fuller Theological Seminary. Journalist and theologian, served with Radio Voice of the Gospel, Addis Ababa, Ethiopia, Lutheran World Federation, Geneva, International Mass Media Institute, Kristiansand, Go out Centre, Hurdal, Norway, Norwegian Church Aid, Mekane Yesus Seminary, Addis Ababa, and mission foundation Areopagos. Until 2010, Dean of Tao Fong Shan, Hong Kong. Adjunct professor at MF Norwegian School of Theology and Lutheran Theological Seminary, Hong Kong. Published several books and articles on journalism, communication, leadership and mission, including 'Equipping for Service: Leadership in Church and Society' (Regnum 2012). An editor of Regnum Edinburgh 2010 Series.

Kari Karsrud Korslien, b. 1958. Assistant professor at Diakonhjemmet University College since 1998. Professional social worker, deacon and lecturer for several years. CanSan from University of Oslo 2003 with thesis on 'Ambiguity in meeting among people. The importance of inter-subjectivity to diakonia and fellowship'. Has contributed to various textbooks in Norwegian about recognition as a central part of *diakonia* (2009), Methodical reflections of diakonia (2011), and The deacon as pilgrim and leader (2012). Working with education in field of *diakonia*, contributed to establishing a Master's in

Diakonia (2004), and developing different subjects for a Master's degree in Diakonia and Christian social practice (2010). Special areas are *diakonia* as science, practical *diakonia*, voluntary work and the liturgical work of a deacon.

Kjell Nordstokke, b. 1946. Professor emeritus at Diakonhjemmet University College in Oslo, Norway; studied theology in Stavanger and Oslo. DrTheol from University of Oslo, 1990, with thesis 'Council and Context in Leonardo Boff's Ecclesiology. The Rebirth of the Church among the Poor'. Lived ten years in Brazil, first serving as pastor with Evangelical Church of Lutheran Confession in Brazil (1974-81) and later (1994-96) as professor of theology at Escola Superior de Teologia in São Leopoldo. Since 1990 employed at Diakonhjemmet in Oslo, mainly responsible for training for diaconal ministry in Church of Norway and for developing science of *diakonia* as an academic discipline. 1998-2005, CEO of Diakonhjemmet Foundation. 2005-09, Director of Department for Mission and Development, Lutheran World Federation, in Geneva, responsible for Diakonia Programme resulting in publication of *Diakonia in Context* in 2009. Since 2009, lecturer in Science of Diakonia. Has published books and articles on *diakonia*, such as 'The Diaconate: Ministry of Prophecy and Transformation', in The Ministry of the Deacon, ANDREP 2 (Nordic Ecumenical Council, 2000), 'Diakonia in Context: Transformation, Reconciliation and Empowerment' in *Mission as Ministry of Reconciliation* (Regnum Books, 2013), and *Liberating Diakonia* (Tapir, 2011).

Contributors

Olav Helge Angell holds a PhD in sociology and is a professor of *diakonia* and professional practice at Diakonhjemmet University College. Teaches social science methodology, welfare state theory, and health and social policy. Main area of research over past years has been in field of religion and welfare services provision, which has also been his main area of publication.

Anders Bäckström is professor emeritus in Sociology of Religion at University of Uppsala. Has directed European research projects, 'Welfare and Religion in a European Perspective', 'Welfare and Values in Europe', and Linneaus Research Programme, 'The Impact of Religion', at Uppsala University where he is a research fellow.

Olav Fanuelsen was, until recently, Vice-Rector of Diakonhjemmet University College, Oslo, and Dean of its Department of Theology and Diakonia. Research and teaching mainly on history and theology of *diakonia* and on diaconate. Latest publication: 'A distinct and independent ministry. The deacon's ministry in the Church of Norway: Answers and questions on the General Synod's decision' (2011).

Carlos Emilio Ham was born in Cuba. Has been a pastor of Presbyterian-Reformed Church in Cuba for more than thirty years and served as its General Secretary 1993-2001. Joined World Council of Churches staff in March 2001 as Program Executive for Evangelism. Served as Co-ordinator of Mission and Ecumenical Formation Team, and later as Program Executive for Diakonia and Latin America-Caribbean until December 2013. Studied theology at Matanzas Theological Seminary in Cuba. 1999, obtained Doctor of Ministry degree at Austin Presbyterian Theological Seminary, Texas, USA, and currently pursuing PhD studies with Free University of Amsterdam.

Hans Morten Haugen, DrJur (PhD in law), has written extensively on how social human rights can influence powerful economic actors – in realm of patent rights, trade and investments. Has also written on role of churches when encountering injustice and hunger, and analyzed accountability and rights-based approaches by diaconal actors and United Nations. Most recent book in English entitled 'Technology and Human Rights: Friends or Foes? Highlighting Innovations Applying to Natural Resources and Medicine' (Republic of Letters Publishing, 2012).

Kari Jordheim is assistant professor and director of Diakonia programme at Department of Diakonia and Leadership at Diakonhjemmet University College. Has experience from practical diaconal work as deacon in congregation in central Oslo, experience with curriculum work, teaching and guidance in relation to one-year programmes and Master's degree in *diakonia*. Has international experience through various networks, particularly on board of DIAKONIA. Her professional focus is on pedagogy and *diakonia*, and how the church at a local level can play a role within social welfare in Norway.

Annette Leis-Peters, PhD in theology, is Associate Professor in Sociology of Religion at University of Uppsala and head of Department for Diakonia and Leadership at Diakonhjemmet University College. Her research focuses on field of welfare and religion. Currently involved in Linneaus Research Programme, 'The Impact of Religion', at Uppsala University.

Anneliese Schäpers, OP, is a Religious Sister working in Durban, South Africa. She is a CPE Supervisor, a Spiritual Director and a Pastoral Counsellor.

Hans Stifoss-Hanssen, DrPhil, is professor of diakonia and professional practice at Centre of Diakonia and Professional Practice, Diakonhjemmet University College. Responsible for PhD education and carries out research in area of *diakonia*, religion and health, whilst teaching in same field. Publishing lately concentrated on uses of rituals and symbols in connection with disasters, and on different aspects of psychology of religion. Was previously associate professor of pastoral care and counselling, and a Research Director in Church Research Institute.

Edwina Ward, PhD, is an Associate Professor and Senior Research Associate for School of Religion, Philosophy and Classics, University of KwaZulu Natal, South Africa. She is a Pastoral Counsellor and specialises in Clinical Pastoral Education.

REGNUM EDINBURGH CENTENARY SERIES

David A. Kerr, Kenneth R. Ross (Eds)
Mission Then and Now
2009 / 978-1-870345-73-6 / 343pp (paperback)
2009 / 978-1-870345-76-7 / 343pp (hardback)

Daryl M. Balia, Kirsteen Kim (Eds)
Witnessing to Christ Today
2010 / 978-1-870345-77-4 / 301pp (hardback)

Claudia Währisch-Oblau, Fidon Mwombeki (Eds)
Mission Continues
Global Impulses for the 21st Century
2010 / 978-1-870345-82-8 / 271pp (hardback)

Brian Woolnough and Wonsuk Ma (Eds)
Holistic Mission
God's Plan for God's People
2010 / 978-1-870345-85-9 / 268pp (hardback)

Kirsteen Kim and Andrew Anderson (Eds)
Mission Today and Tomorrow
2010 / 978-1-870345-91-0 / 450pp (hardback)

Tormod Engelsviken, Erling Lundeby and Dagfinn Solheim (Eds)
The Church Going Glocal
Mission and Globalisation
2011 / 978-1-870345-93-4 / 262pp (hardback)

Marina Ngurusangzeli Behera (Ed)
Interfaith Relations after One Hundred Years
Christian Mission among Other Faiths
2011 / 978-1-870345-96-5 / 338pp (hardback)

Lalsangkima Pachuau and Knud Jørgensen (Eds)
Witnessing to Christ in a Pluralistic Age
Christian Mission among Other Faiths
2011 / 978-1-870345-95-8 / 277pp (hardback)

Beth Snodderly and A Scott Moreau (Eds)
Evangelical Frontier Mission
Perspectives on the Global Progress of the Gospel
2011 / 978-1-870345-98-9 / 312pp (hardback)

Rolv Olsen (Ed)
Mission and Postmodernities
2011 / 978-1-870345-97-2 / 279pp (hardback)

Cathy Ross (Ed)
Life-Widening Mission
2012 / 978-1-908355-00-3 / 163pp (hardback)

Beate Fagerli, Knud Jørgensen, Rolv Olsen, Kari Storstein Haug and Knut Tveitereid (Eds)
A Learning Missional Church
Reflections from Young Missiologists
2012 / 978-1-908355-01-0 / 218pp (hardback)

Emma Wild-Wood & Peniel Rajkumar (Eds)
Foundations for Mission
2012 / 978-1-908355-12-6 / 309pp (hardback)

Wonsuk Ma & Kenneth R Ross (Eds)
Mission Spirituality and Authentic Discipleship
2013 / 978-1-908355-24-9 / 248pp (hardback)

Stephen B Bevans (Ed)
A Century of Catholic Mission
2013 / 978-1-908355-14-0 / 337pp (hardback)

Robert Schreiter & Knud Jørgensen (Eds)
Mission as Ministry of Reconcilation
2013 / 978-1-908355-26-3 / 382pp (hardback)

Petros Vassiliadis, Editor
Orthodox Perspectives on Mission
2013 / 978-1908355-25-6 / 262pp (hardback)

Orthodox Perspectives on Mission is both a humble tribute to some great Orthodox theologians, who in the past have provided substantial contribution to contemporary missiological and ecumenical discussions, and an Orthodox input to the upcoming 2013 Busan WCC General Assembly. The collected volume is divided into two parts: Part I: The Orthodox Heritage consists of Orthodox missiological contributions of the past, whereas Part II includes all the papers presented in the Plenary of the recent Edinburgh 2010 conference, as well as the short studies and contributions prepared, during the Edinburgh 2010 on going study process.

Pauline Hoggarth, Fergus MacDonald, Bill Mitchell & Knud Jørgensen, Editors
Bible in Mission
2013 / 978-1908355-42-3 / 317pp (hardback)

To the authors of Bible in Mission, the Bible is the book of life, and mission is life in the Word. This core reality cuts across the diversity of contexts and hermeneutical strategies represented in these essays. The authors are committed to the boundary-crossings that characterize contemporary mission – and each sees the Bible as foundational to the missio Dei, to God's work in the world.

Wonsuk Ma, Veli-Matti Kärkkäinen
& J Kwabena Asamoah
Pentecostal Mission and Global Christianity
*2014 / 978-1908355-43-0 / 397pp (*hardback)

Although Pentecostalism worldwide represent the most rapidly growing missionary movement in Christian history, only recently scholars from within and outside the movement have begun academic reflection on the mission. This volume represents the coming of age of emerging scholarship of various aspects of the Pentecostal mission, including theological, historical, strategic, and practical aspects.

Afe Adogame, Janice McLean & Anderson Jeremiah, Editors
Engaging the World
Christian Communities in Contemporary Global Societies
*2014 / 978-1908355-21-8 / 235pp (*hardback)

Engaging the World deals with the lived experiences and expressions of Christians in diverse communities across the globe. Christian communities do not live in a vacuum but in complex, diverse social-cultural contexts; within wider communities of different faith and social realities. Power, identity and community are key issues in considering Christian communities in contemporary contexts.

Peniel Jesudason Rufus Rajkumar, Joseph Prabhakar Dayam
& IP Asheervadham, Editors
Mission At and From the Margins
Patterns, Protagonists and Perspectives
*2014 / 978-1908355-13-3 / 283pp (*hardback)

Mission At and From the Margins: Patterns, Protagonists and Perspectives revisits the 'hi-stories' of Mission from the 'bottom up' paying critical attention to people, perspectives and patterns that have often been elided in the construction of mission history. Focusing on the mission story of Christian churches in the South Indian state of Abdhra Pradesh this collection of essays ushers its readers to re-shape their understanding of the landscape of mission history by drawing their attention to the silences and absences within pre-dominant historical accounts.

REGNUM STUDIES IN GLOBAL CHRISTIANITY

David Emmanuel Singh (Ed)
Jesus and the Cross
Reflections of Christians from Islamic Contexts
2008 / 978-1-870345-65-1 / 226pp

Sung-wook Hong
Naming God in Korea
The Case of Protestant Christianity
2008 / 978-1-870345-66-8 / 170pp (hardback)

Hubert van Beek (Ed)
Revisioning Christian Unity
The Global Christian Forum
2009 / 978-1-870345-74-3 / 288pp (hardback)

Young-hoon Lee
The Holy Spirit Movement in Korea
Its Historical and Theological Development
2009 / 978-1-870345-67-5 / 174pp (hardback)

Paul Hang-Sik Cho
Eschatology and Ecology
Experiences of the Korean Church
2010 / 978-1-870345-75-0 / 260pp (hardback)

Dietrich Werner, David Esterline, Namsoon Kang, Joshva Raja (Eds)
The Handbook of Theological Education in World Christianity
Theological Perspectives, Ecumenical Trends, Regional Surveys
2010 / 978-1-870345-80-0 / 759pp

David Emmanuel Singh & Bernard C Farr (Eds)
Christianity and Education
Shaping of Christian Context in Thinking
2010 / 978-1-870345-81-1 / 374pp

J.Andrew Kirk
Civilisations in Conflict?
Islam, the West and Christian Faith
2011 / 978-1-870345-87-3 / 205pp

David Emmanuel Singh (Ed)
Jesus and the Incarnation
Reflections of Christians from Islamic Contexts
2011 / 978-1-870345-90-3 / 245pp

Ivan M Satyavrata
God Has Not left Himself Without Witness
2011 / 978-1-870345-79-8 / 264pp

Bal Krishna Sharma
From this World to the Next
Christian Identity and Funerary Rites in Nepal
2013 / 978-1-908355-08-9 / 238pp

J Kwabena Asamoah-Gyada
Contemporary Pentecostal Christianity
Interpretations from an African Context
2013 / 978-1-908355-07-2 / 194pp

David Emmanuel Singh and Bernard C Farr (Eds)
The Bible and Christian Ethics
2013 / 978-1-908355-20-1 / 217pp

Martin Allaby
Inequality, Corruption and the Church
Challenges & Opportunities in the Global Church
2013 / 978-1-908355-16-4 / 228pp

Paul Alexander and Al Tizon (Eds)
Following Jesus
Journeys in Radical Discipleship – Essays in Honor of Ronald J Sider
2013 / 978-1-908355-27-0 / 228pp

Cawley Bolt
Reluctant or Radical Revolutionaries?
Evangelical Missionaries and Afro-Jamaican Character, 1834-1870
2013 / 978-1-908355-18-8 / 287pp

This study is based on extensive research that challenges traditional ways of understanding some evangelical missionaries of nineteenth century Jamaica and calls for revision of those views. It highlights the strength and character of persons facing various challenges of life in their effort to be faithful to the guiding principles of their existence.

Isabel Apawo Phiri & Dietrich Werner (Eds)
Handbook of Theological Education in Africa
2013 / 978-1-908355-45-4 / 1110pp

The *Handbook of Theological Education in Africa* is a wake-up call for African churches to give proper prominence to theological education institutions and their programmes which serve them. It is unique, comprehensive and ambitious in its aim and scope.

Hope Antone, Wati Longchar, Hyunju Bae, Huang Po Ho, Dietrich Werner (Eds)
Asian Handbook for Theological Education and Ecumenism
2013 / 978-1-908355-30-0 / 675pp (hardback)

This impressive and comprehensive book focuses on key resources for teaching Christian unity and common witness in Asian contexts. It is a collection of articles that reflects the ongoing 'double wrestle' with the texts of biblical tradition as well as with contemporary contexts. It signals an investment towards the future of the ecumenical movement in Asia.

Bernhard Reitsma
The God of My Enemy
The Middle East and the Nature of God
2014 / 978-1-908355-50-8 / 206pp

The establishment of the State of Israel in 1948 for the Church in the West has been the starting point of a rediscovery of its own roots. In the Middle East the effect has been exactly the opposite: Christians have become estranged from their Old Testament roots, because they have been expelled from their land exactly because of an appeal to the Old Testament. The concept of Israel changed from a nation in the Bible, with which they could associate, to an economic, political and military power that was against them

Pantelis Kalaitzidis, Thomas Fitzgerald, Cyril Hovorun, Aikaterini Pekridou, Nikolaos Asproulis, Dietrich Werner & Guy Liagre (Eds)
Orthodox Handbook on Ecumenism
Resources for Theological Education
2014 / 978-1-908355-44-7 / 962pp (hardback)

We highly recommend the publication of this new *Orthodox Handbook* for Teaching Ecumenism edited by a group of orthodox theologians in collaboration with WCC/ETE Program, the Conference of European Churches, Volos Academy for Theological Studies in Greece, and Holy Cross Greek Orthodox School of Theology in Brookline, Massachusetts.

REGNUM STUDIES IN MISSION

Kwame Bediako
Theology and Identity
The Impact of Culture upon Christian Thought in the Second Century and in Modern Africa
1992 / 978-1870345-10-1 / 507pp

Christopher Sugden
Seeking the Asian Face of Jesus
The Practice and Theology of Christian Social Witness in Indonesia and India 1974–1996
1997 / 1-870345-26-6 / 496pp

Keith E. Eitel
Paradigm Wars
The Southern Baptist International Mission Board Faces the Third Millennium
1999 / 1-870345-12-6 / 140pp

Samuel Jayakumar
Dalit Consciousness and Christian Conversion
Historical Resources for a Contemporary Debate
1999 / 81-7214-497-0 / 434pp
(Published jointly with ISPCK)

Vinay Samuel and Christopher Sugden (Eds)
Mission as Transformation
A Theology of the Whole Gospel
1999 / 978-18703455-13-2 / 522pp

Christopher Sugden
Gospel, Culture and Transformation
2000 / 1-870345-32-3 / 152pp
A Reprint, with a New Introduction, of Part Two of Seeking the Asian Face of Jesus

Bernhard Ott
Beyond Fragmentation: Integrating Mission and Theological Education
A Critical Assessment of some Recent Developments in Evangelical Theological Education
2001 / 1-870345-14-9 / 382pp

Gideon Githiga
The Church as the Bulwark against Authoritarianism
Development of Church and State Relations in Kenya, with Particular Reference to the Years after Political Independence 1963-1992
2002 / 1-870345-38-x / 218pp

Myung Sung-Hoon, Hong Young-Gi (Eds)
Charis and Charisma
David Yonggi Cho and the Growth of Yoido Full Gospel Church
2003 / 978-1870345-45-3 / 218pp

Samuel Jayakumar
Mission Reader
Historical Models for Wholistic Mission in the Indian Context
2003 / 1-870345-42-8 / 250pp
(Published jointly with ISPCK)

Bob Robinson
Christians Meeting Hindus
An Analysis and Theological Critique of the Hindu-Christian Encounter in India
2004 / 987-1870345-39-2 / 392pp

Gene Early
Leadership Expectations
How Executive Expectations are Created and Used in a Non-Profit Setting
2005 / 1-870345-30-9 / 276pp

Tharcisse Gatwa
The Churches and Ethnic Ideology in the Rwandan Crises 1900-1994
2005 / 978-1870345-24-8 / 300pp
(Reprinted 2011)

Julie Ma
Mission Possible
Biblical Strategies for Reaching the Lost
2005 / 978-1870345-37-8 / 142pp

I. Mark Beaumont
Christology in Dialogue with Muslims
A Critical Analysis of Christian Presentations of Christ for Muslims from the Ninth and Twentieth Centuries
2005 / 978-1870345-46-0 / 227pp

Thomas Czövek,
Three Seasons of Charismatic Leadership
A Literary-Critical and Theological Interpretation of the Narrative of Saul, David and Solomon
2006 / 978-1870345-48-4 / 272pp

Richard Burgess
Nigeria's Christian Revolution
The Civil War Revival and Its Pentecostal Progeny (1967-2006)
2008 / 978-1-870345-63-7 / 347pp

David Emmanuel Singh & Bernard C Farr (Eds)
Christianity and Cultures
Shaping Christian Thinking in Context
2008 / 978-1-870345-69-9 / 271pp

Tormod Engelsviken, Ernst Harbakk, Rolv Olsen, Thor Strandenæs (Eds)
Mission to the World
Communicating the Gospel in the 21st Century: Essays in Honour of Knud Jørgensen
2008 / 978-1-870345-64-4 / 472pp (hardback)

Al Tizon
Transformation after Lausanne
Radical Evangelical Mission in Global-Local Perspective
2008 / 978-1-870345-68-2 / 281pp

Bambang Budijanto
Values and Participation
Development in Rural Indonesia
2009 / 978-1-870345-70-4 / 237pp

Alan R. Johnson
Leadership in a Slum
A Bangkok Case Study
2009 / 978-1-870345-71-2 / 238pp

Titre Ande
Leadership and Authority
Bula Matari and Life - Community Ecclesiology in Congo
2010 / 978-1-870345-72-9 / 189pp

Frank Kwesi Adams
Odwira and the Gospel
A Study of the Asante Odwira Festival and its Significance for Christianity in Ghana
2010 /978-1-870345-59-0 / 232pp

Bruce Carlton
Strategy Coordinator
Changing the Course of Southern Baptist Missions
2010 / 978-1-870345-78-1 / 273pp

Julie Ma & Wonsuk Ma
Mission in the Spirit:
Towards a Pentecostal/Charismatic Missiology
2010 / 978-1-870345-84-2 / 312pp

Allan Anderson, Edmond Tang (Eds)
Asian and Pentecostal
The Charismatic Face of Christianity in Asia
2011 / 978-1870345-94-1 / 500pp
(Revised Edition)

S. Hun Kim & Wonsuk Ma (Eds)
Korean Diaspora and Christian Mission
2011 / 978-1-870345-89-7 / 301pp (hardback)

Jin Huat Tan
Planting an Indigenous Church
The Case of the Borneo Evangelical Mission
2011 / 978-1-870345-99-6 / 343pp

Bill Prevette
Child, Church and Compassion
Towards Child Theology in Romania
2012 / 978-1-908355-03-4 / 382pp

Samuel Cyuma
Picking up the Pieces
The Church and Conflict Resolution in South Africa and Rwanda
2012 / 978-1-908355-02-7 / 373pp

Peter Rowan
Proclaiming the Peacemaker
The Malaysian Church as an Agent of Reconciliation in a Multicultural Society
2012 / 978-1-908355-05-8 / 268pp

Edward Ontita
Resources and Opportunity
The Architecture of Livelihoods in Rural Kenya
2012 / 978-1-908355-04-1 / 328pp

Kathryn Kraft
Searching for Heaven in the Real World
A Sociological Discussion of Conversion in the Arab World
2012 / 978-1-908355-15-7 / 142pp

Wessley Lukose
Contextual Missiology of the Spirit
Pentecostalism in Rajasthan, India
2013 / 978-1-908355-09-6 / 256pp

Paul M Miller
Evangelical Mission in Co-operation with Catholics
A Study of Evangelical Tensions
2013 / 978-1-908355-17-1 / 291pp

Alemayehu Mekonnen

Culture Change in Ethiopia

An Evangelical Perspective

2013 / 978-1-908355-39-3 / 199pp

This book addresses the causes and consequences of culture change in Ethiopia, from Haile Selassie to the present, based on thorough academic research. Although written from an evangelical perspective, this book invites Ethiopians from all religions, ideological, and ethnic backgrounds to reflect on their past, to analyse their present and to engage in unity with diversity to face the future.

Godwin Lekundayo

The Cosmic Christ

Towards Effective Mission Among the Maasai

2013 / 978-1-908355-28- 7 / 259 pp

This book reveals a complex interaction between the Christian gospel brought by western missionaries and the nomadic Massai culture of Tanzania … an important insider's voice courageously questioning the approach to condemn some critical Maasai practices, particularly polygamy, and its missionary consequences. This is a rare study from a Maasai Christian leader.

Philippe Ouedraogo

Female Education and Mission

A Burkina Faso Experience

2014 / 978-1-908355-11-9 / 263pp

This volume is the result of six years research in 'Overcoming Obstacles to Female Education in Burkina Faso'. It narrates how Christians and religious groups can speed up female education and contribute to the socio-economic growth of Burkina Faso. Religious culture and traditions were seen as a problem to female education. However, the evidence from this research shows that Christianity is also part of the solution to a quality female education, thus a key factor of socio economic growth of the country.

Haw Yung

Mangoes or Bananas?

The Quest for an Authentic Asian Christian Theology

(Second Edition)

2014 / 978-1-908355-47-8 / 232pp

Over the past few decades there has been a growing awareness of the need for contextual theologies throughout Asia. But how genuinely contextual are these? Based on the premise that theology and mission are inseparable, the author applies four missiological criteria to representative examples of Protestant Asian writings to assess their adequacy or otherwise as contextual theologies.

Daniel Taichoul Yang

Called Out for Witness

The Missionary Journey of Grace Korean Church

2014 / 978-1-908355-49-2 / 167pp

This book investigates the theological motivation for GKC's missions: Reformed theology, Presbyterian theology, and mission theology. The book also shows the extent of the church's mission engagement by continents. Finally, the book turns its attention to the future with an evaluation of the church's missionary journey.

REGNUM RESOURCES FOR MISSION

Knud Jørgensen
Equipping for Service
Christian Leadership in Church and Society
2012 / 978-1-908355-06-5 / 150pp

Mary Miller
What does Love have to do with Leadership?
2013 / 978-1-908355-10-2 / 100pp

Mary Miller (Ed)
Faces of Holistic Mission
Stories of the OCMS Family
2013 / 978-1-908355-32-4 / 104pp

David Cranston and Ruth Padilla DeBorst (Eds)
Mission as Transformation
Learning from Catalysts
2013 / 978-1-908355-34-8 / 77pp

This book is the product of the first Stott-Bediako Forum, held in 2012 with the title *Portraits of Catalysts*. Its aim was to learn from the stories of Christian leaders whose lives and work have served as catalysts for transformation as each, in his or her particular way, facilitated the intersection between the Good News of Jesus Christ and the context in which they lived, in particular amongst people who are suffering.

Brian Woolnough (Ed)
Good News from Africa
Community Transformation Through the Church
2013 / 978-1-908355-33-1 / 123pp

This book discusses how sustainable, holistic, community development can be, and is being, achieved through the work of the local church. Leading African development practitioners describe different aspects of development through their own experience.

Makonen Getu (Ed)
Transforming Microfinance
A Christian Approach
2013 / 978-1-908355-31-7 / 264pp

"This book highlights the important role that Christian-based organisations bring to the delivery of financial services for the poor. It is times, significant and important and deserves a wide circulation".

Lord Carey of Clifton, former Archbishop of Canterbury

Jonathan Ingleby, Tan Kand San, Tan Loun Ling, (Eds)
Contextualisation & Mission Training
Engaging Asia's Religious Worlds
2013 / 978-1-908355-40-9 / 109pp

Contextualisation & Mission Training, offers "contextual frameworks" and "explorations" in order to enhance deeper engagement with the complexity of Asian social, cultural and religious systems.

On Eagle's Wings
Models in Mentoring
2013 / 978-1-908355-46-1 / 105pp

David Cranston writes unashamedly as a Christian for whom no account of mentoring would be complete without placing it in the biggest context of all – that of the relationship between humans and God.

John Lennox, Professor of Mathematics, University of Oxford
Fellow in Mathematics and Philosophy of Science

GENERAL REGNUM TITLES

Vinay Samuel, Chris Sugden (Eds)
The Church in Response to Human Need
1987 / 1870345045 / xii+268pp

Philip Sampson, Vinay Samuel, Chris Sugden (Eds)
Faith and Modernity
Essays in modernity and post-modernity
1994 / 1870345177 / 352pp

Klaus Fiedler
The Story of Faith Missions
1994 / 0745926878 / 428pp

Douglas Peterson
Not by Might nor by Power
A Pentecostal Theology of Social Concern in Latin America
1996 / 1870345207 / xvi+260pp

David Gitari
In Season and Out of Season
Sermons to a Nation
1996 / 1870345118 / 155pp

David. W. Virtue
A Vision of Hope
The Story of Samuel Habib
1996 / 1870345169 / xiv+137pp

Everett A Wilson
Strategy of the Spirit
J.Philip Hogan and the Growth of the Assemblies of God Worldwide, 1960 - 1990
1997 /1870345231/214

Murray Dempster, Byron Klaus, Douglas Petersen (Eds)
The Globalization of Pentecostalism
A Religion Made to Travel
1999 / 1870345290 / xvii+406pp

Peter Johnson, Chris Sugden (Eds)
Markets, Fair Trade and the Kingdom of God
Essays to Celebrate Traidcraft's 21st Birthday
2001 / 1870345193 / xii+155pp

Robert Hillman, Coral Chamberlain, Linda Harding
Healing & Wholeness
Reflections on the Healing Ministry
2002 / 978-1- 870345-35- 4 / xvii+283pp

David Bussau, Russell Mask
Christian Microenterprise Development
An Introduction
2003 / 1870345282 / xiii+142pp

David Singh
Sainthood and Revelatory Discourse
An Examination of the Basis for the Authority of Bayan in Mahdawi Islam
2003 / 8172147285 / xxiv+485pp

REGNUM AFRICA TITLES

Kwame Bediako
Jesus in Africa, The Christian Gospel in African History and Experience
(2000) (Theological Reflections from the South series)
SECOND EDITION FORTHCOMING 2013

Mercy Amba Oduyoye
Beads and Strands, Reflections of an African Woman on Christianity in Africa
(Theological Reflections from the South series)
2002 / 1-870345-41-X / 114pp

Kä Mana
Christians and Churches of Africa Envisioning the Future, Salvation in Christ and the Building of a new African Society
(Theological Reflections from the South series)
2002 / 1-870345-27-4 / 119pp

Ype Schaaf
On Their Way Rejoicing, The History and Role of the Bible in Africa
2002 / 1-870345-35-9 / 252pp

E.A.W. Engmann
Kpawo-Kpawo Toi Kpawo – Vol. 1, Adesai, Oboade, Lalai, Ajenui ke Shwemoi (Folklore of the Ga People)
(Gbotsui Series - Indigenous Sources of Knowledge in Ghanaian Languages)
2009 / 978-9988-1-2296-6 / 70pp

Philip Tetteh Laryea
Yesu Homowo Nuntso (Jesus, Lord of Homowo)
(Nyamedua series in Mother-tongue Theology)
(reprinted 2011) / 1-870345-54-1 / 176pp

E.A.W. Engmann
Kpawo-Kpawo Toi Kpawo – Vol. 2, Kusumii (Folklore of the Ga People)
(Gbotsui Series - Indigenous Sources of Knowledge in Ghanaian Languages)
2012 / 978-9988-1-2294-2, 186pp

Philip T. Laryea
Ephraim Amu: Nationalist, Poet and Theologian (1899–1995)
2012 / 978-9988-1-2293-5, 425pp

Jon P. Kirby
The Power and the Glory, Popular Christianity in Northern Ghana
(Trends in African Christianity Series)
2012 / 978-9988-1-2295-9, 350pp

For the up-to-date listing of the Regnum books visit www.ocms.ac.uk/regnum

Regnum Books International
Regnum is an Imprint of The Oxford Centre for Mission Studies
St. Philip and St. James Church
Woodstock Road
Oxford, OX2 6HR

regnum